I think it was Mother who first suggested that we bought Carneddi. At first the idea of farming in the hills seemed quite impracticable. My father was fifty, I was seventeen and we had lived in the city all our lives. It was true that Carneddi was to be sold cheaply, but even so we had little money to cover any mistakes that we might make. Yet somehow we were unwilling to settle back into a suburban routine once more. We talked, wondered, and at last decided. We bought the farm, and burned the boats of the life we had always known.

'She is full of determination and of an energetic and quite unsentimental love of the life she has taken up. She makes her daily work seem as real and as tangible as the stones after which her farm is named . . . quite free from the townee giggle and the townee rapture, yet the townsman will enjoy it as much as anybody'
The Times Literary Supplement

Place of Stones

Ruth Janette Ruck
with a foreword by
George Henderson

CORGI BOOKS

PLACE OF STONES

A CORGI BOOK 0 552 12577 6

Originally published in Great Britain by Faber and Faber Limited

PRINTING HISTORY

Faber and Faber edition published 1961
Faber and Faber revised edition published 1970
Faber and Faber revised edition reprinted 1975
Corgi edition published 1985

This book is set in 10/11 Cheltenham

Corgi Books are published by
Transworld Publishers Ltd.,
Century House, 61–63 Uxbridge Road,
Ealing, London W5 5SA

Made and printed in Great Britain by
Hunt Barnard Printing Ltd., Aylesbury, Bucks.

*Y mae y llyfr hwn yn gyflwynedig
i'm cyfeillion a'm cymdogion Cymreig,
yn arbennig felly i bobl Nantmor,
am eu caredigrwydd yn ein cynorthwyo
i amaethu yn eu cwmwd godidog*

Foreword
by GEORGE HENDERSON

This book delights me. Not only is it well written, which means that interest is steadily built up throughout, but it drives home many of my cherished principles of farming without appearing to do so. This true and modestly told story shows once again that given the will, courage, faith, patience, ingenuity, and certain basic equipment, and no matter how stony the soil, how steep the terrain, or heavy the rainfall, a living can be wrested from the poorest mountainside, and often proving in the process that 'life is sweetest nearer the bone'.

For many years I have had the cause of the small farm at heart. I have been privileged to teach, help and encourage those who would farm well in a small way. As a farming author I have advised many of my pupils that they too should write a book, in due course, on their experiences, to tell others how worth while it has all been. Miss Ruck is the first to take my advice in this direction. Her simply told story could be duplicated a score of times by others, each with his own adventure of overcoming the difficulties, and finding the effort in itself a reward. I know that there is a temptation to be so happy and busy in farming that there seems no time to refute the economists, who knowing all the answers are content to remain economists, but have never seen the sunrise on the Welsh mountains, or met the kindly neighbours who say they keep sheep for fun, and give golden sovereigns for wedding presents. The truth of the matter is that farming is a happy way of life for those who enjoy it, who are content with a modest standard of living, but usually have a considerable appreciation in the value of their farm over their working lifetime. It is this reserve which enables them to withstand the bad times when they come.

If we seek to analyse this success, we find a basic system adapted to soil and climate – in this case sheep and cattle – and an attempt to grade up to make the best of that stock, with perhaps a sale of sheepdogs as a sideline. Then once this has been established, superimposed other departments, whether it be laying hens, turkey rearing, strawberry runners or seed potatoes, and without neglecting the basic system of farming, on which one can always fall back if any new department fails. If there is a relationship between the departments so much the better. The poultry manure enriches the soil for strawberry runners, the intensive cultivation of which gives better crops of seed potatoes, and so on.

Any system of farming that succeeds must depend on the character and intelligence of the people who work it. I have the greatest admiration and respect for the Ruck family, who identify themselves so closely with the neighbourhood, who are accepted by the community, and yet in many respects retain the standards of gracious living they have known elsewhere. I have visited Carneddi a score of times, and have seen the steady progress which has been made. I have taken part in two sheep shearings, and remember with special pleasure a party there one evening, where with two harpists to play, and a group of neighbours to sing, an age-old tradition was maintained on what is now one of the most up-to-date farms in the whole district.

Acknowledgments

My thanks are due to Jones Williams, Gardd-llygaid-y-dydd, for help with the Welsh language, and also to my sister Mary for even more help with the English. Brian Nicholson and Paul Orkney-Work have shared in producing all the illustrations and it is hard to thank them enough.

For readers unacquainted with the Welsh language,
Carneddi is pronounced Carnethi,
with the 'th' hard as in 'the'.

Preface

Carneddi means the place of stones or cairns. Behind the house is a cliff with gullies down which boulders and broken slabs of slate have tumbled to form a clutter of rocks at its foot. It was from these rocks that the house itself was built, and the old cottage before it. It was from the stones of the place that walls were made and sheds built, and from the rocky land men have earned their daily bread for many generations.

Contents

Illustrations

1 Beginning a Menagerie

I always wanted to have a farm. It seemed the most sensible and pleasant way to live and, from the age of seven, I began to acquire animals and to grow vegetables in our town garden. It did not concern me that there was nothing but brick and concrete outside the garden walls; my imagination supplied a different scene. We lived in a house not far from the centre of the city, my parents and I, my sister Mary and Nanny whom we nicknamed Fred. It must have been Fred who first made me interested in farming. She was a splendid story-teller and her answers to cries of: 'Tell us a story' usually began: 'When I was a little girl . . .' and went on to tell of her country upbringing as one of a large family. She was always enthusiastic about my projects and was a great ally in the farming idea. She seemed to see our town garden as a farm, just as I did, and was passionately devoted to the animals, particularly Waggles. He was the first pet, a black and white mongrel dog. Then I had Bunlop, a pedigree white Angora rabbit, with one ear upright and one hanging down, bought cheaply on this account. Then there were six hens. Here my father came into his own. As a carpenter he was very ingenious and everything he made was intended to last till Doomsday and bear strains verging on earthquake violence. Saturday afternoons were spent happily in holding hammers, passing nails and watching an interesting hen palace being made out of an old pigeon cote. Mother knew what hens needed. She used to keep prize-winning Blue Orpingtons when she was a girl. Daddy and I produced, to her specifications, the scratching pen, the upstairs sleeping quarters and the nest-boxes and perches, all very strong and rigid, out of bits of old wood.

Then the war came and food production was all-important. 'DIG FOR VICTORY' and 'BACK TO THE LAND' posters appeared on every hoarding, offering an encouragement that I hardly needed. Although our house was on the main road there was quite a large garden in front of it, enclosed by trees and a jungle of privet bushes and variegated laurels. The back garden was even better, having a small lily pond, potting shed and a range of dilapidated wooden sheds and wire runs which once had been an aviary. It was surrounded by more trees and a high red brick wall topped with flat sandstone slabs. Parts of the garden were an intriguing jungle for a small girl but, as I grew older, camp-fires and explorers' games seemed less important than growing food. I decided to dig up the back lawn. I was then twelve and my parents approved of the idea. I bought a book on vegetable growing, saw in it a diagram of how to trench two spits deep and decided that this was the treatment to give the ground. The lawn had been laid over the foundations of an old building and as I went deeper and deeper, determined to do the job properly, a lot of old bricks were unearthed and piled up on the edge of the trenches. When I had made a good deal of progress I became aware of Cyril looking at me intently over the wall. He was our neighbour's gardener and a friend of mine. When I felt like a chat I could reach the sandstone slabs on the wall-top by climbing an adjacent tree, or from the aviary roof. Here I would sit, after scraping off some of the bird messes, and admire the neat professional garden over the other side, and perhaps be given some of its fruit to sample. When Cyril wanted to talk to me he would stand on the corner of a cold-frame—the level of their garden was higher than ours—and his head would just appear above the wall. This he did now.

'What are you doing down there?' he asked.

I told him I was making a vegetable garden.

'Oh,' he said, 'I thought you were digging an air-raid shelter.'

I felt slightly mortified, but the vegetables I grew on that deeply-dug plot supplied the house throughout the war.

The next venture was goat-keeping. New pets were not always received enthusiastically as there were times when

Mother or Fred found themselves left with my animals to feed, and I tried to introduce further livestock into the family as inconspicuously as possible. It was easier, I thought, for my parents to forbid the arrival of new pets than to turn them out after they had been installed. Fred, of course, backed me up. For some time she and I had been going to visit her sister on Thursday afternoons and I would study the goats in the orchard there. Then we heard of two kids for sale. One afternoon we brought them back with us on the top of the bus, paid for with 30s. from my savings account. The consternation was soon over; the kids were elegant little animals with an impudent manner and wistful eyes. Before long my father was making very strong hayracks, feeding-troughs and stalls for them. With me as his tool-passer, he turned part of the aviary into an original and functional goat house on successive Saturday afternoons.

The two kids were called Horns and Chloe. Horns was white, a tough extrovert character; Chloe was a light beige, hornless and timid. Their coming was a step towards real farming, I felt, since they required hay in bales and feeding-stuffs in sacks. The goat manure, together with contributions from the hens, had a good effect on the vegetable garden, the waste from which the goats consumed. It was a natural cycle and seemed like proper farming, a big step, this, from the time when I believed, as a small child, that the world was made of solid concrete and tarmac, and that people's gardens were only soil-filled pockets in its surface.

As a change from being tethered on the lawn I took the goats for walks down the side roads. If I ran they would career after me, bouncing on and off the low garden walls or shooting quickly up someone's path, their small tails erect with excitement. At first the district was rather surprised, and a local paper even included an article on the goat girl. After a while the neigbours took a more practical and less romantic view of the goats and I began to get requests to tether them on overgrown lawns. Gardeners were now in the Army and mowing machines rusted in idleness. Goats are not generally considered to be good grazers but our two neatly reduced several lawns, and it was only when the grass was really short that they pulled out their tethering pins and started on the rose trees and ornamental shrubs. Even then their hosts generally forgave them.

In due time and after a visit to a pedigree billy and much speculation on my part, Horns produced triplets, Chloe twins. I saw them born and was filled with wonder and amazement at the neat and satisfactory arrangements of Nature. The kids were sold easily and I managed to milk. I had a bucket and strainer and, in the summer at least, our family had plenty of milk when the rest of the city were living on rationed half-pints.

About this time the house in Bournemouth, where we had always spent our holidays, was sold and the beach and promenade were no longer our summer playground. We had fields and farmyards instead. Sometimes the whole family camped. Here my father's army training came in useful and he had us all smartly organized for pitching and striking the tent, digging latrines, carrying water and for the various other camp duties. I loved it, particularly as Waggles always came. I loved the cheery roar of the primus and the awareness of the stretching night outside, the sound of cattle grazing in the darkness and the feeling of being really in the country.

On these camping holidays Mary and I used to make for the nearest farm as soon as possible. At morning and evening milkings we were always there, absorbing the scene with intense interest and not heeding the manure oozing over the welts of our sandals. These farms were mostly small, not very progressive, where children were welcome and we were soon begging for permission to try to milk the cows. It was on these holiday farms, when I was about thirteen or fourteen, that I learnt to milk properly—cows were much harder than goats. Uncle Fred, an elderly Derbyshire smallholder, gave us the best tuition. He let us milk a whole cow each, twice a day.

'Keep on squeezing until their tits are flamp,' he would say. Flampness became our aim, and we squeezed and squeezed until the desired state of flampness was reached and we had milked our cows.

Mary was very interested in bulls. Whenever we found one in a field, we sat in a place of safety and watched it for hours.

Sometimes we furtively displayed Mother's red mackintosh to it but always with disappointing results. A fierce bull chained in a shed was even more of a fascination. I liked farm horses and would scramble unobserved on to their backs as they grazed, and sit there for a long as I dared. Mary would come to watch and give me a leg up, but horses were not really in her line. From the age of eight I had been having riding lessons whenever someone could be induced to pay for them. I became moderately proficient and after a while was allowed to exercise the horses and take out younger children in return for doing stable work at week-ends. Horses became my passion. 'I wish I could have a pony,' I said over and over again during my childhood, but it was no use because we had neither the space nor the money to keep one.

One day I spent all my savings on a pedigree white Alsatian puppy and called him Zenda. In some ways his beauty and strength satisfied my longing to own a larger animal. Waggles was getting fat and old and liked to lead a lazy life. Although he was never replaced by Zenda in my affections, it was nice to have a young dog to accompany me and join in games.

I found school a place of excruciating boredom. I tilted my chair, sighed, shuffled and gazed out of the window until the final bell rang. Then I streaked down the stairs, battled in the cloakroom for coat, hat and outdoor shoes, and was out and away as soon as possible. Science and biology were sometimes interesting but more often dull, since I had already learnt much from my nature books at home. English I liked, but the rest was so boring that I made the most of colds and headaches to stay at home and follow more interesting pursuits. The teachers looked at me with suspicion. My class work they labelled 'careless' but I managed somehow to pass exams. Mother expected a good academic standard from Mary and me, and near exam time, feeling guilty, I worked hard. The best that school life gave me was the friendship that I had with Paula and Anne. After twenty years it is still as flourishing. At school we were three apart from all the others of whom the clever girls, destined for academic careers, left us stiff with boredom, while the dunces with their chatter of boy friends seemed merely silly.

When I was sixteen, in 1944, I passed matric and wondered what I should do next. The obvious thing in our family was to take a degree in something or other. Medicine attracted me a little, but Mother was discouraging. I caught infection easily, and quickly became ill. As a doctor I might not, she thought, survive for long. Also I felt the prospect of dissection rooms was repellent, and since my vocational urge did not seem strong I gave up any more thoughts of becoming a doctor. The openings for a girl in farming were not attractive. The Women's Land Army seemed to lead nowhere and agricultural colleges to be more productive of farmers' wives than women farmers. Miserably I stayed on at school to take the Higher Certificate. Now my back garden farming had lost its charm. I hardly knew what I wanted do and life was pointless and lacked its old zest. I wanted change and suddenly, as if in answer to my wish, it came.

2   Hill Farm

The war ended, and in the midst of victory celebrations I became ill with diphtheria and nearly died in hospital. For a few days it was uncertain whether I would live and our family was in turmoil. Then slowly I improved and was taken home. I had to lie flat on my back for two months and my work for exams was over. Later I was to go away for a long holiday.

The holiday was arranged in North Wales where we had often been before. We stayed as usual in Nantmor village and took familiar walks on the lower slopes of the mountain. My heart was still weak and we had to go slowly. During the holiday we heard that Carneddi was for sale, a small hill farm of eighty-three rocky acres, high on the mountainside. We had often walked past it. It was the home of Richard Griffiths, a Welsh writer and bard, and his wife who was almost a recluse and seldom went farther than her cowshed. He had farmed the land—there was a small hill flock and a few hardy cattle—with the help of his son, Hywel, but when Hywel was found dead that summer, drowned in the lake on the other side of the mountain, the old man was unable to go on farming alone. The couple were to leave Carneddi, home of the Griffiths family for many generations, and live with their eldest son in England.

There was a bardic sign over the front door of the house. Mary and I had once been inside and talked with Mrs. Griffiths in the brown-painted, book-lined parlour. There was no fire in the grate but a smell of coal smoke clung about the room and a haze of it was visible in the kitchen. We had heard that Carneddi was notorious for its smoky chimneys. Above the parlour fire place was a placard with NO SMOKING on it in large letters, but whether this was intended for visitors or as a silent injunction to the grate we did not know. We could see that here learning mixed with living conditions which were primitive by city standards, and culture with a way of life that was almost as ancient as the hills themselves. Tuberculosis had reduced the Griffiths family until only Richard Griffiths, poet and scholar, survived among numerous brothers and sisters who had been born in the old cottage adjoining the present house. The house itself stood under the lee of a crag and was surrounded by a huddle of fir trees and one huge cedar. It could be seen from miles away, alone on the spur, with ridge after ridge of hills piling up to the summit of Snowdon behind. A stony track twisted and turned upwards, in places fading into wheel ruts through patches of bog. It threaded through small stone-walled fields and ended at last by the clump of trees and the house above. The farm was different from the English farms where we had played as small children; it seemed alien and austere to us, and yet there was a sense of ancient tradition and security about it that was absent from city life.

I think it was Mother who first suggested that we bought Carneddi. The thread of our normal existence seemed to have been broken by the end of the war, which made my father's work redundant, and by my sudden illness. A moment of pause and choice had come to us. In a restless state ourselves, it was as though we were more receptive to the changelessness and peace of the mountains. At first the idea of farming in the hills seemed quite impracticable. My father was fifty, I was seventeen and we had lived in the city all our lives. It was true that Carneddi was to be sold cheaply, but even so we had little money to cover any mistakes that we might make. Yet somehow we were unwilling to settle back into a suburban routine once more. We talked, wondered, and at last decided. We bought the farm, and burned the boats of the life we had always known.

A month of packing and organizing followed. It was difficult to decide what we should need for the farm. In the end we took everything: our furniture; old clothes, long since put away and now useful for farm work, we said; the movable fitments from the goat house, hay-racks, mangers, gates and milking stand; the Christmas decorations; the garden tools and work bench; the beehives and all our books. It seemed impossible to leave anything behind.

Meanwhile Mother and I wondered what we could do to fit ourselves for the new life ahead. While Daddy was making lists and Fred packing boxes, we spent a day at a nearby agricultural college learning how to make butter. We knew that buttermaking was traditional on hill farms. We had seen farmers' wives churning, and now we determined to learn how to make it ourselves. We received much kindness and help at the college, and were allowed to operate one of a row of end-over-end churns which were being used by some of the girl students. Butter was still rationed but here we saw gallons of cream being made into pounds and pounds of it. The college had an impressive array of dairy equipment, a steam sterilizer, a refrigerator and butter-working tables. Carefully measured quantities of lactic acid were used to turn the cream to just the right degree of sourness, and we thought of Carneddi on its bare mountain slope, without piped water and without electricity, and wondered how we should ever manage there.

We had been told to turn our churn until the observation window in its lid had cleared and the butter inside had formed into grains the size of rice. We turned conscientiously but our little window continued to remain coated in yellow cream. We saw the contents of one churn after another turn to grains the size of rice and finally into pats of butter before the dairy instructress arrived to look into our churn.

'Your cream had gone to sleep,' she said.

We watched, surprised. The cream had thickened and clung to the sides of the churn, travelling round with it instead of concussing with each revolution. A little water was added, a few brisk turns of the handle given, and the window was suddenly clear.

'Now a few more turns,' the instructress told us.

We turned, this time too vigorously. When the lid was lifted again we found our grains of butter were now the size of hens' eggs. But, as we made it into decorated pats, we felt that we had gained some useful experience.

25

At the beginning of that December in 1945 we were ready to leave the city behind us, perhaps for ever. Mary was now at Cambridge University but, in her long vacations, she would share the new life in the mountains for part of the year. Fred said good-bye to her relatives. After twenty years in our family it was impossible to imagine life without her and, of course, she was coming too. The furniture vans arrived and everything we possessed was stowed inside. We spent one night in the stripped and echoing house and on the following morning the last of the bedding and cooking utensils were packed into one of the vans. We set off for Wales by train, the family and all our animals. Our exodus to the mountains had begun.

That train ride had a nightmarish quality. We had too many animals and too much luggage with us to enjoy the prospect before us. It was only with difficulty that the goats were prevented from plucking off and eating the labels on luggage in the guard's van. The hens cackled and poked alarmed heads through the bars of their crate. Zenda was hot and restless. We arrived at last, late and exhausted, and the animals were taken to the farm while we spent the first night in the village. The next day we were to move into Carneddi.

In the morning the furniture vans arrived in Nantmor but they were too big to negotiate the track to the farm. They were unloaded half a mile down the road and all our familiar possessions were piled on to a neighour's cart and tractor to finish the rest of the journey up the hill. A few stray bees had escaped and were pinging round the van, harassing the men as they worked. It began to rain softly and the mountains were hidden in mist. Mother and Fred had gone up to the house to receive the furniture as it arrived and to make tea for the workers. They were spared the sight of upholstery in the rain, and polished tables and wardrobes grating and scraping against the sides of the manure cart as it mounted the hill. They waited for pots and pans, bedding and cups and saucers so that the empty little house could be turned into a home, but the first thing which appeared and was carried in through the rain was my old dolls' house.

Somehow we settled in. Our life was now like a camping

holiday of indefinite length. It was winter but, even in the sombre colours of the year's end, the mountains were beautiful. It was strange and delightful to wake up each morning to the seemingly infinite silence and emptiness of the countryside, to milk our new cows and to look with pleasure at our grazing sheep. The hens settled down quickly in their new surroundings but the goats hung round the farmhouse door, bemused with freedom and at a loss to decide what to do with it.

Indoors we arranged ourselves as best we could. The house had been built in 1914 and was just a square box with four little rooms downstairs and four up, the stairs in the middle. All the interior walls were painted dark brown and made of match-board. So were the ceilings. The black-lead range in the kitchen smoked badly and so did the sitting-room grate. In the garden was a sentry-box privy which none of us cared to approach. Water had to be carried from fifty yards away. Candles and paraffin lamps provided our light. Perhaps our worst difficulty was the furniture. We had brought all we possessed from a house twice the size of Carneddi, and now it filled those eight little rooms almost to the exclusion of the occupants. Daily life was something of an obstacle race but through it all Fred was splendid. Country life was no new experience for her, and soon she produced a homelike atmosphere in those strange surroundings.

One of the first tasks was to prevent the chimneys from smoking so that we could have a fire. It was a cold, damp December that year and paraffin heaters were an unsatisfactory substitute. We borrowed a sweep's brush and set to work. There appeared to be an old jack-daw's nest in the sitting-room chimney. In turn my father and I struggled to get the brush up but it always stuck half-way. Mary watched in the garden for the brush to come out of the chimney-pot but nothing appeared. We poked and poked, with trickles of soot descending on us, but it was no use; the brush would not go through.

'What about getting up on the roof and sweeping downwards?' I suggested.

The prospect of never being able to have a fire seemed a

grim one and I was ready to try anything. Being the youngest, I climbed on to the roof and inserted the brush down into the chimney-pot. It went in and I screwed on another length of cane, then a second and then the brush stuck.

'It won't go any farther,' I called down the chimney.

My father was in the sitting-room, waiting for something to happen.

'What did you say?' he shouted.

'The brush is stuck.'

'What?'

I gave another poke. Down below, my father approached the fire-place to hear better. I poked again and the brush suddenly moved the blockage, shooting a cascade of soot, mortar, twigs and dirty sheep's wool into the room below. When I climbed down my father was a blackened figure waiting in the doorway, but from then onwards the fire drew well.

The kitchen chimney was not improved by sweeping and dense smoke poured into the room whenever we tried to light a fire. The cliff behind the house seemed to create a permanent down-draught and, that first winter, we never managed to have a kitchen fire. On Christmas Day Fred created an artificial one of shiny paper which, if it did nothing to warm the room, at least looked cheerful.

We cooked on a paraffin stove. It was satisfactory and efficient and surprisingly, we did not miss electricity. For some months we reached automatically for a non-existent switch on entering a dark room, but even this gesture of habit passed. Filling lamps and trimming wicks was an extra task, but soon it became part of our daily routine and the 'paraffinalia' was established in the old dairy.

We had brought an old-fashioned hip bath with us, previously used for bathing dogs. Now humans took baths in it with a bucket of boiling water from the stove and a bucket of cold from the spring. The vaunted simplicity of country life, we found, was genuine. Life here really was simpler in some ways. On a remote mountain farm with no mechanization and no amenities, there was less to go wrong. There was no pipes to burst, no fuses to blow, no breakdowns, nothing in fact which could not be fixed with a hammer and nail, or a bit of string.

Soon after our arrival Paula and Anne, my school friends, came to stay, and they entered into our curious camp life with zest. One of the little upstairs rooms served as a bathroom, and here the hip bath was kept. There was also an old-fashioned washstand with tooth mugs, a fluted jug and basin, slop pail and the chemical closet. By the light of one candle visitors and family took it in turns to wash themselves in cold spring water, and then all retired to their brown-painted, box-like bedrooms to fall asleep to the sound of the wind in the cedar and owl calls from the wood below.

On the first morning of their visit various bumping sounds could be heard through the match-board partition of the bathroom. My father was washing, but obviously something was wrong. Then, in aggrieved tones, he called out: 'Who's moved my teeth?' Nobody remembered moving his teeth. We all looked for them in the bathroom, but they were not to be found. Then we began to search in unlikely places. Suddenly Paula recollected that she had tipped water out of a tooth mug in the candle-lit bathroom the night before. We dredged in the slop pail and the teeth were retrieved. This was the sort of happening that was peculiar to our early days at Carneddi.

The farm buildings were few. The land was so rough and poor that it did not support much stock. The mountain sheep needed no man-made shelter, and kept themselves alive in winter on the sparse herbage without stored fodder. We had a cowshed, however, a long, low, windowless building, perhaps a hundred and fifty years old. The roof was covered with thick hand-made slates fixed to the timbers with oak pegs. The cattle occupied one end of it with hay in the other, so that both beasts and fodder were under one roof.

The old cottage provided a store for the tools, and next to it stood a stable and pigsty. These were built in dry stone walling of crude workmanship and in places they bulged ominously. Time and weather had produced cracks in the long slate lintels above windows and doors, and in the thinnest of the wall stones, causing the masonry to shift in the passage of years and only the immense thickness of the walls held it up.

The best building on the farm was Capel Anwes, our lower barn. Here the masonry was excellent, with two arched doorways of a design unusual in the district. The roof slates had been replaced in recent times but the original oak timbers remained, purlins, rafters and two big trusses made from single trees. No nails were used in the construction and dowel pegs held the great beams in place. The barn was sited on our lower boundary, a couple of hundred yards from the house. We learnt that it was an ancient monument and that in medieval times it had been an open hall, home of some Welsh chieftain. Later it was divided into two. Half belonged to the little farm of Ty Mawr, half to Carneddi. On our side of the interior dividing wall was an old cottage fireplace, the inglenook beam bearing the date 1519. Here, in what once was a family kitchen, the hay was now stored. Oak panelling of in-and-out design divided the barn again, and on the farther side were standings for cattle.

The ruins of a third barn stood in our lowest field, Gors Goch, the Red Marsh. Here eight or nine acres of deep peat land were cupped in a narrow valley between steep ground on either side. It was the only flat land on the farm, bog land drained by deep sluggishly-flowing ditches. There was no way for a wheeled vehicle to reach it, and the barn was a relic of the days when hay was cut with scythes for wintering a few store cattle from the hill. Now rushes, bracken and bog myrtle grew there and, even as rough grazing land, it was poor.

We had bought all the livestock and the tools and implements which belonged to the farm. They had been listed and valued, and the whole came to £410. The flock of a hundred and fifty Welsh Mountain ewes and lambs were priced at 30s. a head, a low figure at that time. Grazing rights on the mountain for a hundred and thirty-three ewes went with possession of the farm, and the Carneddi ewes had the extra value of being acclimatized. The flock had grazed a particular area of the mountain for generations and were now attached to it by a deep hereditary instinct. Any new sheep turned on to the unfenced mountain would soon have strayed and caused endless trouble to their owner and other farmers. *Cynefin* is the word used for this hereditary homeground and is derived from the Welsh for familiar or customary. Up in the mountains there are innumerable small sheep-pens said to date back to the days before flocks were acclimatized. The sheep were penned in at night and watched during the day by women and children. Many farms still have the names *hafod* and *hendref* attached to them. *Hafod*, the summer dwelling, was occupied during the good weather while the sheep were on the open mountain. In winter they were brought down to *hendref*, the winter dwelling, and the enclosed fields below.

For £38 we became the owners of three Welsh Black milking cows. These we named Betty, Brute and Grandma. Grandma was not with us for long. She appeared to have a chronic kidney complaint and was sent to the slaughter-house straight away. I was surprised by the cheque we received for her—15s. 3d., the value of her hide. In life she had looked a fine animal with great sweeping horns, but her carcass was not fit even for sausages. Betty and Brute were healthy but gave only a dribble of milk and, as nobody had taken them to the bull, it would be a long time before we had any more from them. Also on the list were two bullocks, a black and white heifer named Prim, a young black calf and the sheep-dog Nell.

The tools and implements were laid out neatly in the old house. This was a single-story stone cottage where the Griffiths family had lived before the new house was built. Now it was used as a stone shed. The slate roof had been replaced by corrugated iron but the old fireplace and oak beam remained. Very little light came through the cobweb-covered windows set deep in the wall. List in hand, my father and I checked over the tools of our new trade. Apart from the horse mower, all of them were hand tools: light wooden hay-rakes; a *telyn*, which is also the Welsh word for a harp, and is a cleverly designed hay-rake with long curved tines for dragging along the ground; hayforks; a chaff cutter and hand shears. There were long straight scythes with a *stric* on their handles. The *stric* is used for sharpening in this district in preference to a carborundum stone. It is made of wood, four-sided and tapering. It is rubbed with pig fat and then coated with powdered sandstone and will keep a scythe blade razor-sharp. There were two long saws with T-shaped handles at one end, for use in the old saw-pit. There were cow chains, a mildewed set of harness, hurricane lamps, sheep dip and a variety of different coloured drenches for curing every sort of animal illness. There were barbed wire and netting, axes, a crowbar and two mole traps. The summer's wool clip, packed into a great bulging wool-sheet, stood in one corner.

We checked down the list.

'What are "pig rings and pilers 3s."?' I asked. 'Can you see any?'

'Pilers?'

'That's what it says here. "Pig rings and pilers." '

We looked anxiously for the pilers. They had a sinister sound. Probably pilers were indispensable on a well-run farm, and we did not know even what they were.

After more searching my father exclaimed: 'Here they are! It means "pig rings and pliers".'

Another difficulty arose.

'Have you found "grasping corns and cutter 15s 4d."?' I asked.

The grasping corn was more difficult to locate. After eliminating everything else, we decided it was the long fork with tines bent at a right angle. The cutter was its partner, a blade on a long handle for cutting out ditches on peat land. I never found out quite what grasping corns meant. It may have been another misprint.

The butter-making utensils were in the dairy. There was a big dasher churn, several earthenware crocks, a pair of scotch hands and two circular butter prints, blackberries and leaves for the one pound pats and a cow for the half pounds.

A sense of the past clung to the farm, indeed to the whole district. Most of the people lived where they had been born and where their families had lived for generations. Many had not travelled farther than the Welsh border. The ways of farming were still traditional. Though farmers were quick to learn and adapt modern methods, the hills remained the same and the old wisdom of shepherding had been found out long ago. Hill land does not lend itself well to mechanization and generally the old practical methods were the only workable ones on land so steep and rocky that a lowland farmer would be aghast at the prospect of making a living from it. Money was scarce too, and a man had to get his shilling's worth out of every eleven-pence ha'penny if he were to keep his family. I asked John Williams. our neighbour, if there was money to be made from mountain sheep. At that time, in 1945, lambs sold for £1 each and wool was controlled at 1s 5d. a pound.

'I don't look to get rich,' he said, 'I keep my sheep for the pleasure.'

Carneddi is in the sun. The first morning rays touched the house and buildings and warmed the sloping fields. Day long we enjoyed its heat until it slipped down behind the shoulder of Moel Hebog. Long after the valley was in shadow, we caught the pink evening glow. There were many farms on the northward-facing slopes where the sun never shone for a couple of months in winter. On a bright cold day one could see the grass white with frost and the air blue in the mountains' shadow, while half a field away the ground was thawed and the air warm. The best sheep farms face the morning sun. The thin grass and heather is quickly thawed after a night of frost and the ewes are able to get a bellyful of dry herbage before the sun goes down.

Perched on the spur with an airy view of the world spread out before us, we always had a feeling of height and space. Visitors were surprised to learn that the house was only 450 feet above sea level, for it looked much higher. The upper limits of our land reached to 750 feet, while the lower fields descended to 350 feet. Though the altitude was not great, the steep track to the house, the naked rock rising in one outcrop after another and the piles of boulders showed Carneddi for what it was, a mountain farm of rock and shallow acid soil. The illusion of height was given by the flat, sea-level valley below. In the past tidal flats had stretched where fields are now, and present inland villages once had a boat-building industry. A seawall was built at Portmadoc in 1811 and during the next hundred and fifty years the sand-banks were reclaimed and now are farm lands.

And so, in that New Year of 1946, we came to know our

new acres, walking over the rough land to look at the flock, trying out our new tools with inexperienced hands, experimenting with our new life. In a few months my daydreams of having a farm had suddenly been realized, but it was the sort of farm which had never figured in those dreams. A year ago none of us would have imagined ourselves living on that remote spur of the mountains.

3 Cow-Keepers

Betty, Brute and Grandma lived in the cowshed. The store cattle were wintered in Capel Anwes. Our initiation into farm life began with the cows, and morning and evening milking established the start of a farmer's routine.

The cowshed was floored with huge slabs of natural slate, worn smooth over the years by generations of cloven hooves and the scrapings of muck shovels. The skylight in the roof, perhaps six inches square, gave enough light to make the animals inside faintly discernible while more light came in through the open doorway. Garlands of cobwebs hung from the apex of the roof like tattered black rags, and cloaked the walls. If a calf pen were required, an old gate could be jammed into the angle of the wall, but there were no loose-boxes or accommodation for calving cows. We brushed the cobwebs away and whitewashed the rough wall-stones, but the place always retained a cosy darkness and I enjoyed milking there by lantern light on a cold winter's morning. Agricultural officials advised us to pull down the old shed and build a new one, but we liked our cowshed as it was. We found it satisfactory; the cattle were comfortable and did well there, milk-selling regulations did not govern us and so our cows continued to march in and out through the low doorway as cows had done for the past hundred years or more.

My father began to learn to milk but he found it hard work. Usually I did the milking for I was fairly expert. Betty and Brute were both going dry and, though Betty was now in calf again, Brute remained obstinately barren. We hoped to join the Welsh Black Cattle Society and have pedigree cows eventually, but first we needed to learn how to manage the stock we already had. William Owen, our neighbour at Corlwyni on the northern boundary of Carneddi, helped us when he found that we wanted to learn. He displayed a bundle of hay in his arms.

'This much,' he said, 'one feed to the cow.' He also drew our attention to Grandma's complaint—'the black water'—and said it was best to get rid of her. When she had gone to the slaughter house, an empty stall was left and we decided to buy a new cow. As we had no experience, we were grateful when a local farmer, who was also a lay preacher, offered to purchase one for us. He wanted no commission. Here was an instance of the great kindness of the Welsh farmers. In the past poverty had left its mark here, and there was a tradition of co-operation which seemed to extend naturally to include us. Although we were foreigners, we were made welcome.

There was always a welcome at Beudy Newydd, the farm below, and I often called to talk to Mary Alice and her father John Williams. One evening I set out to visit them. It was market day at Brynkir and we had been wondering all day if the kindly lay preacher would see a suitable cow at the sale and buy it for us. So far we had received no message but we waited eagerly, excited at the thought of adding another cow to our stock. It was a dark night but not cold. I hurried down the track, swinging a hurricane lantern. The sweep of valley and mountain were shut out under an inky sky, but here and there a farmhouse window glowed and far away by the sea were the twinkling lights of Harlech. I moved in a little world of lantern light, walled by the darkness and crossed and recrossed by giant shadow legs, walking as I walked. It was a world filled only by the sound of my own crunching footsteps. When I stopped there was absolute silence. Then I became aware of the small sounds of the night, the faint rushing of a distant stream, the cropping of a near-at-hand sheep and the owls in the wood over the hill. Here, if you were afraid to go out in the dark, you stayed in. There were no street lamps and no company till you reached the next farmhouse, only a lonely road.

The lighted windows of Beudy Newydd were round the next bend. I tapped at the door.

'*Dowch i mewn,*' called Mary Alice's voice. 'Come in.'

I went in. Their door was never locked. John Williams said that someone coming down from the mountain might be glad of a cup of tea and a rest sometime, and were welcome to take it, whether the family were in or not.

Mary Alice's son, Robin, now two years old, was in a tin bath before the fire. The bath was a present from the U.S. Army when encamped in the valley before the invasion of Normandy. All the farms round about had equipment dating from those days and marked 'made in U.S.A.' The chewing-gum, the Life Savers and the Camels that found their way into those lonely Welsh farmhouses had been consumed long ago but the sturdy tinware remained. It was strange not to be able to speak to Robin. He did not understand my language and I did not speak his. He looked at me with bright, dark eyes, knowing all about the new people at Carneddi, as Mary Alice lifted him from the bath. He was already heir to the cowshed and sheepfold and all the things that were still so new to me. Although only as high as their bellies, he could drive the cows with a big stick. At shearing this year he would be old enough to gather up snippets of wool and pass ties to the shearers. Now he stumped up the stairs in his flannel sleeping-suit, peeping at me through the banisters, with Mary shooing him from behind. I sat and chatted with John Williams. The fire burned brightly and two big kettles steamed on the hob. The clock ticked on the dresser, with a Bible and a mass of letters and agricultural returns tucked behind it. Mando, the sheep-dog, peeped out from under the tablecloth, not quite sure if he ought to be there.

Mary Alice came downstairs. The number of her daily chores was enormous and she had no tap or drains, no gas or electricity to help her. She also did the milking, fed the calves, made butter and helped her father with the general work. In no time the dirty dishes from Robin's supper were washed, and basin emptied through the front door and clean ones for our supper appeared in their place on the oil-cloth. Down came the side of bacon from a hook on the rafters, and soon long rashers were frying over the fire. A mountainous pile of bread and butter was cut. While she worked, Mary kept up a flow of chat, telling me the Welsh names of the articles she put on the table, now and again breaking off to direct a quick stream of Welsh at her father. He had taken his Bible down from behind the clock and was proceeding with his eighth reading of it from beginning to end. On the completion of each reading he marked the date on the back fly-leaf.

'It's no good,' said Mary Alice, 'you must learn Welsh. Now what's this?'—holding up a knife.

'*Cyllell*,' I said. My vocabulary was slowly increasing.

We sat there eating our meal in the kitchen. I was grateful to them for making me feel a part of it, and sharing in friendship their country life of hard work.

Then a new sound reached our ears, the sound of a heavy engine grinding upwards in low gear.

'Now who can that be?' said Mary.

The engine came to a stop outside the house and there was a knock at the door. John Williams went to open it. After talk in Welsh with the newcomer, he turned back to us.

'Your new cow's here, Ruth.'

I jumped up, excited. With the talk and pleasant heat from the fire, all thought of a new cow had gone from my mind. John Williams said the lorry was too wide to go right up to Carneddi, we should have to unload the cow here and he and Mary Alice would help me to drive her home. The lorry driver was given tea, and then we all went out with our lanterns and the back of the truck was lowered. There were thumpings, pushings, a flash of horns, a rattle of hooves and the cow was down on the grass beside us. By lantern light it was hard to see what she was like, but she seemed larger, fatter and trimmer than the gaunt milkless Betty and Brute in the cowshed at home. She was grey, with smaller horns than the Welsh Blacks, and John Willams said she had some Shorthorn blood. The three of us drove her slowly up the track in the darkness. She was heavily in calf and stopped, panting, every few yards or started to turn the wrong way, sniffing and snorting at her new surroundings. At last we got her to the cowshed and chained her in Grandma's empty stall. The rest of the family came out to admire, and for a while we all stayed talking in the shadowy cowshed. The arrival of a new animal is an important event on isolated mountain holdings, and the unfamiliar grey cow, plucking at her hay, would be part of our daily life now.

We named her Jane and waited eagerly for the birth of her calf, the first since our arrival at Carneddi. William Owen was ready to supervise the calving, and we were grateful for his support. In those days our ignorance was the source of many anxieties and we knew nothing about calvings. William Owen, however, was reassuring. Each day he came to examine the cow and stood thoughtfully feeling the pelvic bones and pinching her udder. 'He not come tonight' was the verdict. Then one evening it was 'I think he come'. We had had Jane about three weeks and were beginning to think the calf was overdue. With no other shed or loose-box to use, she would have to calve chained in her stall as her predecessors had done. Someone would have to be with her at the time of the birth as the calf might get an infection or become chilled if left unattended in the dung channel, and so my father and William Owen prepared for an evening vigil. I did not see this first calving. It appeared that the midwifery was to be an all-male event on this occasion, and so I went to bed. By morning the calf had arrived, not a black or grey one as we had expected it to be, but a very large bull calf which was pure white.

'I not see such a big one before,' said William Owen.

It seemed fitting that our first calf should be spectacular in size and colour. My father was very pleased with it, though slightly fractious through loss of sleep. He and William Owen leant over the calf pen gate like two proud parents. It was a good feeling to take a stool to a cow with a full udder and come away with a deep pail of milk. We could make butter now and avoid the ignominy of being farmers who bought their milk.

The mountain holdings were too far from the road for milk-selling and the old ways of butter-making and calf-rearing were still practised. The Welsh Black cows had been selected for their butterfat and the richness of their milk is second only to the Channel Island breeds. The milk was kept in earthenware crocks, holding six or eight gallons, until it was sour and then churned. This accounted for the large size of the churns and made churning heavy work, sometimes taking an hour or more. William Owen churned by water power. A stream flowed past his house and could be diverted into a small dam on the slope behind. The dam held enough water to turn the old water wheel on the gable end of his dairy for the hour or so needed, and then the sluice could be closed with a bit of turf and a stone or two and the water level allowed to rise again ready for the next churning. Many of the mountain farms had a derelict water wheel but Corlwyni was one of the last with a wheel in working order. There were no such neat arrangements at Carneddi; the huge dasher churn was cumbersome to operate and so I bought a small end-over-end churn of the type we had used in the college dairy. It was not big enough to churn the whole milk, and so pans of milk, set for the cream to rise for hand skimming, occupied every corner of our cramped little dairy and kitchen. Often we had not enough vessels to hold it all, for Jane was milking well and the cream took twenty-four hours to rise. A separator was needed but in 1946 it was difficult to buy. As food was still rationed, it was, perhaps, unfair to have cream and butter of one's own and most of the separators were for export only. However, butter-making and calf-rearing seemed natural to Carneddi's economy and finally I managed to buy one. With advice from Mary Alice I was soon making farmhouse butter of good quality in traditional circular pats, with a print of the blackberries or the cow on its pale yellow surface. I never quite mastered Mary Alice's technique of making pats by tossing a lump of butter round in one hand. The butter either stuck to my fingers or fell on the floor and I returned to using the wooden scotch hands in the way we had been taught in the college dairy. Now the day began and ended with the cheery humming of the separator, and I felt that here was one branch of farming in which I was becoming proficient. But there was still much we did not know.

Experience is of great value in farming and of this we had none. Our policy, so far as we had one, was to farm Carneddi as it had been farmed in the past, rather than to embark on untried schemes until we knew what we were doing. We had experts in the traditional methods of hill sheep farming on every side, and from them we took our guidance. An uncomfortable lack of understanding can arise when a newcomer appears to be rich, eccentric and foreign, and disregards the steady, time-honoured methods of his new home.

I also read as many books on farming as I could get. One of these, *The Farming Ladder* by George Henderson, made a deep impression on me. At times I felt depressed by the complexities of farming and the insecurity which faced a beginner with little capital, but *The Farming Ladder* was most encouraging. The author showed that hard work, common sense and a liking for the life could produce successful results in the face of many disadvantages. He himself had a prosperous farm which had been built from the very smallest beginnings. Although his was an Oxfordshire mixed farm, very different from the Welsh mountains, his principles seemed to be universal and I resolved to follow them as far as I could. Our adventure into Wales seemed less rash and our chances of making a success of the life much better in the light of Mr. Henderson's book.

The gap between theory and practice, however, had to be bridged. This I did by going down to Beudy Newydd and asking John Williams what we ought to do next. When he told me I would go home and try to do it. We also watched other people's farming activities with an eager eye. Carneddi is ideally placed for this. By sitting on the cowshed roof I could clearly see the work in progress on five different farms in the valley below. Having seen, I would slide down the cement roof and hurry in.

'Daniel Evans is carting manure. If the ground is dry enough for him, it must be all right for us.'

Later in the season it would be: 'All the Cwm Caeth family are turning their hay. Evidently they don't think it's going to rain this afternoon.'

The result of this was that for the first year we were always a little behind our neigbours, but we learnt a great deal in that year.

4   Keeping Sheep for the Pleasure

We felt we could not attempt to shepherd our wild mountain flock without some expert help. Nell, the sheepdog, was bought with the farm but she understood only Welsh and was several years old. She was black with a white muzzle and paws, long hair and many ticks, and she did not understand anything we said to her. She lived a private, outdoor Welsh life and was quite unlike the lapdogs we had always kept before. Without her help we could do nothing with the sheep, even had we known more about them, and so John Williams suggested that we ask his nephew, Thomas Williams, if he would shepherd the flock for us in his spare time.

Tom arrived one evening to talk it over. Small, wiry, nearing sixty, stick in hand, cloth cap on head, he inspired confidence. He was willing to help us, he said, but at present had no dog and so we offered the use of Nell. Perhaps she would respond to a fellow-countryman where we had failed to make her work. Tom was willing to have a try with her and agreed to gather the sheep when necessary, to wash, shear, dip, dose and look round the flock for foot-rot, maggots and lambing troubles. We were to help as much as we were able.

Tom and Nell took to one another from the start and soon established a working partnership. He was always good with his dogs, and a man without a dog is helpless in dealing with mountain sheep. A man with a well-trained dog can gather the flock smoothly and easily over the rough land, the scree, heather and bog and waist-high patches of bracken. The ones and twos merge into dozens, the dozens become a steady stream of slowly-moving sheep and the streams converge into a tight-packed woolly mass, bleating in the pens. Yet a

43

man without a dog is the most futile of figures on the hill. To try to drive the sheep alone is like bailing a boat with a teaspoon or mowing the lawn with nail scissors. On those first mountain gatherings we tried to help, hurrying over the tussocky ground, hot and over-eager, but our shooings were of small avail. Half a dozen sheep would bunch and start in the right direction, then, as we passed on over the dips and rises of the ground and before we had turned a few more sheep towards the first, they would already be spreading out again, grazing and drifting back the way they had come. On the other hand a dog that is too keen and wild can make pandemonium of gathering. The flocking instinct is shattered when sheep become really terrified. They burst out from the bunch in all directions, like the debris from an explosion, pouring out over the rocks in frantic cascades and not stopping until they are dots on the horizon.

The spring of 1946 was mild and the sun shone. Our lambs were born into a world of green grass, blue skies and bursting catkins. Tom walked up in the lengthening spring evenings, with Nell at his heel, to see how the lambing was progressing. I was amazed at how much his experienced eye could see. He could distinguish the ear-mark of a distant sheep while I was still looking for the paint brand on its fleece. He could tell its age, condition and when it was due to lamb, and probably remember something of its history too. At first they all looked alike to me. Later I began to distinguish between them and even know where to look for a particular ewe. I would walk round with Tom and began to learn a little about the flock as I watched and listened.

He told me that the ewes are brought down from above the mountain wall in October, and the rams turned out to them at the end of the month. Through the winter they graze on the fields round the farmhouse and the enclosed *fridd*, getting no extra feeding. If hay is put out in very severe weather, few of them will touch it and most prefer to survive on heather, gorse and ivy which is not covered by the snow, getting thinner beneath the heavy, grey fleeces. March comes and the five-months' gestation period is over. As the grass begins to grow again the lambs are born and the extra feeding helps the ewe to produce her milk. A bad spell of weather now can bring disastrous results. Heavy rain will so chill a weak lamb that it never rises to its feet after birth and flooded streams will drown others. Lack of grass can cause the ewes to give birth with little or no milk and so abandon their offspring to the attacks of foxes and carrion crows. As the flock is spread out over many acres of rough land, the shepherd has to be constantly on the move to protect it from danger.

In mountain conditions the Welsh ewe generally has a single lamb. Her struggle for survival is too hard for her to bear and rear twins. By May the doubled flock is through its worst difficulties, and sheep and lambs are moved up to the open mountain to allow for a hay crop to be taken from the lower fields. Before the introduction of D.D.T. sheep dips, this was the danger time for maggots. The sheep were in full fleece, often scouring from the new grass, and the weather was warm. The flies would lay their eggs in the soiled wool of the tail or a damp patch on the shoulder; the eggs hatched and the resultant maggots, if not caught in time, ate their hosts alive. With D.D.T. the position was changed, and many lives and much shepherding was saved. The sheep could be dipped just before they were put on the mountain in May and the six weeks' protection would last until they were washed in the middle of June. A few days after washing, the ewes are shorn and the whole flock returned to the mountain. In July they are gathered again. Any cuts received at shearing time have now healed, the wool has grown a little and they are ready for another fly-dip to protect them for the rest of the season.

Selling time comes in the summer and early autumn. The season's best wether lambs are the first to go, sold to lowland farmers for fattening before Christmas. The smaller lambs go next and may be wintered on the new farms before selling fat in the spring. Then the ewes are gathered from the mountain and their teeth examined to determine their age. At four years old a ewe has eight permanent incisors in the lower jaw and is termed 'full-mouthed'. These old ewes are sorted out and sold to valley farmers where, in more favourable conditions, they will rear another crop or two of lambs before going

45

on for slaughter. With these go a few of the two- and three-year-old sheep, picked out for poor characteristics which will unfit them for the rigorous mountain conditions, for wool that is too fine and short, for stunted growth or bad conformation. About a quarter of the flock is drafted each autumn, its place being taken by the maiden yearlings.

At the end of October the ewe lambs are sent off for wintering on lowland farms. Here they grow well, unhampered by competition with adult sheep and the strain of pregnancy, and are ready to return to their own mountain the following April. At home the ewe flock is brought down and the rams, one to every thirty or forty females, are turned out among them and the cycle of the sheep year begins again.

All this was new to me that first spring, and I learnt the traditional pattern of mountain sheep-farming only as it was unfolded before my eyes. Carneddi is a small sheep farm by comparison with the majority in Snowdonia, with a permanent flock of only eighty or ninety ewes, but it was a thrilling experience for me to see the flock double itself during March and April.

Our very first lamb was a black one, the daughter and first lamb of a two-year-old ewe. There it was, ears drooping, tight black curls still damp, bleating plaintively. The mother, marked by the blood on her tail, grazed unconcernedly a few yards away. When I came nearer, she bounded off in a panic, disregarding her lamb. I retreated in haste but the mother would not return to her offspring.

All day the black lamb bleated sadly. I came for many anxious looks but never saw it feeding from its mother. It was clear that something was wrong. Sunset streamers were flaring in the west when I saw Tom's figure approaching up the hill. I hurried down to tell him.

'We'd better have a look on her,' he said.

He sent the dog round quietly, and the mother and her still-pregnant sisters bunched together in a corner. The black lamb did not know which way to run and stayed where it was, crying more wretchedly than ever. With a quick movement Tom had his crook round the ewe's throat, caught her by the wool and up-ended her. A glance at her tiny udder satisfied him.

'She had no milk. It's no good messing with her.'

He let her go disgustedly and walked to the lamb which thought maybe here is mother, and began to nuzzle at his trousers, wiggling its tail expectantly. He picked it up and gave it to me, a feather-weight bundle of black plushy wool.

'You'll have to give it the bottle. If we find another ewe that's lost her lamb, we can get her to adopt it.'

He shot another glance of disapproval at the ewe which was grazing again in an off-hand manner.

We had a good lambing season and there was no ewe to act as foster-mother to the black orphan. I reared her on the table. We named her Topsy and she became a great pet. Never having known a sheep for parent, she was tame from the start and looked anywhere and everywhere for milk. The cats hated her and would retire to the window-sill with tails like Christmas trees when she approached. As she grew bigger she took every opportunity of hastening into the house when the front door was opened. She would tip-tap across the tiled kitchen floor, giving a loud demanding bleat, and express her cleverness at getting in by leaving a little trail of pellets behind. Fred, who was very fond of her, would clear them up hastily before any other member of the family could notice and complain. When she was a full-grown sheep and too old for bottles, she still hankered for the pleasures of indoor life. The family were on guard against her door-entering strategies and so she learnt to lurk in the garden, waiting for the arrival of callers, when she would bull-doze her way in past their unsuspecting legs.

She grew very bold and quite unafraid of any sheepdog. Often she spoiled a gather by shooting off in the wrong direction and leading the other sheep with her. Her worst fault was her invincible tactics with wire-netting, barbed wire and stone walls. There were never any of these which could either fence her in or keep her out. She could always worm her way under, climb over or bore her way through the most stoutly-made fence. She could always mount the highest wall, with a raucous bleat and a clatter of falling stones. Her talent in this direction made gardening a depressing occupation. Willam Owen had ploughed the small enclosure just below the house and I was attempting to establish a kitchen garden there. Topsy found that she liked vegetables better than the natural herbage and periodically forced her way in and ate everything in sight.

We kept Topsy for four years and at last it became clear that one could not afford to run a farm and a circus at the same time, particularly as she tried to teach her lambs these cunning methods of entering. We sold her and tried to stifle the traitorous feelings in our hearts. It was not the last we saw of Topsy. For three subsequent years she arrived at Carneddi at the end of March and gave birth to twins before the harassed owner discovered her whereabouts and came to fetch her.

During our first summer at Carneddi, Topsy was only a lamb and we knew nothing of the tiresome ways she was later to develop. Everything about the sheep was new to us then and I looked forward eagerly to our first shearing. Already I had privately selected a pair of shears from the pile in the old house. I was determined to learn to shear and hoped that I could practise on a sheep or two under the tuition of Tom or John Williams.

The washing and the shearing are communal events in the mountains; your neighbours help you and you help them; much gossip and farming news are exchanged and large dinners and teas are eaten. It also provides the first real opportunity for our neighbours to look us over, for naturally they are interested to see what we are making of life at Carneddi.

Tom fixes our washing day. We are the first farm to begin. The sheep are washed five to ten days before shearing and are plunged into a mountain pool and allowed to swim to the bank. This ducking removes grit, bits of bracken and heather tangled in the wool, and part of the natural grease. I was puzzled to understand how cold water could remove the grease, but it is true that it does and the swiftly-flowing water in the washing pool turns greyish white and pours out over the rocks like dirty milk. It used to be the custom for all sheep to be washed; the wool merchants preferred clean fleeces. Now only the mountain flocks are washed, and those not always. The loss of weight in the wool of a fat sheep offsets the higher prices paid for clean wool and so it is worthwhile to wash only the lean, hill ewes.

On the morning of our washing day, I wake and look out to find the sun is not yet through the mist which veils the mountains. Fred is astir, with the kettle already singing on the stove. I dress quickly and take the milk bucket out to the cowshed. There has been a heavy dew in the night and my sandals are soaked as I drive Betty and Jane down the rocky slopes of Clwt yr Wyn, the Lambs' Patch, and into the cowshed. Betty is dry but she is heavily in-calf, so I let her in to have a handful of cow cake. We have sold Brute as a barren. The milking done, I feed the calf, let the cows out again and return to the house for breakfast. My father is in from feeding the hens; Mother and Fred are already preparing the meals for the day.

Breakfast over, we go out and there coming up the track are Tom, John Williams and Jones. Daddy gets Mot, our new sheepdog puppy, and slips the lead on his collar. He is untrained as yet and may spoil the gather if left free, but we want him to see the other dogs at work.

Tom is in command for the day. We do not know enough to direct operations and leave it all to him. William Owen and his son Gwilym are going straight up from Corlwyni to sweep the flock down towards us from the crest of Moel Dyniewyd. Tom is circling the great bog, Gors Hafody, which lies in the hollow of the cwm below the crags, and there will join William Owen. My father goes with him. John Williams and Jones take the lower boundary wall and I, the weakest link in the chain, am left near the mountain pen to prevent the flock from over-running the gap and escaping downwards to the slopes which have already been cleared of sheep.

The others move off and I take up my post. They are lost to sight among the undulations of the ground, and there is no sound now but the piping of a curlew and the singing of the wind. The morning mist has all dispersed and a few big cumulus clouds blow by, chasing their shadows up and down the mountains. I stroll to a cone-shaped eminence and climb to the top for a better view. This is called Pig yr Wylfa and is said to have been the look-out point for Roman soldiers from the camp at Beudy Newydd. I can see the camp from where I stand, three sides of a square clearly visible in John William's mowing grass, two hundred feet below. For a moment I am a Roman soldier and see the valley as it must have been then, the sea covering all of Traeth Mawr, no houses and no chapel but a few round mud and wattle huts, no snaking stone walls sectioning the mountains as they do now, and no road except the Roman one below.

A far, faint whistle catches my attention and I turn towards the north again to face the vast, lonely cwm below Moel Dyniewyd's summit. High on a distant crag I can see grey dots shooting downwards. William Owen's dog is notoriously keen and the sheep are coming at a great speed. Tom is visible too, a tiny figure picking its way along the edge of the bog. Now my father is in sight, a little behind Tom, and I can hear very faint but impassioned cries of 'Mot, MOT!' as a black dot scatters the white dots far and wide. I am relieved to see Tom's dog collect the sheep neatly once more and Mot being brought to heel. In a minute the figures are gone again and I look at the sea, the sky, the mountains, sit down, stand up, stroll round, then sit down again and look at the sky. I am almost taken by surprise as the first bunch of sheep come scuttling over the nearest rise, stop short and look at me suspiciously. More join them and the foremost ewe stamps her foot and snorts with annoyance at finding the way barred. She is about to turn and make off to the left when Mando, John Williams's dog, appears over the crest, drops flat and fixes her with a menacing stare. Now the men are all converging and the sheep have no choice but to pour into the pen in a tight-packed mass. The lambs are less used to the dogs and have lost their mothers in the throng. They hang back until the last, ready to make a wild dash for freedom but we are prepared and close in on them rapidly. At length all are in and now comes the task of picking out the strangers. Tom and Jones wade in among the sheep, seize any which do not bear our mark and turn them out. The dogs, excited by the morning's work, do not want to let them go and converge in a menacing circle round the gate. William Owen threatens Mick with his stick and John Williams ties Mando up beside Mot. The others call their dogs away.

There is one sheep which John Williams says comes from the other side of Beddgelert. We must take her down to the farm with our flock and telephone her owner as, if turned back to the mountain, she may stray even farther afield. I open the gate into the Allt, the highest part of our enclosed land, and the lambs and ewes stream through. Here Tom turns off and goes to collect a few of the weaker ewes which have been left below the wall. The others follow the flock down and I hurry on ahead to warn Mother and Fred that we are ready for our dinner. The heifer and the bullock, which have been put on this high pasture for the summer, are delighted to see me and come careering over the heather in search of cattle nuts but I have no time for them now and hurry on.

In the house everything is ready. Soon the men come in and we sit down to eat. The talk is mostly about Carneddi and everyone is very interested in the changes we have made. By now the dark, interior walls have been painted; the kitchen and pantry are knocked into one to give more room, and we are hoping to have a bathroom soon. When the meal is over, all rise as at an invisible signal and clump out, thanking Mother for their dinner as they go.

It is arranged that John Williams and Jones shall stay behind to earmark all the lambs and castrate the ram lambs while the rest of us go down to the river to wash the ewes. I am glad to miss the ear-marking and castrating this year as I am not yet hardened to the more gruesome sides of farming.

The lambs and ewes are separated and we drive the ewes down past the house, across William Owen's lower fields and ford the Nantmor river. At first the ewes are unwilling to cross, so Tom grabs one and pulls her over. He holds her on the far bank and makes realistic bleating noises. The rest of the flock, governed by the ancient, follow-my-leader instinct, are soon splashing through the shallows. We follow the road for a short distance, past Tanrhiw farmhouse and then join the river higher up where the washing pool lies.

It is a place overhung with hazel bushes, the June leaves freshly green, the sunlight filtering through them and dancing on the pool. According to custom we have sent down previously to ask Owen Jones, Tanrhiw, if we may wash there. Carneddi sheep have been washed in that pool for generations but it would be impolite if we did not ask for permission. William Owen has been there a few days earlier and thrown up a rough, stone dam to raise the water level. There are pens on the bank, one side open to the water and one side formed by a moss-covered bastion of natural rock. The babble of the running water makes endless background music to the bleating sheep, barking dogs and the shouts of the men.

The sheep are hustled into the pen and Tom takes up position by the water's edge. I am told to stand on a stone which juts out into the pool and given a long pole with a T-shaped head. My job is to push the sheep under as they swim by downstream in order to make sure the fleeces get thoroughly soaked. The work begins. The other men pass the ewes rapidly up to Tom who plunges them into the water and I give them an extra dousing as they swim by. They are strong swimmers and their white heads rise far out of the water with the power of their strokes. In five yards they reach the shallows and scramble out, stumbling a little with the unaccustomed weight of water in their wool.

The work is hard and after a while Jones takes Tom's place. He begins to throw the sheep in nearer to my rock and I am cascaded with spray. It is a few moments before I realize he is doing it on purpose, and noticing his lurking smile, I dip my long pole into the water and sweep it up, showering him with a cascade of sparkling drops. The men roar at this retaliation and a truce is called.

At last the final sheep has taken her plunge and we drive the flock out of the gorge into the sunlight. I feel very happy as I trudge behind in squelching gum-boots. The sheep move slowly now, stringing out along the path and now and then stopping to shake themselves. Their fleeces are still heavy with water. The dogs, too, seem subdued.

We ford the river again and the ewes go over quietly, and then slowly up the hill to the house. 'We must let them have their time,' says Tom. They are reunited with their offspring and we go in for tea. Afterwards the whole flock is returned to the mountain, the men hurry off to get their milking done and I call in our cows. It seems much more than twelve hours since I took my stool to the dark shed and milked with Jane's grey flank near my cheek. A lot has happened today and I feel tired and very peaceful.

Our shearing day was to be a week later. The larger the farm, the more shearers are required to finish the work in a day, and the more days a farmer must give to his neighbours in return, to repay them for their help. Carneddi, with its small flock, does not need many men, but that year there was a big gathering. The reason for this, I suspect, was partly for a close view of Carneddi's new occupants and their antics, but chiefly because mountain farmers are always courteous and helpful to a newcomer. Tom was in charge again. The flock was gathered from the mountain, and the lambs sorted out and let loose in the field adjoining the pens. A row of benches was set out along the field wall where the shearers would be partly protected from the hot, June sunshine, and the men took their seats. Besides the helpers of washing day there were Jones's father, William Williams, portly Hugh Roberts from Tylyrni and Jack Humphrey Ty Newydd. There was lanky Arthur from Cwm Caeth who preferred to shear standing, doubled hairpin fashion, but who could turn out shorn sheep faster than anyone else. There was Owen Jones Tanrhiw who did not shear but who was kept busy all day long rolling the fleeces, and Frank Hughes who had come all the way from Oerddwr, the lonely, beautiful sheep farm on the flanks of Moel Hebog.

Tom was catching the sheep to supply the shearers, and my father had the job of stamping the shorn ewes with our wool-mark, the letter H on the left shoulder. The Griffiths family had been at Carneddi for generations and the H stood for Hywel, a family Christian name. We saw no reason for changing it now, particularly as it was known to farmers for miles around as the Carneddi mark, and our strays would be quickly returned to us. The occupants might change but the farm and the flock was always there.

'Come on Ruth, where be your shears?' cries John Williams suddenly. 'Let's see what you can do.'

I had not thought to shear before all these watching eyes but before I know what is happening I am firmly seated on a bench beside him, with William Williams on my other side. A ewe is plonked into my lap and I begin to work under the paternal instructions of the two of them. The wool is first trimmed from the belly and legs, and the legs tied. The sheep is then turned on its right side and the left side, starting from the neck, is clipped in long sweeps from belly to spine so that rain will be shed easily instead of soaking into the skin. About half an inch of wool is left to protect the ewe. If a bad spell of weather comes immediately after shearing and a ewe is badly shorn, she may die of exposure. The sheep is then turned over so that the free half of the fleece falls clear, and the right side is shorn. The fleece comes away in one piece, creamy-white on the inner side, grey and ragged on the outer, and is rolled into a neat bundle by Owen Jones, with the grey side inwards, and lapped with a band of twisted wool. The shorn ewe, with feet still tied, is dumped on the ground to be carried away, stamped and released by my father. If Tom keeps a shearer waiting even for a minute there are loud cries of '*Eto*, another' or '*Llwdn*, a wether'; this last because the wethers are in better condition than ewes which have had the strain of pregnancy and rearing lambs, and so are easier to shear.

I work away with concentration and, being afraid of nipping the skin, I am very slow. I look up to find Jones by my side with a bunch of grass in his hand.

'What's that for?' I ask.

'Why, for the ewe, of course. She must be getting hungry after all this long time!'

This produces a roar of laughter from the others but I do not mind. I feel they are pleased to see me learning and John Williams says that in the old times the womenfolk always came out to shear, although none do so now. At last my ewe is finished and I take another and another. I notice that Tom is picking the easy ones for me, with bare bellies and the wool rising well from the skin. I am glad as I have a horror of cutting the sheep, but John Williams sees this and tells me: 'It won't harm them none to get a button-hole or two.'

We go in for lunch when about half the flock is done. It is

hotter when we come out again and there is less talk now, only the steady click-click of the shears and the rustle and bleat of the sheep in the pen. Tom is having more difficulty in catching them; they are no longer so tightly packed and race round and round the wire. He hauls out the two rams and gives one each to Jones and Arthur. It is a compliment to be given a ram to shear as its appearance at the autumn sales depends much on the way it is shorn now. With the heavy fleeces gone, the rams look much smaller, and trot away, half indignant, half ashamed, like old gentlemen turned out in the street in their long winter underwear.

The last sheep is done and we troop to the house for a late tea. It is Midsummer's Day and although the sun is sloping towards Hebog there is plenty of daylight left. The men are talking about their own shearing days in the coming week. Will Ruth come to Corlwyni, to Beudy Newydd, to Cwm Caeth, to Garddllygaid-y-dydd to give a hand? She certainly will, and is pleased and honoured to be asked to take a part in the work. Tom will be the real representative of Carneddi, skilled and experienced, who will return some of the skill and experience which has been so willingly given today, but Ruth will come and do as much as she can.

And so it turned out. I helped at the shearing of all the neighbouring flocks and the standard of my work began to improve. I counted the sheep I sheared that season and they numbered eighty. I was often given the easiest ones and indeed some of them were nearly nude, having lost their wool in the mountain, but all the same this seemed to be a satisfactory beginning.

5 Grey Skies

By that summer we had made improvement to the farm-house. Piped water had been carried to the house and cowshed, and sinks, basins, a bath and w.c. installed. Even with the aid of a grant we had found it a costly and worrying business. Labour was hard to obtain and materials controlled and expensive. A tank of a thousand gallons capacity had been built just below the spring, the source of our water. This was a hundred and fifty yards away up the slope of the mountain behind the house, but it provided a natural gravity feed and there was a good pressure of water in the taps. The congestion of furniture in the house was now further aggravated by the fact that one of the tiny bedrooms had been turned into a bathroom. We said good-bye to the hip bath and our endless white-enamel pails almost with regret. Their going was a step away from the classic simplicities of country life, but the result was practical and increased the efficiency of the farm.

One change that we did not regret was the departure of the old, black, maddening kitchen range. We were completely thankful when, after months of waiting, it was replaced by a large slow-combustion stove, an ideal-home dream of stainless steel and vitreous enamel. This cooked perfectly, heated the kitchen and the bedroom above, and never once puffed furious, black smoke in our direction as had been the custom of the range.

We had bought a horse, Corwen, with the help of the farmer who had purchased Jane for us. One of the first jobs for which Corwen had been used was the carting of the stove. The lorry could get no farther than Beudy Newydd and there dumped the crates, weighing a hundredweight apiece, on the side of the road. These were heaved into the cart and carried, one at a time, up the track to Carneddi.

Corwen was a great delight to me. She satisfied my longing to have a horse of my own, although she was only a carthorse with a docked tail. The management and ways of a horse, the handling and harness were all familiar to me from childhood days at the riding school. Here was a side to farming at which I was not a complete beginner, and I took great pleasure in looking after Corwen, keeping her well groomed, and the elderly cart and harness, with its joining bits of string, as smart as possible. She might be long in the tooth, her back might sag and her tail be a mere wisp, but she was a real horse. She had a velvety nose and a stiff little moustache on the upper lip. She had a pleasant whinny of welcome when I opened the stable door and she was also reputed to be in-foal.

She was invaluable to us. The road to Carneddi degenerated beyond Beudy Newydd into a couple of ruts over the grass, with loose shale in the steep places. In wet weather it was hard for a horse and all the times impassable for any vehicle without four-wheel drive. The improvements we hoped to make at Carneddi would require materials, and these had to be transported somehow up the road. My father had begun to write anguished letters to the Rural District Council about the non-existent state of the road, our isolation, the depopulation of mountain areas and anything else which he thought might persuade them to take action. In the meantime we had Corwen, and she and I thoroughly enjoyed being the lifeline to the farm.

Then in that summer of 1946 I fell in love. It was a state I had never much considered, never sought and never longed for, except as a possible occurrence in the far-distant future. The inspirer of this deep emotion was not a native of the British Isles nor staying in them long. There was no happy ending, nor need there have been. If he saw youth, beauty and love in me that summer, as I believe he did, it was because he bestowed them. But one person, one time and one place were only a part of life and the world to him, the whole of which he found fascinating, and so there came an end. This occurrence is only of importance to the story of Carneddi in that it left me profoundly unsettled. The mountains are not a good place for the untranquil. Their unchanging form and grave beauty turn the mind inwards and one needs long roots of calm and spiritual integrity to come to terms with them. There are few distractions and palliatives here and one is left face to face with oneself.

I was unsettled. I began to feel that after all I had imprisoned myself in the hills and that life, youth and enjoyment would pass me by. I had frequent letters from Anne and Paula and they both seemed to be having a better time than I. They sent accounts of parties and excitements of which I had none. Mary was at Girton in a world of culture and learning. Perhaps I was not yet quite better from my illness for everyone seemed to be doing something better than I. I would stagnate and become a yokel. Feverishly I longed to circulate again. The pleasures and interests of the farm and the added comforts of Carneddi were as nothing to my sudden feelings of loneliness and longing. I decided, since I could think of nothing better, to go to college. This necessitated my studying Latin to School Certificate standard and taking an entrance examination. I went back to town leaving my father, mother and Fred to farm Carneddi as best they could, and took up residence with Paula, there to begin studying.

It is strange how the mind wanders from the pages of a Latin book to thoughts of a bleak little farm on the mountainside; strange how all these interesting people at the party seem a little unreal, their values a little false, their amusements a little futile. The snowflakes that winter, falling past the window and whitening the street outside, make me ponder their effect in the mountains. How are the sheep bearing this hard frost that grips the country, and these fierce blizzards? Strange how I feel all the time that I am in the wrong place.

The work, however, had to be done. I applied myself to study all through that cold winter, but when spring came and I had passed my Latin examination with distinctions, and also had passed the entrance examination to a Scottish university, I went home. I had done what I set out to do but, what is more important, I had proved to myself that none of it was what I wanted. Everyone was very much surprised; even Paula's father, a tolerant man, was moved to remark: 'Ruth is an odd person', but I was quite clear now; I wanted to farm Carneddi.

The destruction on the farm, caused by that grim winter, was not at first very obvious. We were not yet experienced enough to see the signs. My father said that eight or nine ewes had died while I was away, and he had buried them. There had been no spectacular snowdrifts, such as one hears about, burying dozens of sheep at a time, just day after day of iron-hard frost, covering the ground with a glaze of ice. The bitter winds had swept the snow clear from most of the farm, and where it did pile up there were no sheep sheltering. The walls and the gaps in them are well placed at Carneddi so that the flock can move round and keep clear of the snow. But there was nothing for the sheep to eat. Even the heather and gorse which stuck out from the white ground and coated in a hard glaze of ice. The sheep slowly starved all through the winter, with the heavy fleeces masking the skeleton bodies. It was at lambing time that the effects of the winter became apparent. A few ewes were so weak that they died in giving birth to their lambs, but it was among the lambs themselves that there were the greatest losses. Many were born dead, some only partly developed. Many more were so weak that they quickly fell a prey to the foxes and carrion crows. The ewes had little milk for them and, long after they should have been safe from these menaces, we found their unthrifty little bodies with the eyes and tongue pecked out or the head bitten off by a fox.

In spite of our inexperience the Carneddi flock did not seem to have suffered worse than others in the neighbourhood. In fact we had lost fewer ewes than had some, but it was a great set-back to us. There were only nine ewe lambs to send away to wintering that autumn; the wool cheque in the summer was less; there was only a quarter of the usual number of wether lambs to sell and it would be three or four years before we could bring the flock up to strength again. A relief fund was instituted and from this we received £25, help indeed, but only a fraction of the loss we were to feel for several years.

We had also suffered losses among the poultry. We had reared about three dozen chickens, under broody hens, the year before and they had just begun to lay well when the cold weather came. Snug houses and careful management would have kept egg production up, even in the worst weather, but there were the foxes. The hard winter seemed to make them particularly bold and they raided the poultry-yard regularly. Even one or two hens missing from such a small flock made a difference, but foxes are wanton killers and maul bird after bird until disturbed. Mot became alert to the least flutter from the hen-house and would rush from his bed in the cowshed and drive the marauders away. Even so we lost most of our birds that year.

Besides the damage that the hard weather had caused, it was clear that my parents could not manage the work without me and, even more important, they had reached a time of life when the responsiblity for this changed life and the initiative it required were a burden to them. I began to feel that it was no longer a case of my helping them, but of their helping me. That I knew I should get so much help spurred me on. Both of them loved the life, and the thought of taking work in town again was anathema to my father; he liked doing jobs about the farm. I took over the accounts and filled in the forms, and I opened a bank account. I was now nineteen.

Farming was still feeling the post-war prosperity and prices were reasonably high; also in our favour was the fact that we had bought Carneddi, with its live- and dead-stock, at a surprisingly low figure; there were few farmers in business who had laid out so little capital as had we. On the other hand Carneddi was small, the type of farming was limited by the nature of the land and it had never provided more than a very low standard of living for its occupants. And we had been used to a high standard of living. It was fatally easy to drain away the last of the precious capital on the day to day luxury-necessities that we had always had. It was painfully hard to adjust our ideas to this.

But I was beginning to realize it. We should have to farm more intensively than is the usual practice on hill farms in order to maintain a standard of living even approaching that

61

which we had in the past. Here I was confronted by my own ignorance. How was I to do it? Then I thought of the book I had read two years ago, *The Farming Ladder*. Mr. Henderson had begun farming with no capital at all and, over the years, by hard work and careful planning, had built up a business that was extremely prosperous. Here was a man who obviously knew his job. And his farm was worked by pupil labour. If I could become one of his pupils, I was sure I could exchange ignorance for experience and afterwards use my knowledge to turn the financial tide at Carneddi before it left us high and dry. The situation was not yet desperate, but I had a feeling it might be later if we made too many mistakes or had more bad luck. I wanted to be prepared. I loved the mountains now but I had seen their harshness and I needed strength to meet it when the time came.

I wrote to Mr. Henderson asking him to take me as a pupil, and setting out my modest qualifications as attractively as I could. Then I waited. In a few days the reply came. I opened it. There was my own hopeful letter inside and, printed across the top with a rubber stamp, were the words: 'NO VACANCIES. Number of applicants make more formal reply impossible.' It seemed very final. I was only one of hundreds who had had the same idea as I. There was no hope for me here.

I read *The Farming Ladder* through again. Perhaps I could gain the elusive secret of success from its pages. It was an astonishing story of personal achievement, and an inspiration to agriculture generally. If only I could learn its lessons. Before he began to farm on his own, Mr. Henderson had occupied the post of pupil on various farms and learnt his job thoroughly. This is where I had gone wrong, I thought, but perhaps it was not yet too late to put it right. I decided that since I could not go as a pupil to Oathill, Mr. Henderson's farm, I would try another place and learn what I could. A year away from Carneddi might not make too much difference at this stage, and we should reap the benefits of my extra knowledge later. If my parents could only keep the farm going in a modest way for another year, I could fit myself to run it more profitably on my return.

I advertised in the farming press and, after much thought,

chose a farm in the Isle of Wight from among my replies. In the New Year of 1948 I went there. It was a farm on rich land suitable, among other crops, for growing early potatoes, and there was a well-managed, pedigree herd of Jersey and Guernsey milking cows. The farmer and his wife were most pleasant, the sort of people I had met before, but in this was a disadvantage. They had not been born to farming; the capital they had invested in the farm had not been earned from the land, and they had not lived from the land through the lean times as well as the good. I had no means of knowing if the farm really was a business proposition, and they had many luxuries which I suspected a real working farmer could not afford. I felt that after all I might not get the hard type of education that I needed.

But there was much to learn that would be useful. It was revealing to be employed for a change, instead of being the boss. Here I learnt to operate a milking-machine, manage high-yielding cows—so unlike our Welsh Blacks which were tough enough to put up with anything—and I saw artificial insemination used. Much of what I learnt would not be directly applicable to Carneddi, but it would provide a background and a yardstick to assess my progress.

It was the first time I had been away from home for more than a holiday—Paula's house always seemed like a second home. I was painfully homesick all the while, but there was a sort of fierce pleasure in measuring myself against the outside world after the sheltered family background that had been mine for all of my twenty years. I found I was making the grade. My employer seemed to think I was quite satisfactory in the post I filled, and even praised me from time to time. I learnt to hide my homesickness under a calm exterior. The worst time was in the early morning. I was up and out in the cowshed by half-past five. A chill sea-mist shrouded the buildings on those dark February mornings. Far away the muffled hoot of a fog-horn sounded, where unseen ships passed in the Solent. The smell of the sea was everywhere and it was bitterly cold. Glaring electric-light, the hard concrete expanse of the cowshed, the pulsating of the milking-machines and throbbing engine were a background to my heavy heart. I thought longingly of my own stuffy cowshed on the Welsh hills, where milking seemed a delightful task under its aged beams, where work was preceded by a cup of tea drunk sleepily over the warmth of the Aga, where it was followed by the lovely freedom of self-imposed tasks about my own farm. But I was learning to work harder here than I had done at Carneddi. Self is often an indulgent task-master, but now I would work twice as hard when I was home again. Also I was earning good money, and so I determined to stick it out.

But suddenly I found I was losing more on the roudabouts than I was gaining on the swings. Mother wrote to me from home saying that Corwen was dead. She had developed pneumonia and died in a couple of days in spite of the vet's attention. I had insured her for £40, the price we had paid for her, but the insurance period had just expired. The company would gives us an *ex gratia* payment of £25 and that was all. It was a loss. I wondered if I could have saved her, had I been at home. Perhaps I might have noticed the signs of illness sooner. It was a tormenting thought. There were other difficulties too. The goats had died from liver-fluke, without the family's guessing what was the matter. They were not an important part of the farm, but they were old friends. My father was finding he could not keep up with the farm work, everything was getting behind. And they missed me.

It seemed that my plans for learning more about farming were going awry. If I stayed away much longer the benefits I already had would all have drained away. It seemed that after all I must learn in the slowest and the hardest way, at home, by trial and error. I gave in my notice to my employer, and went back to Carneddi for the second time.

6   Hens and Hay

It was wonderful to be at home again. At last I was convinced that no other life would suit me so well as farming in the mountains, and that there was no quick and foolproof way, now that we had already begun, of learning how to do it. My two departures from Carneddi had taught me this. I still longed for a short training period at Oathill, but of this there seemed no chance. However, the workings of a hill farm were beginning to seem less unfamiliar; already I had made progress and mastered many of the tasks, I was resigned to the fact that I would meet few people, that indeed I should live a very quiet life, but the great interest of the farm and the goodness of our neighbours more than compensated for this. Indeed as time went on, odd and interesting people, perhaps to be found only in out-of-the-way places, could be discovered wandering on our mountainside. If, occasionally, the responsibilities of running the farm seemed heavy, they were also a sign that I had reached the pleasant state of being grown-up. In spite of financial worries in the background we had so much that money could not buy—good health, freedom and creative work in a beautiful setting.

The first step towards more intensive farming and a better income appeared to be an increase in the number of our poultry. A well-managed hen would pay for herself and show a profit in twelve months, while it would take three years for a heifer to show a return. I did not want to neglect the sheep and cattle, mainstay of a hill farm, so the hens were to be a sideline, and I hoped to develop a long-term policy while netting in some quick returns.

The greatest difficulty was the lack of feeding-stuffs. Our

65

hill land was quite unsuitable for growing poultry food. Land which could be ploughed was only to be found in half-acre patches in the dips of the mountainside, and even these were studded with huge, glacial boulders which snapped the ploughshares, while the cool wet climate of the hills was unfavourable for ripening grain. Purchased feeding-stuffs were rationed and Carneddi, as an upland sheep farm, received an allocation which would just about support nine hens—and nine hens would do little to solve my problems. If my poultry were accredited under the Poultry Stock Improvement Plan I could draw a ration for the birds I kept, but starting an accredited flock also presented problems. At least fifty home-reared, pure-bred birds were required to qualify, and these would have to be reared on nothing more substantial than fresh air and a beautiful view. Since this seemed to be the only way to get a food ration, I determined to do it.

I bought some day-old pullets, hatched from Henderson eggs. If Henderson Light Sussex were profitable in Oxfordshire they might be profitable in Wales too. I reared them in a home-made, hay-box brooder, being anxious to save as much on equipment as I could. The capital costs of starting a poultry unit can be high with all the odds and ends, the nest-boxes, the perches, drinking vessels and feeding troughs that are required besides a good house. At the same time I wanted to avoid the make-shift appearance which so many poultry units assume, and I ordered a well-made poultry cabin to house the fifty birds.

The chicks grew and did well. I lavished attention on them and had almost no losses. I boiled large pans full of potatoes; I simmered fish heads and tails until they were reduced to jelly, and used a minimum of meal to make a mash out of the brew. The kitchen reeked, but it was worth it. Even the cows gave up their concentrates so that the hens could have something to eat.

The foxes were a menace still. It was necessary to let the birds range as far as possible to pick up some natural food to help balance their unorthodox diet, but I confined them to their house until after breakfast. Meal times were a danger period. With everyone inside and the dogs near the farmhouse, a fox could slip down from the hill unseen. Sometimes my father sat waiting with the gun, but the fox never appeared when he was ready for it and so, discouraged, he gave up. At my request, he taught me to fire the gun. I hated it. After a few sessions with tin cans on a wall, I retired from the practice with a bruised shoulder and a deafened right ear. It seemed we were not a sporting family. We developed a more successful method of keeping the foxes at bay. On misty days when visibility was bad, or when nobody was working near the poultry field, we would go as far as the cowshed and let out a few piercing shrieks from time to time. This appeared to be highly effective in discouraging a raid, and we never lost a bird on days when this was done regularly.

One day when mist hung low, Fred volunteered to make the fox-frightening noises. A heavy drizzle had begun so she put on her mackintosh as she went out. Mother and I were making marmalade in the kitchen. After a few minutes, Fred returned looking shocked.

'I've just had a horrible experience,' she said.

She seemed so overcome for a moment that we could hardly get the story from her. She had gone out to the cowshed and, looking up through the mist, had seen the hens sheltering peacefully under the henhouse. She had shouted and hallooed in her very best manner and was about to return to the house, thinking the hens would be safe again for a time, when she found herself looking into the eyes of three hikers, sheltering under the wall. She had not noticed them before. The look of fascinated terror on their faces caused her to flee into the house without saying a word. We laughed, but it was no joking matter to Fred. It was days before she ceased to worry about what those hikers must have thought of her.

Foxes were not a constant menace however. There were hundreds of them living in rock dens in the mountain, but it was only the occasional one that took to killing our poultry. If it were destroyed, we had peace of quite long periods. The £1 a head reward for a dead fox made their destruction quite profitable, and some of the local boys were expert at killing them with gun and terriers.

We lost only three or four hens to foxes that season and the rest grew into good birds. Mr. Ephraim, the County Poultry Advisory Officer, inspected them, seemed to think they were satisfactory and I applied to become a probationer on the Ministry of Agriculture's accreditation scheme. At the end of June two officials came to see the flock. I had made the henhouse look as tidy and efficient as possible, but I wondered if they would find the scale of my poultry-keeping too insignificant and my arrangements too simple. I had no incubator, no elaborate brooders, only fifty sprightly, red-combed pullets and the house they lived in. The panel inspected, greatly admired the view and went away again. They could give a recommendation to a higher official, but not the final verdict. In the meantime I boiled the fish heads and potatoes, scrounged a bushel of corn here and a parcel of stale crust there, for it was not until October that the ultimate expert would arrive. Sometimes I hardly knew where the next day's feed was coming from, but somehow it was produced and the pullets not only lived but laid. The days were shortening and leaves in the wood turning yellow, when Mr. Ephraim and the last inspector arrived. The birds were viewed, tea was drunk and then they left, but not before Mr. Ephraim had murmured that he thought my birds would qualify for accreditation. And so it was. I was accepted into the Poultry Stock Improvement Plan, and every month a fat envelope of food coupons arrived by post. I could expand as I chose.

Later in the month Mr. Ephraim told me that George Henderson was coming to give a talk at Pwellheli. Here at last was an apportunity to see the man whose book had encouraged me so much, and to listen to words of wisdom from his own lips. The town where he was to lecture was twenty miles away. The connections of the country bus service were poor, so Mother and I decided to go for the day. We started early in the morning. It was pleasant to look round new shops together and eat a hotel meal. Farm life, our isolation and infrequent buses usually allowed only for a brief, weekly shopping trip to Portmadoc, so we enjoyed this full day out. We were in our seats in the lecture hall early for it seemed an important moment in my farming progress.

When George Henderson came on the platform he began

by quietly recounting some of his farming experiences at Oathill; he spoke of his early days as a farm pupil, and went on to give advice to young people who were just beginning. Work, Muck and Thought was the magic formula he offered to us, simple and straightforward, and yet I thought there must be something extra which made him succeed where others, with seemingly equal advantages, had failed. His methods were irreproachable, his timing perfect; all sounded so simple, but perhaps there was a touch of genius as well. Indeed I had much to think about.

After the talk was over Mr. Ephraim, who knew something of my preoccupation with Henderson methods, brought him over to speak to me. It seemed they had been to Carneddi while Mother and I were out. I regretted the lost opportunity of reopening the subject of working at Oathill as a pupil, but there was no help for it now. People were leaving the hall, time was running out and I had not the courage to ask again in that atmosphere of departure. Then Mr. Emphraim said: 'You missed a good pupil in Miss Ruck.' My hopes rose for a moment, but Mr. Henderson was smiling and saying goodbye. It was obvious that I was not considered particularly suitable for the coveted position of an Oathill student. But it had been an interesting afternoon, and, before I left, Mr. Ephraim told me that he was leaving his post as Poultry Advisory Officer to begin a hatchery. He would like to buy my eggs for hatching if I wanted to sell. This was good news. Hatching eggs usually command a third more in price than eggs for eating, and this could make the difference between a good profit and a bare one, or between a profit and a loss. Also Mr. Ephraim was knowledgeable and he was fair. I felt I could deal with him happily. It had been a satisfactory day.

My poultry scheme was well under way now. With a local market, sufficient food and good stock, I began to make progress. In the isolation and rigorous mountain conditions of Carneddi the birds remained healthy and hardy, and we were, perhaps, unique in keeping an accredited flock in so wild a situation. Over the next two years I expanded to two more units of fifty, making a hundred and fifty birds in all, and bought two more hen-cabins. A hundred of these birds were pullets, the third house being made up of the best yearling birds from the previous season. Each spring I raised a hundred pullets and sold fifty yearlings and fifty two-year-old birds, so keeping the numbers constant. The pullets were mated to Brown Leghorn cockerels to produce a sex-linked chick, very popular for commercial egg production, and the mature birds were mated to Light Sussex cockerels to provide pure-bred chicks for my own replacements.

I sited the hen-cabins on rocky ground of the rough-grazing land. Our tiny hayfields, although flatter, were too precious for poultry, for we needed all the hay we could get. Also the hens, with busy, scratching feet and widely-distributed, fertile droppings, wrought an amazing change in the turf in places where no machinery could have reached it. They combined diminutive but effective harrowing and manure-spreading operations with their business of egg-layings. They scratched out the moss and broke down the stiff tussocks of molinia grass, while sweeter grasses and wild white clover came in its place. The improvement was so marked that I was asked to send turf to the Royal Welsh Agriculture Show for a demonstration of the effects of poultry-keeping on grassland. Two sections of turf were taken early in the spring, one from near the poultry house, one from similar ground where the hens had not ranged. These were grown on large wooden trays until the time of the Show, when they were exhibited with samples from a lowland farm and also a marginal farm. The improvement after poultry was marked, but the Carneddi mountain turf showed the most striking difference of all.

The wind was our enemy. We drove oak stakes into the ground at the corners of each house, and lashed the houses down with a double strand of twisted fencing-wire. I did not want to see the huts and hens whirled away in the fury of the gales which strike this ridge in wintertime. The houses were also chocked up on stones so that the birds could find extra shelter underneath in driving rain. After ten years they still stand, buffeted by wind, drenched by rainstorms and sometimes drifted over with snow. Quantities of eggs continue to be produced within, and in winter, spring and early summer they go each week to the hatchery in Anglesey to become chicks which are sold to farms far from the mountain where they first began.

We spread the manure from the hen-houses on the hay fields. With the coming of early summer the grass was growing lush and brilliantly green, a heavy crop for mountain fields, and I was glad that the poultry, while being profitable themselves, were helping to increase the productivity of the rest of the farm. Hay was a valuable crop, and the cows were an important part of the farm's economy. Although milk yields were low and there could be no monthly milk cheque because of our distance from the road, the cows provided us with good calves for rearing, and cream, butter and milk for the house. They were tough, compact little animals, not much to look at, but extremely healthy. When tuberculin-tested cattle were rare in the county, we had ours tested, and they passed both tests with a clean bill of health. Our scrubby cattle now had the distinction of being an attested herd, and they were ideal for the farm. They climbed the rocks with the agility of goats, and scraped a living and produced milk from the heather and mountain grass in the summer, but in winter we had to feed them.

In those early days hay-making was a time of mixed anxieties and pleasures. To buy the £100 worth of hay necessary to keep the cattle over the winter would have been too great a drain on the farm's economy, and we worked our hardest to snatch in the short mountain grass before the fickle weather ruined it. The hay harvest is late here. The sheep flock does not leave the lower fields until first or second week in May, and so the mowing grass is not mature until July. Hay-making is a laborious job too. The steeply-sloping fields, with big boulders poking blunt snouts through the turf, do not lend themselves well to mechanization. In some places the gradient exceeds one in three, and the fields are all shapes. Wherever there was a patch of ground which could conceivably yield hay, those bygone farmers looped their walls to enclose it. In the middle of the fields there are rock outcrops, with a scrubby oak tree or two, and piles of stones, picked from the ground long ago when the fields were first made. Here and there rise the humpy backs of underground, slate-covered drains, obstruction to any mowing-machine.

At first we had used Corwen in the old Deering horse-mower. It was hard work, and I had to take the steepest slopes on the diagonal to prevent the mower bearing too hard on her on the downward cuts and the pull being too heavy on the upward ones. This meant that I was perched at a crazy angle on my iron seat. When we hit a rock, which happened often, Corwen would stop of her own accord while I raised the mower blade, and then start off with a rush when I was ready again. When she died in the spring of 1949 we were left without motive power. We considered the question and decided regretfully against having another horse. The work for a horse was only seasonal and we could more profitably keep a cow in its place. Also we needed road transport. The long walk up and down to the road and bus route took much time, and there was an increasing number of hatching eggs to deliver and poultry food to fetch. And so we bought a jeep. It was an ex-American Army vehicle with CRASH RESCUE TENDER painted in white letters on the front bumper. With a trailer it cost £200. I learnt to drive and my horizons widened with its coming. My father's repeated appeals to the Rural District Council had produced results; hard-core had been put on the track and in places it had been widened a little. It was still just as steep as ever and the surface was loose, but the danger of being bogged down in the peaty stretches was gone.

In preparation for the hay-making we took the shafts off the horse-mower and fitted a tow-bar. We adapted the hay-frames from the cart to go on the trailer. It was exciting work cutting the hay that year. My father drove the jeep and I perched precariously on the iron seat of the mower, ready to work the lever which raised the blade, when danger appeared. This came in the shape of the hump-backed drains, the rocks and the large moss-covered ant-heaps. There was no release mechanism on the mower arm as there is on a tractor-mounted mower, and when we hit a rock it was with a shuddering impact that sent me toppling from the seat. What seemed a painfully slow pace to my father, seated in the jeep, was a dizzy speed to me with the iron wheels of the mower bucketing over the rough ground. The machine, meant to proceed at a sedate two or three miles an hour, was now careering along at three times the speed, with the knife chattering madly through the grass. The obstacles approached at a frightening rate and it took all my strength to heave up the blade, with its weight of cut grass, in time to clear them. Sometimes the danger was not visible and it was not until we hit the rock that we knew it was there. The mower shuddered to immobility. The jeep's engine stalled and my father's hot and alarmed face was looking round to see where his daughter was. Stops for minor repairs were frequent but no irrevocable damage was done. It was amazing how the old mower stood its maltreatment.

For jeep mowing we found that the cut swath had to be raked back from the growing grass, otherwise it piled on to the blade and choked the knife on the next trip round. Mother, Mary and Fred were set to do this and they worked like slaves in hot sunshine to keep the path clear for the jeep as it came relentlessly round. If the patch we were cutting was large, each had a long stint to do and their rakes became a blur as they went faster and faster to keep ahead of the approaching jeep.

We could not turn sharply with a trailer mower; large pieces of uncut hay were left in the corners, and the fields were all corners. We hired John Jones to cut these with a scythe, and to mow the very steep places where it was dangerous to take the jeep. He was small, nearing seventy and had immensely powerful arms and shoulders. He liked to take seasonal work, moving from farm to farm and taking a job here and a job there. He had worked occasionally at Carneddi for many years and at Clogwyn higher up the valley. He was wise in country ways, knew all the farms for miles around and was very skilled at his job. We never had to tell him what to do; he would be cutting out the next corner before we had decided that it was the right one. He worked steadily all day long, with only an occasional pause for brow-mopping, a swig at his bottle of cold water and a few moments to sharpen his scythe. Each Monday morning he would arrive at the front door with his copy of the *News of the World* which he handed in 'for Miss Brown'. Fred was slightly indignant for the paper was not to her taste, but nevertheless she was seen to scan through it.

After the grass was mown we let it dry in the swath for a while. Then we spread it out, turned it again and collected it into big piles with our wooden hand-rakes. In hot weather, the short hay would be dry in thirty-six hours and we would cart it off rapidly to the barn. Every load under cover was a step nearer to peace of mind for us and good feeding for our cattle in the wintertime. But the mountains attract the rain. Three miles away on the slopes of Snowdon is a rain-gauge which records an average of two hundreds inches a year. At Carneddi we have about ninety inches, but the storm clouds which gather round the peaks shut out the sunshine and, though no rain is falling, our hay does not dry. It is maddening to look down to Harlech and see the sun shining brightly while we ourselves are under the umbrella of cloud. At such times Fred, who was always aware of the urgency of beating bad weather, found it hard to quell an impulse to heap armloads of partly-dry hay over the kitchen cooker so that some of it, at least, would be saved. It was a time of dilemma, of wondering whether we should carry this load which is still greenish, or leave it till tomorrow when it may be drier. We cannot be sure if the heavy, grey clouds now flocking up from the sea will thicken and give us steady rain for two or three days, or will disperse by evening and be followed by a dry night and a sunny day. In the hills our eyes are constantly turned towards the sky. With the meagre equipment of a mountain farm one cannot fight the weather, one must outwit it. The crucial week, day or hour of favourable conditions must be seized and exploited with all our resources, so that when the fury of the mountain weather breaks it is too late, the work is done and the labourers have departed.

The valley farmers also have floods. The rain which falls on the high ground collects in the hurrying streams and pours down to the river which can rise and flood in a single night. After a summer cloud-burst I have seen whole fields of cut hay swirled away down the rivers to the sea, and oat sheaves stranded two or three feet from the ground in the scrub of alder bushes which grow along the river's margin. After the river has subsided, a fine, gritty deposit is left on the fields, making the grass unpalatable to cattle for some time.

I learnt to use a scythe so that we could be independent of outside labour. Bracken-cutting is easy enough. The tough, succulent stalks stand up against the scythe blade and are soon sliced through, but grass flattens under the inexpert choppings of a beginner and springs up again after the blade has passed. 'If you don't sweat sharpening, you'll sweat cutting,' said John Williams, watching my attempts one warm evening. 'This is how we do get an edge on it,' and with a few skilled strokes with the grit-covered *stric*, the blade was razor-sharp again. He demonstrated its fine edge with some swinging cuts which sliced through the grass at ground level and heaped it neatly on his left.

Gradually I mastered the rhythm. It was heavy work but the muscles soon became used to it. We all grew tough and sunburned. Summer uniform on the farm was khaki shorts and a shirt. Arms and legs were brown, and my hair bleached nearly white in the sunshine. Calluses developed on our hands in that first year and have never since left them. After a while it was difficult not to become too much a creature of wide-open spaces and hard-working appearance. It was easy to say: 'The cows and sheep won't notice what I wear' and find one had become a little uncouth when suddenly faced with polite usages and social conversation.

Paula and Anne came to visit us each year in the summer. Old friendship was renewed with every visit and we talked till midnight every night. They were intolerant of dowdiness on my part. 'Really, Ruth,' they would exclaim, 'you can't wear this old thing any more,' and on the boiler it would go. Their friendship was invaluable to me. I was often lonely. The Welsh language was a barrier between myself and others in the district, although in time I learned enough to get the gist of conversation, and all were kind and friendly. Between jobs on the farm, Paula, Anne and I swam in the rivers, lakes and sea and climbed mountains together. They quickly became adept at farm work, and popular with the neighbouring farmers for their gameness and glamour. Anne achieved popularity one year at shearing time by stamping William Owen's pitch mark, the letter O, on to Arthur's defenceless rear as he stooped over a sheep. Their help at hay time was great and a couple of extra rakes in use made all the difference in getting the crop safely under cover.

We found that mowing with the jeep was wasteful in labour. With one to drive, one on the machine and two or three to rake back the swath, it was impossible to begin to turn the previous day's cut until we had mown enough for the day. With our limited tools we could not handle a large area, so we cut a small piece at a time and then, if the weather were bad, there was less hay to be spoiled by the drenching summer rain. But the work trailed on for a very long time. Most of the summer was occupied with gathering our hay crop and it was a relief when the final load was carried. Then Morris Williams of Dolfriog bought a tractor and Gwilym, his son, used it for contract work. It was a help to get our grass mown quickly and efficiently, and well worth the few extra pounds that it cost, for we were left free to toss the hay and cart it. We had to take our turn, however, among the other farms which hired the tractor, and often on a fine morning I would wait impatiently for the sound of the tractor coming up the hill. Sometimes it did not come, a repair was required or there was too much work elsewhere, and a fine day was lost. Gwilym worked hard to keep his clients satisfied, from dawn to late at night, but he could not give the same service as a tractor of our own. One day we would have a tractor, I thought, but at the moment it seemed far out of reach. In farming with little capital, I found, one has to learn patience, and so we waited and improvised.

7 Improvements

On the whole women do not make good employers, or so I felt. By nature they prefer to follow rather than to lead and the thought of employing a man can be a horrifying one. I now faced the prospect with reluctance. John Jones was different, and it did not worry me to give instructions to him. If they happened to be the wrong ones, he would tactfully point it out and offer an alternative course. He did a good day's work whether I were there or not, and belonged to the mountain setting as completely as if he had grown there, as indeed he had, while he stooped day-long over his scythe. But he was getting old. He was now entitled to his pension and so he gave up work. Now that I had acquired the skill of scything, he was no longer necessary at hay-time, but I had a new idea which would need extra labour.

In 1946 an Act had been passed to grant hill farmers 50 per cent of the cost of capital improvements to their holdings. The war had emphasized the importance of agriculture; and the mountains, last stronghold of a nation in adversity, were to be made more prosperous. Hill farmers, in their constant struggle with weather, rock and meagre, acid soils, were not often in a position to accumulate wealth and invest capital in their land and buildings. They had to accept a low standard of living or else retreat to the lowlands. Government grants, it was hoped, would give a new life to neglected hills and prevent the mountain folk from drifting away to join an already top-heavy urban population.

The grant scheme was just what we needed for Carneddi. Here was a chance to improve our land and buildings, decayed over long years of agricultural depression; a chance too of combining the best of the modern world with an old way of life, so that Carneddi would not be just a picturesque anachronism but a vital unit. There was a thousand pounds in trust for me, left by a great-aunt. It was the only financial security I had, but buildings and field gates, sheep netting, lime and fertilizers seemed infinitely more satisfying than bonds, however secure, and so we terminated the trust and I drew the cash. With careful planning and the aid of the grant I would get, the improvements would double the value of the money I spent. The scheme was also an incentive to begin to put our farm to rights in an orderly manner.

The Hill Farming Act required that the improvements should be comprehensive, covering all the capital needs of the holding. No grant, however, was available for enterprises that were not traditional to mountain farms. Sheep, calves and store cattle were approved, while poultry-keeping and milk production were not. This suited me. The hens were paying their way and showing enough profit to allow for gradual expansion, and milk production at Carneddi would never be worthwhile.

In the summer of 1949 the Hill Farming Officer came to see our land. Together we walked the rough acres, noting all their dilapidations and deficiencies, the smallness of the house, the collapsing stone walls, the gateways stopped with bedsteads and rusting iron sheets. Soil tests were taken and a recommendation made for the amounts of lime and fertilizer that were needed on the fields. The estimated cost and amount of work to be done was frightening, but it seemed difficult to leave out any of the items. The improvements could, however, be carried out over a period of five years and this limit was later extended.

All the work was to be done by direct labour. At that time it was impossible to get anything done by contract except at very high cost. Builders and materials were still scarce and it was difficult to lure workmen to anywhere as inaccessible as Carneddi when there was plenty of work to be had in more convenient places. My name was typed beside each item in a column headed 'Name of person responsible for having work done'. It seemed that I would have plenty to do. Now I needed to find a good handyman. I was now twenty-one and wanted to begin these major improvements to the farm without delay.

The preliminary draft read like this:

Description of proposed work	Estimated cost	
	£	s.
1. FARM BUILDINGS. Erect implement and store shed	180	0
2. FARM HOUSE. Recondition and enlarge farmhouse, including provision of an additional bedroom, dairy, pantry, sink and w.c.	1,200	0
3. ROAD. Improve about 100 yds. of access road	55	0
4. DIPPING ACCOMMODATION. Recondition dipping bath and pens	30	0
5. FENCING. Erect about 1,315 yds. of fencing with gates	207	16
6. LIMING. Apply lime to 10 acres of land	90	0
7. MANURING. Apply artificial manures to about 10 acres of land	38	15
8. SILO. Construct silo	30	0
	£1,831	11

The summer passed and still I had found no one to work on the scheme. My father and I were busy with the normal running of the farm. We were still rather slow and inexperienced; there seemed little spare time to give to major improvements, and also our own labour would not qualify for the grant. Then one day a friend of ours told me that she knew of a man in Beddgelert who kept a guest house, but wanted outside work for the wintertime. He was also a mountain guide and rock climber but was finding, as so many had before, that making a living in the shadow of the hills could be a grim struggle. He was, she said, a responsible type of person, he was English and his name was Paul Work. This took my fancy as being most suitable and I agreed to interview him.

And so Paul came on the scene. He arrived at the farm one

morning in October, a small, dark man in the middle thirties, with kind hazel eyes and a sudden, cheery smile. It was easy to talk to him; hours, wages and the work to be done were discussed and settled. We drank a cup of coffee; it was all decided; he would begin on the following Monday. I felt I had sailed through the interview with a fair degree of calm and authority; it had not been too bad after all.

The first task to tackle was the improvement of the road. The County Council had made it serviceable to within a hundred yards of the house, but there had stopped, and said the rest was our responsibility. Old parish boundaries seemed to be the reason for this abrupt halt. The remaining stretch was barely wide enough for the jeep to go up and down, and would not take heavy lorries which we hoped would one day bring anthracite, feeding-stuffs, lime and building materials right to our door. My father, now inspired by thoughts of progress, and Paul began the task of widening it. They hacked two feet of earth from the upper bank and wheeled it away in endless barrow loads to fill a depression by the roadside farther down the hill. It was a damp autumn and winter with low hanging clouds and days of drizzle, but still two mackintoshed figures worked tenaciously away in the wet, and little by little the bank was nibbled back. In places there was a patch of *suntur* in the soil they moved and this was spread on the road. It was sticky, grey gravel, left behind by glaciers long ago, and made a good natural dressing for an unmetalled track. As they worked, jutting shoulders of solid rock were exposed, forming obstacles across the newly-widened part. We asked Harry from Nantmor to put a charge in the three largest rocks for us. He came one afternoon. A hole was drilled in each, according to its grain and cleavage, the charge tamped down and big tree branches laid on top to break the force of flying fragments. The fuses were lighted and we retired to the top of the hill to watch. One after another the charges went off with a dull boom that echoed among the surrounding crags, and a shower of twigs, branches and shattered rock cascaded upwards against the dull sky of the winter's afternoon, and rattled down again in a wide circle. A large part of our work had been done in a few minutes but there was still much to do with a hammer and chisel. Sharp fangs of slate projected where the rocks had been blasted and would have to be knocked down. Slate splits easily. It is formed from the fine dark mud laid down thousands of millions of years ago on the floor of the Cambrian seas. Age after age of pressure and subterranean upheaval have compressed and hardened it, giving a wafer-thin cleavage to the rock which is the source of the roofing-slate industry in these mountains. Delicate trinkets such as the fans made from paper-thin leaves of slate, artistry of a quarryman's skill, are to be seen on some of the local cottage window-sills.

And so my father and Paul chipped and hammered away at those slate obstructions, and at last the road was widened. The way was now clear for heavy lorries to come up the hill.

Next we began to enlarge the sheep-dip from a capacity of thirty or forty gallons to a hundred and fifty gallons, and to repair and put new gates on the pens. The old pen gates had fallen to pieces every time we opened them, and were reinforced with bits of string and baling wire. Gatherings, shearings and dippings had been complicated by outbursts of sheep through frail places in the fencing, and by wether lambs hooking off their baby horns on stray pieces of wire. Now we made new gates which opened with ease; strengthened the fencing, and put sheets of corrugated iron round the lower part of it, making a strong barrier for our athletic ewes and guarding the lambs from entanglement. The small dip, made from slate slabs cleverly cemented together, was knocked apart, excavated and relined with concrete so that it would hold enough dip for the whole flock without refilling. In the New Year our pens became neat and business-like as befitted a hill farm.

Then spring came and lambs were everywhere. The outhouse was filled with chicks. Kale must be planted, the fields closed for hay and bracken must be cut. Also the tourist season was beginning and it was time for Paul to reopen his guest house. We should have to leave our improvement scheme until the autumn.

Carneddi was only one farm of many which benefited from

the Hill Farming Act. Aga cookers and porcelain baths were trundled up rough roads to farmhouses in the hills, where coal fires and buckets of spring water had been in use before. Miles of new fencing appeared, bracken was cut and lime spread. There were more cattle on the mountain and more sheep. Bright, white asbestos roofs were to be seen where none had been before, as old buildings were repaired and new ones put up. Some farms even had a new house to replace the old, now tumbledown, dark and cramped, and to be used in future for hens and calves. It was satisfying to see increased prosperity and production coming to the mountains. The Welsh dressers and china dogs could remain in the possession of their rightful owners and preside over shearing teas as of old. The Bed-and-Breakfast signs and Welsh Lady postcards still had a solid foundation of hill farming behind them.

When autumn came again Paul was back at Carneddi. Now we turned our attention to fencing the mountain wall which divided our farm from the open mountain and Crown land above. There was nearly a mile of this, dry stone walling made of loose blocks that once had lain scattered over the hillside. In places it had fallen over and the careless hooves of generations of sheep had further widened and enlarged the gaps. Here and there, on the better parts, some fencing was still standing and needed only a little new wire and a few staples to make it sound again. The oak standards which carry the wire will bear the weather for twenty, thirty or forty years, and even after the outer layers have crumbled the inner core remains as durable as iron. We felled a few of our tallest and straightest oak trees and cut them into seven-foot lengths. Then we split them with wedges and a heavy hammer, getting as many as forty standards from each of the best lengths. All day long the sound of Paul's hammer and axe rang from the wooded slopes below the house and, with autumn leaves drifting round me, I would go down with the cross-cut saw to assist with the felling of another tree. We became skilled at dropping the big oaks exactly into the desired position for trimming and cutting. When all the stakes were made we carried them, two by two, up to the highest crest of our land, three hundred and fifty feet above the place where once they had been growing. Each was fastened in position at four-yard intervals by a wire passed through the stone wall and tourniqueted on to the post. Then we strained two strands of barbed wire from post to post above the top of the wall, making a defence seven feet high and impegnable even to our athletic ewes.

Like us, Paul was inexperienced in the ways of a hill farm but he kept his eyes open, and between us we produced good and workman-like results, and we learnt fast as we went along. Having found someone pleasant and energetic, I did not now want to employ other and perhaps less congenial labour to speed the work. With occasional help from my father and me, Paul could do everything for our improvement scheme except the extension of the farmhouse which we felt was a builder's and architect's job. There was a great deal to be done but I was content for it to be spread over a long period. The bills did not come in at such an alarming rate, and all the time our experience was growing. We knew better what we needed and how it should be done, and so we proceeded cautiously and during the winter when Paul was free to work for us. In the end it took us eight years to finish the scheme. We lined the four roofless walls of a derelict hut by the cowshed with a sloping face of concrete to make a small silo. I did not want to be over-ambitious with silage-making. This method of grass conservation was new to the district and we had heard alarming stories of the contents of a silo becoming, not silage, but a sticky sort of compost. Our grass was too precious to be turned into manure without first having been eaten by an animal and, for a start, the experiment was to be a small one. We covered the silo with a sectional and removable roof for easy filling. If the venture was a failure the roof could be fastened down permanently and the hut used as a calf pen or food store.

The house extension job proved easier than I had imagined. As I was puzzling how it should be tackled, an architect friend of ours who lived across the valley offered to help. He drew plans, found builders and the work was begun. All I had to do was say what we wanted and cart the materials with jeep and trailer. We extended the house on the west side to make a sitting-room. No grant was allowed for this but it seemed a pity to miss the opportunity of making the house really comfortable when architect, builders and materials were all assembled together. I hoped I could spin out the money to cover it. On the east side, as part of the Hill Farming Scheme, a ground floor room was built for me with a long view over our lower fields to the woods and mountains beyond. This I used as office, sitting-room and bedroom. There was a second room, a scullery, dairy and downstairs w.c. After months of banging, of holes being knocked in walls, of cement on the kitchen floor and ladders and planks outside the front door, the little house had almost doubled itself and at last there was room to perform our growing activities. The churn no longer had to be dragged from under the stairs for butter-making. Piled trays of eggs were not constantly endangered by Mother and Fred as they swept and scrubbed. We could put our possessions away in cupboards instead of tidying them away from one spot to another. The overcrowded furniture was dispersed about the new rooms and became useful instead of merely an embarrassment.

William Owen came to see the improvements and was taken round the house. He looked at everything with silent admiration and nodded in approval at each change. Carned-dog, the bard, would scarcely have recognized his old home now. William Owen seemed pleased with the size of the new rooms.

'Plenty of place,' he said, 'plenty of place in Carneddi.'

So I invested everything I had in the farm. It was a long-term policy and time alone would show whether I had enough skill to make it produce returns. The inherent harshness of the land and the weather was still there but I felt we were better armed to face it now.

8 Climbing Novitiate

One day Paul and I were spreading lime. The work was part of our farm improvement programme. It was a mild day in January, so deceptively warm that one felt that spring had come already. With the jeep we had dropped bags of lime all over Buarth Ty Mawr, our best field. We loaded up from the big stack of bags which a lorry had dumped by the roadside and, as I drove, Paul heaved them off at ten-yard intervals to give a dressing of two and a half tons to the acre. Now we were slashing their paper coverings and scattering the pinkish ground limestone with our shovels. The finer dust swirled up round us in a light wind and the field began to take on a snowy appearance. After a while we paused to collect the empty bags and set fire to them. As the flames curled up through the paper and smoke wafted round us, we chatted lazily about the coming season and the time when Paul would stop work on the farm and begin his mountain guiding again. He offered to take me climbing one day, if I would like to try it. I was eager to go. It was impossible to live in the district and be unaware of the rock climbers; young men with coiled ropes were to be seen every week-end and sometimes the R.A.F. Mountain Rescue truck driving purposefully along; the hotels had a mountaineering aura and there was much talk of climbing. It was quite new to me and I was beginning to think it was time I ventured on to the crags.

Later in the week Paul took an old pair of hobnailed boots which I seldom wore and replaced the toe-plates with a few tricouni climbing nails and put two more into each instep. These, he said, would do for a start.

Then the weather changed again. For days an icy north wind swept down the Nantmor valley bringing snow and sleet. The land, which had stirred with a feeling of spring in those first warm days of January, now disappeared under a blanket of whiteness. We were back in winter again. Each day I walked round the farm stripping ivy from the trees to provide a bite for the disgruntled sheep. They were much put out by the disappearance of the grass and trailed along the sheep-paths in aimless files, hunched under the dirty greyness of their fleeces and bleating forlornly.

Early in February the snow melted in the valleys but the summits remained chilly and distant-looking in cloaks of white. The lower land was drab in contrast, with its shades of olive green and dun, and just below the snowline lay a dappled band of half-melted drifts with the turf showing through in grey-green patches.

One day Paul told me he had arranged a day's climbing with Bill Staunton and Brian Nicholson later in the week, and asked if I would like to join them. I said I would. We were to meet in Beddgelert and Bill would take us all to the Ogwen valley in his car, an open, liver-coloured 1921 Bugatti. I already knew Bill who lived at Aberglaslyn Hall and who was often to be seen zooming along the winding mountain roads in a succession of different sports cars. Brian Nicholson, it seemed, was a male nurse and, Paul said, a fine climber.

The day came and I arrived in the village to find the others already there. After greetings were exchanged and many athletic turns of the starting handle performed by Bill, the car's engine roared and we were off. Soon the speedometer needle was fluttering towards eighty miles an hour and the air, icy from the snowfields above, screamed past. Bill shouted that at slower speeds the car's plugs might oil up. The mountains, lakes, streams and stone walls flew by; this was exciting. The others were talking and laughing behind but their words were snatched away by the wind and lost in the din of our speed.

Now we were flying down the Helyg Straight, now past the Climbers' Club Hut, past the shores of Llyn Ogwen which was leaden under a cloudy sky, and finally came to a stop outside Ogwen Cottage. We climbed out and ropes, ice-axes and rucksacks were collected from the back of the Bugatti. We walked up the rocky path to Cwm Idwal. The air was icy and almost took one's breath away. We were already high; the waters of Llyn Ogwen are 1,000 feet above sea-level and the temperature falls one degree with every 300 feet of altitude. I was tough and fit from climbing Moel Dyniewyd after our sheep and could keep up with the men easily enough. Here the scenery was much grander than the foothills of our farm. Three thousand foot summits rose all around and it was bleak and treeless. Giant blocks of stone were heaped in confusion everywhere, and the bare bones of the rock stuck up through the turf. There was nothing to relieve the harshness of the scene, with its forlorn patches of snow merging into unbroken whiteness higher up.

We reached the shores of Llyn Idwal, cupped in the hollow of the cwm. Dead sedges were immobilized in ice, round its shallow margin, and high on the crag above was the great, black gash of the Devil's Kitchen. Paul made tea over a spirit stove in the shelter of an over-hanging boulder, and we talked and ate our sandwiches. We were going to climb the 400-foot Slabs, he said. The rock appeared to slope back at an easy angle but, as I looked up, I began to be apprehensive at the thought of scaling it.

Our lunch was finished and we prepared to rope together. Brian and Bill were going to climb Hope, and Paul and I the easier Ordinary Route. I began to take off my jacket ready for the exertions ahead, but Paul noticed and told me to put it on again: it would be colder still up there. Indeed the others had brought extra sweaters and were now putting them on.

Brian and Bill began their climb a few yards to the right and Paul started up the Ordinary Route. I stood below, an end of the nylon rope tied round my waist with a bowline, the other end attached to Paul now climbing rapidly upwards. About a hundred feet from the ground he stopped, belayed the rope to a flake of rock and hauled in the slack. It was my turn. I stepped into the crack and slowly worked my way up to where he stood. It was not so difficult; the rock was cold with icy water trickling down it but there were plenty of hand- and foot-holds. Paul showed me how to tie myself on to the flake, and then climbed up again and disappeared over a bulge. It suddenly seemed lonely. I looked down and saw that was nothing but air between myself and the lake, two hundred feet below. I found my knees were trembling. The cheery voices of Brian and Bill, lower down and away to the right, seemed only to heighten my isolation. Suddenly rock climbing had become a terrifying sport.

Then there was a gentle tug at the rope; Paul was ready for me to climb on. I could not see him and it seemed useless to shout: 'I feel sick' into that vast space of air and emptiness. With trembling fingers I untied the belay and began to crawl upwards again. There was a comforting tautness about the rope but it was obvious that nobody was going to haul me up; I must rely on my own buckling legs and shaking arms. Then Paul came in sight, a faint smile of pleasure on his face. I realized that it would spoil the day's sport for all three men if I asked to be returned, somehow, on to the ground again.

'Enjoying yourself?' said Paul as I arrived at his stance.

'Yes, thank you,' I heard myself reply through chattering teeth.

In another minute I was again belayed to the rock, and Paul was climbing rapidly and relentlessly upwards. The chance of declaring my fright had been missed, and every second made it more difficult to return to the safety of the ground. Another peep downwards, and the lake seemed infinitely far below at the bottom of a giddy space. I must go on after all, until faintness really overcame me. At that moment Bill's face appeared over a ledge, a few yards lower down. He shouted that they had found Hope too difficult in the cold and icy conditions and were following us up the Ordinary Route. It was a little more comforting to have them close behind.

It was my turn to climb again. I crept upwards expecting to fall off at any moment, but still my frozen fingers and trembling legs took me on. I kept as close to the rock as possible and the icy water streaming down it entered the cuffs of my groping arms, ran down my sleeves, down my body and out at the turn-ups of my slacks. The soaking material dragged at my knees and made every step up an effort. There seemed an endless number of pitches to the climb; first Paul would go up, then I would join him; one of us was always belayed while the other climbed. The final mists of vertigo never completely closed over my head, although I expected them to do so at any moment. I had ceased to look down now and concentrated instead on the few yards of rock in front, on the next crevice that would support a boot-nail, the next knob of rock that would provide a hand-hold; up like a spent caterpillar with the single idea of remaining attached to the rock.

At last I joined Paul on a ledge that seemed wider than usual. He made no move to go on but sat in the snow lighting his pipe.

'Well,' he said, 'this is the top. The rest is quite easy.'

I flopped down exhausted on a rock as far from the edge as possible. In spite of soaking clothes and limbs trembling with tiredness, a strange feeling of elation was bubbling inside me. It was possible to look down now at the lake and the great hollow of the cwm nearly 1,000 feet below without giddiness, but only a tingling sense of achievement. Two ravens, uttering their harsh croak, flew past, skimming and gliding on the icy down-draft from the mountain tops, yet they were still below our level.

Presently Bill and Brian arrived over the lip of the precipice, and there was a lighting of cigarettes, a coiling of ropes and a general discussion of the pleasures of the climb. I felt strangely detached. For the last hour I had had no thought for any part of my life, past, present or future except the simple, encompassing need to defy the laws of gravity. My mind felt washed clear of every past accumulation of worry and emerged tremendously alive. I saw the world with a new eye from this airy ledge. The massive significance of the mountains was dawning in my consciousness. This rock, this thin turf, this granite and slate, the kind of land from which I had been attempting to make a living for the past seven years, appeared in the different light. Having intimately tested their height on the plummeting rock-face, a new relationship with the mountains appeared, one that was destined, I felt, to stay with me.

Then it was time to go. I followed the men up the Senior's Ridge into the Nameless Cwm, then up a snow *couloir* and on to the Gribin. It was colder here and the snow was crisp with frost. A huge vista of white peaks half draped with cloud was spread out on every side, a wonderful world won by our own hard efforts. The sun, lost behind the mist, had sunk and it was getting dark. We began to descend, glissading down the hard snow in a flurry of ice particles and at exhilarating speed. Elated by the beauty of the evening, we shouted and laughed as we shot downwards from our white world towards the browns and greens of the snowless valley below. Glorious to go down so fast after having ascended with such infinite slowness, yet sad to leave the remote fortress of those chilly peaks.

It was almost dark as we reached the Bugatti and climbed in. Bill cranked the starting handle vigorously but nothing happened. Brian and Paul tried but still there was no result. Here was anticlimax after the ethereal world of snow and summits which we had left behind us. The four of us began to trot down the darkening road pushing the car but the gradient was gentle and we could not get much speed. Bill jumped into the driver's seat and let in the clutch. The Bugatti shuddered to a halt without firing once. We trotted once more, our boot nails striking sparks on the tarmac. The hill steepened but still the car would not fire; the threatened oiling up must have taken place. Soon the three men had their heads under the bonnet and were unscrewing the plugs. Bill slopped a puddle of petrol from a spare tin on to the road and lighted it, tossing the plugs into the flames. I stood on the roadside, soaking clothes clinging to my body and teeth chattering uncontrollably. It had been a wonderful day. I stood in a daze of physical exhaustion and discomfort but feeling tremendously happy. The others in their balaclavas and anoraks stood round the petrol fire until it died down. There was another delay while the plugs cooled enough to be handled but at last they were screwed back and the Bugatti's engine roared into life. Soon we were heading back along the road to Beddgelert. Ahead lay hot baths, food and fireside reminiscences. Later I found that I was so stiff after the day's experiences that I could not laugh with comfort for a week.

Now I longed to climb again. Brian suggested that I accompanied him a few days later and we went to Lliwedd, the 1,000-foot rockface that towers above Llyn Llydaw. It was again new ground and the immense crag, far steeper than the Idwal Slabs, looked unclimbable to me. Brian seemed quite confident however, and from the guide book we found the start of the Horned Crag Route. Once on the climb I felt more assured and all my attention was fixed on climbing well. I really enjoyed myself. The pause for sandwiches on an airy ledge with a great view all around, the sight of the little figures of hikers plodding up the Pig Track far away on the other side of the cwm, my increasing confidence, the stops for enthusiastic photography by Brian, the feeling of new-found esoteric intimacy with the mountains and the final stepping up from the shadows of the cold north-facing cliff into the sunshine at the top, were all new delights.

After this I climbed quite often, with Brian in his holidays and with Paul when he could spare the time. It was a long while before I overcame the first feeling of fright at the beginning of a climb but gradually and with experience it wore off. Soon I began to lead some of the easier routes but I found that I had not enough daring ever to be a brilliant rock-climber, or enough time to become even very practised. Even so we did many of the best classic routes and rock climbing became part of my life.

I was fortunate to have Brian and Paul for my teachers. Both were kind, patient, reliable and good company. Sometimes we went to the Ogwen valley. At week-ends climbers from Manchester and Liverpool were out in their hordes and the rocks were studded with figures in brightly coloured anoraks and woolly hats, in various stages of ascent and descent, in minor difficulties or progressing with practised ease, shouting instructions, complaints and encouragements to one another. In every direction the rocks were festooned with nylon ropes and parties queued at the foot of the most popular climbs. A string of parked cars would line the road with picnicking tourists watching the antics going on above. Usually we avoided the week-end crowds and climbed in more secluded areas or in winter went out in the middle of the week when the hills were silent and lonely, with only the sheep and the huddled grey farms blending into their ancient mountain setting. Now and then we enjoyed the sociability of the energetic town youngsters who loved the mountains as much as we did. It was on these occasions that I sometimes saw a beginner getting unsympathetic treatment and being bumped and bullied up a climb too hard for him. Then I was thankful that I had had Paul's or Brian's kind instruction.

Paul had been climbing since he was fourteen years old and had enjoyed the golden climbing era of the 1930s, when guide books were being compiled and the pioneering routes taken on Clogwyn Du'r Arddu, when climbing was a sport of the select few. He had climbed with Colin Kirkus and Menlove Edwards and led some of the severest climbs of those days, when the hemp line he used protected only the second man, never the leader. His reminiscences came out modestly, bit by bit. He had done two thousand different climbs and then given up the count some years before I met him. Recently he had found several new climbs in the Beddgelert district, a number on the Moel Hebog rockface overlooking Carneddi and one in the Aberglaslyn Pass. This gave an aerial view of the larch tree tips and the river roaring through the gorge, and was marred only by the cars which would gather on the road below, their occupants craning necks in the expectation of someone's falling off. There was another climb of his, Christmas Buttress, on Moel Dyniewyd, only ten minutes' walk from our house. It was a steep and difficult, three-pitch route on sound rock, which caught the morning sunshine and commanded a view of the elegant peak of Cnicht, the Moelwyns and Traeth Mawr stretching down to the sea. This crag I regarded as belonging to Carneddi. It was well away from popular walks and provided a perfect place to take friends for a private view of climbing.

Now Paul was devoting more of his time to introducing beginners to the mountains and less in climbing severe routes himself. He had helped Brian towards becoming a proficient mountaineer, as later he had helped me. Brian had rapidly taken to climbing and had linked it to his hobby of photography. Two cameras slung round his neck, one for colour and one for black-and-white pictures, were always part of his climbing equipment. On a minute ledge several hundred feet from the ground the cameras would come out, accurate adjustments be made and stupendous photographs captured. Diversions for photography were frequent. Once we came on a group of red-topped, white-speckled toadstools, a perfect subject for colour photography. After rearranging them into a more natural-looking group, Brian photographed them with great satisfaction. He also liked to take photographs about the farm, and it was not unusual to be startled at some task by a triumphant exclamation of: 'Captured for ever in Ferrania Colour.' He photographed every sort of subject, but his favourites were undoubtedly the mountain views. All were home-processed, beautifully and accurately reproduced and of professional standard; the valleys, the streams, the peaks and the fierce rock formations, a record of dozens of perfect days spent in the hills.

One of our climbs was particularly memorable. We went up to Llyn Llydaw on a grey day in September. It was showery, and we were late in setting out.

'Let's do something easy,' said Brian. 'It gets dark quite early now and it's rather cold.'

We looked through the Lliwedd guide book but it was difficult to find anything suitable. After some consultation we decided on the Slanting Wall, a climb of moderate difficulty. Brian led up. It was cold and I concentrated on the climbing which after all seemed quite hard. We ascended several hundred feet and paused for a rest underneath an overhang while Brian studied the guide book. At last he returned it to his breast pocket and stood up. The greyness of late afternoon was in the air and a light rain was falling. He cast an odd sort of look in my direction, said, 'I'll tell you something at the top,' then began to climb out of the niche and vanished over a ledge up on the left. By myself, I studied Crib Goch, fringed with a tattered edge of cloud, away over the cwm and paid out the rope. I hoped we were near the top by now or I should be late home for milking. It was odd how the rope slithered up so slowly, inch by inch, then a pause, then another few inches slipping up over the rock edge above my head. I wished he would go more quickly. Then my turn came. Up over the edge, and there was a great exposed slab ahead, veined with quartz and with a bow-shaped crack in the angle of a vertical wall. Brian was looking down encouragingly from a stance above. It was clear now why he had been so slow. The holds were nothing more than a roughness in the rock and the lower edge of the slab finished in airy space. The crack was of little help as the bulging vertical wall forced the climber's weight out again on to the naked slab. For the moderate climb I was finding it surprisingly difficult. In fact I was feeling a little frightened. Perhaps it was the cold and the thin trickles of water running down over the holds which made it seem so hard, but I said nothing and kept on inching upwards till I reached Brian's stance. Presently the route became easier and we finished the climb in near-darkness, and paused for a few moments to sit on a rock and watch light finally fading out of the sky.

'Well, that was hard,' I said.

Brian was smiling.

'Do you know what climb it was? It was the Slanting Gully, not Slanting Wall. I found out half-way up and it seemed too late to turn back then. There was a man killed on that climb once.'

Eagerly I read the account of Slanting Gully in the guide book. It was one of the big classic routes of Lliwedd although among the first to be climbed. It was classed as severe in wet conditions and was the hardest route that I had yet done. We had a feeling of deep satisfaction as we picked our way down the mountain in the darkness.

Other memories flock forward from the corners of the mind; that exposed ledge on the Gambit, described by the guide book as 'a situation of great charm'; the day on the Rocker route of Lliwedd when I split the seams of my slacks and found it difficult to climb in such circumstances; the Cave Pitch in the Great Gully of Craig yr Ysfa where the guide book suggests 'a pirouette to the south' as being the best means of reaching the chockstone; wet weather contortions in the depths of Lockwood's Chimney; fine weather delicacy and poise on big open slabs—a host of memories of sunshine and shadow, rain and mist, space and silence and the broken rocks of those ancient mountains.

9 With the Hendersons at Oathill

The Hill Farming Scheme was progressing steadily, the poultry were laying well and showing a useful profit, and the cattle and sheep were healthy and thriving. Gradually the pattern of hill farming was falling into place and the year's routine was being mastered. It was possible to plan ahead now as the sum of day-to-day experience added up to form a useful total. I was working less in the dark and we were also becoming less dependent on our neighbours for help. Now the mountains felt like home. The Welsh villages, with their slate and stone houses and four-square chapels, no longer seemed alien and depressing at times but expressive of the asceticism of the hills with their ever-present hint of austerity and struggle. The clear mountain air had given us a taste for space and freedom and town life had little to offer us now.

But my bank balance continued to flicker from red to black and back to red again. The cost of living was still rising and the flush of farming prosperity that came at the end of the war was over. The hundred mountain sheep, three milking cows with store cattle and calves, and the small breeding flock of poultry were still only a slender source of income. The stock we had was profitable but I felt there were a hundred ways we could produce more and save more if only I were wiser.

About this time I paid a visit to Oathill Farm. My longing to work there still bordered on obsession but it did not seem to produce corresponding signs of eagerness to employ me in Mr. Henderson. However, he agreed to show me round the farm when I was having a holiday in Oxfordshire. Knowing only a limited circle of relations and family friends until this time, it was stimulating to meet the famous and successful on my own account. Oathill Farm was familiar through the pages of *The Farming Ladder* and I recognized it from the photographs in the book. It was set in a saucer-shaped depression in the gently undulating countryside. Many buildings were clustered near the mellowed brick farmhouse, rows of poultry folds strung out over the fields and the land dotted with grazing cattle and sheep, and specked with the whiteness of innumerable hens. There was an air of dense concentration about the farm which was surprising after the eye had become used to the big blank Oxfordshire fields I had already passed, where only an occasional tractor at work or a bunch of cattle focused the attention. Mr. Henderson took me on a brisk tour of the farm. In my preoccupation with farming and its problems, and in particular their relationship with my own land and capabilities, I was intensely interested in all I saw. There was much modern machinery and many electric motors to take the hard work out of farming, but a flail and also a yoke for carrying milk pails still hung in the barn. Oathill had progressed from the simplest horse and hand tools to the latest farm equipment and yet the basic tradition of mixed farming remained. One felt that if the modern inventions of petrol and electricity were suddenly cut off, a few easy adjustments would keep the farm running much as before.

I met Mr. Henderson's fair-haired wife, Elizabeth, and had lunch with the family; I saw the farm pupils at work and felt I could be happy here. Before I left Mr. Henderson said he would put me on the waiting list in case he had a vacancy; at last I had visited Oathill and now I felt I had got a foot in the door.

We had been at Carneddi for five years and a change was to come; Fred was going to Australia. She was taking her mother out to visit a married sister who lived in Victoria. To lose Fred, even for a year, was an occasion for bewailing. Mother had engaged her as a nanny for Mary two years before I was born, and for twenty-five years she had scolded and loved us and regarded us as her own children. All the family depended on her; we considered her to be essential for our happiness; her fiery streak of originality was prized by us; we did not want her to go, and yet we had a sneaking feeling that since we had monopolized her for twenty-five years her own family ought to share her sometimes. We could not try to discourage her, although at heart we wanted to. I was Fred's own special darling and she had given me the happiest childhood. She was a most exceptional nanny. She had enormous dark eyes and long brown hair which she wore either plaited round her head or tucked in a ribbon in what we called her 'bowler hat' style. Occasionally she had allowed me the thrilling experience of cutting off large pieces of it when she considered it had grown too long. She had read to me for hours at night and had devised the most spectacular games. Once Mother had opened the front door to see, with astonished eyes, Fred whizzing down the stairs on a tea-tray to the sounds of shrieking delight from Mary and me. She was a good toboganner. She would roar down the wintry slopes of the park, her nurse's veil streaming out behind, a joyful light in her eyes, while all the small children gathered round to gaze in fascination at this enthralling adult.

As we grew up she supported our activities with a deep and prejudiced interest. We always knew that Fred would be on our side. When we moved to Carneddi the advantages of her country upbringing were apparent. She was an expert with paraffin lamps, at cooking under difficulties and nursing ill animals. She made hay with a devoted fervour that recognized the need to snatch every wisp into the barn before the storm clouds broke. She did not miss the lack of town amenities, but went on living in that nun-like seclusion which had always discounted the rest of the world except in so far as it affected us.

Now she was to sail ten thousand miles and leave an empty place in our family. It seemed an eternity before we would see her again. We watched her go, bumping slowly down the road on a dull autumn day, with my father driving the jeep. She waved till the last, torn by dividing loyalties, and then a turn in the road had hidden the jeep and we went sadly back into the house.

We exchanged letters but I missed Fred's encouragement in person. Patient listener to grumbles and complaints, joyful participant in new schemes and happy occasions, her presence was needed; letters were not the same. In the New Year she wrote to say that she was unable to get a berth on the next homeward-bound ship and would have to stay a month or two longer. The delay seemed unbearable but there was nothing to do but wait. April passed to May, and May to June. The lambs grew big and were turned up the mountain with their mothers. Fallen stones were picked up and put back on the walls and the fields closed for hay. The cattle lost their rough ginger-tinged winter coats and grew black and glossy, while the woods below the house were a spread of summer leaves. Even the mountains lost some of their harshness and attracted only harmless little white clouds out of the blue June sky. The shearing would soon be upon us, and Fred would be on her way home.

I wrote a joyful letter to Fremantle welcoming her on the first stage of the journey. She never received it. She wrote to say she would not be coming back. The passage on the boat was cancelled. She was going to be married.

Our first feeling was that it couldn't be true; Fred, who loved us and was part of our life and the farm, never to come back; Fred, who had regarded men only as a necessary evil and had had no truck with them before, was to be married. It was unbelievable. Then other feelings crept in. After all she had given us more than half her life, surely now she had the right to live one of her own. To have a husband and home would be a great happiness. We could not want to deny her that after all she had been to us. We rejoiced for Fred, but selfishly we mourned for ourselves as well.

It was strange to pack wedding presents for her, among them the silver cake basket that she had polished with energy so many times. It was difficult to get used to her absence, to know that it was useless to save up all our experiences to tell her, that we should have to write about them in letters or she would never know. I had an odd feeling that some vital part of myself had been amputated. I kept forgetting that she had gone for good and it was painful when remembrance came back; no more absurd jokes, no more crazy fits of laughter, no more visions of Fred crossly wrestling with the icing of a birthday cake, no more birthday poems and flowers, no more love and lectures and comfort to be gained from Fred in person.

And so some of the zest went out of my farming that year, and some of the colour and life of the family was lost. But the changing seasons were not halted and the shearing was followed by hay-making, and then came the bracken harvest and potato-lifting; the lambs went off to wintering and the rams were turned to the sheep, and all the tasks of a hill farm were performed in their order.

Then something new happened, something which helped to lighten the weight of sadness caused by Fred's going; a letter arrived from Oathill saying that now there was a vacancy there for me. Elizabeth Henderson was expecting her fourth baby and if I were willing to work indoors in the mornings I could spend the rest of the day on the farm. I was to go as soon as possible. My chance had come at last. It was a hard moment for my parents. With Fred gone, the running of the farm would mean even more extra work for them in my absence, but since I had set my heart on going to Oathill, since I was sure that the effort would be worthwhile, they were willing to manage.

Then there was a washing, mending and packing of my working clothes. I made a list of the farm tasks to be done at home, the details of calf and hen feeding, when this cow should calve or that one go to the bull. The urgent summer work was done and what my parents could not manage would have to be left until I came home again. I expected to be away for about six months. I felt that any neglect or losses at Carneddi that might happen would be justified in the end.

It was hard to say good-bye to the dogs and cats, to the sheep-dotted mountains now russet with dying bracken, to the harsh beautiful country that was home, and hardest of all to say good-bye to my parents and leave them with so much to do. I was glad that Paul had promised to come to Carneddi once or twice a week to help my father while I was gone. And so I left, hoping to bring back a store of knowledge, skill and experience that would help us all.

But it was an adventure. That first night at Oathill I hardly slept at all, knowing that I must be awake again at five. The moonlight crept across the floor of the unfamiliar room and I lay awake looking at my watch every hour or so and listening to the cockerels outside my window crowing all night long. The farm noises were different from the ones at home, and the smells too. There was not the acute hush of the mountain darkness with its owl calls and lonely night-flying curlew's note, but a rustle and stir of living, a bumping of animals in the buildings, the distant bark of a dog, cows mooing, the hint of cat life pursuing mouse life through a labyrinth of hay and straw and corn. There was an ordour of silage and barn-stored fodder rather than the wind smells swept down from heather and rock. It was a new life.

Then an alarm clock shrilled somewhere in the house and presently footsteps went down the stairs. Morning was replacing moonlight at the windows. It was a quarter to five and time to get up. I went out into the shuddering greyness where the farm was waking up. Lights were going on in the buildings and there was the roar of the tractor starting up as Frank Henderson prepared to take mash and water round to the laying houses. One of the pupils was feeding the pigs and suddenly a clamour of grunts and squeals came from the pig-house. I went to the cowshed. New to almost everything else, at least I could milk. David, the youngest pupil, was bringing the cows in. Mr. George was there with the milk buckets. The numerous Oathill cats were silently flitting into the cowshed from their noctural haunts to line up expectantly. I was given a bucket, allotted a cow to milk, and so began my first work on the farm.

Oathill Farm covers eighty-five acres. The Henderson brothers began to farm there in 1924 when the land was practically derelict and both were under the age of twenty-one. They had only the meagrest capital behind them but, in a time when experienced and formerly wealthy farmers were going bankrupt in the depression, they made money, stocked the farm with pedigree animals and extended the buildings until Oathill was one of the most productive farms in the country. I wanted to see how they had done it. I did not expect to equal their brains and dedication but I thought I could learn something. Soon I noticed a phrase which often appeared in the Oathill conversation—'It's quite simple.' When giving an explanation even the children began by saying: 'It's quite simple.' Here was an outlook that did not recognize difficulties as insuperable and which was not limited by barriers of muddle-headedness or laziness. It was one which I wanted to learn.

The most important branch of the farm was perhaps the poultry. A flock of nearly two thousand hens was kept in ten laying houses on the permanent grassland. They were line-bred on a closed flock system which ensured that the birds were genetically homogeneous and their progeny always of a reliable standard quality. Here, as elsewhere on the farm, the time taken in management was reduced to the minimum. The morning feed was rapidly delivered by tractor; the square buckets each containing a measured quantity of mash fitted neatly into the link box in front and a water tank was carried at the back. Corn and pellets were stored in rat-proof bins inside the houses and the pupil who did the midday and evening feeds had nothing to carry but his bucket of eggs.

Replacements for the breeding flock, pullets for sale and fattening cockerels were hatched and reared on the farm. They began life in paraffin hovers in a small cosy brooder-house where it was easy to keep the air temperature at an even sixty degrees although it was freezing outside. With thirty years' experience, Mr. George still preferred paraffin lamps for the first critical week of the chicks' life. It was possible to keep the temperature of the hovers more delicately adjusted than with electricity and he always attended to the wicks himself. The little brooder-house was a haven of warmth on cold days and work there was pleasant, with the promise of spring in the yellow fluffiness of the chicks as they trotted out to peck at their food and take sips at the water founts. After the first week they were moved to the big brooder-house, holding a thousand young birds, with its sunny windows and uniform pens which made the management very simple. Peat was used for litter, clean and absorbent material that did not need to be changed until the chicks were again moved on. At six to eight weeks old they were put out into the aluminium folds and moved daily across the grassland until they were sold or replaced the breeding stock in the laying houses.

The Oathill cattle were pedigree Jerseys and numbered a herd of forty or fifty, descendants of the two animals which the Henderson brothers bought in 1924. About twenty calves were reared each year on the milk from four or five cows. Heifers were sold when they calved at two years old and their calves retained.

There was a large Danish pig house. Six or eight pedigree Large White breeding sows were kept, and their progeny went off as bacon pigs after a number of the best gilts and boars had been sold for breeding stock. Monday nights were a pigs' red-letter day at Oathill; then we had the offal from the incubators to feed to them. Infertile eggs, dead-in-shell and dead chickens were scrunched up with equal delight. The pigs jostled forward for the treat like squabbling children, giving sly pokes and bites at one another. Charlie, the boar, was a pet of David's and had a large share of the scrumptious infertiles. He learnt to stand with his trotters over the side of the pen and, with yolk trickling down his chops, would wait while egg after egg was popped into his mouth. In the evening the little piglets, tiny and silky, would lie stretched out by the bulk of their sleeping mothers under the warmth of the infra-red lamps, and the hulla-balloo of feeding time was hushed. Then the pig-house was a good place for farming discussions among the pupils.

Also there were sheep, a flock of thirty or forty pedigree Clun Forests, a sideline but profitable. The eight-stone ewes seemed enormous to me after our little sixty- or seventy-pound Welsh Mountain sheep, and it was odd to see dusky twins or triplets trotting after their mothers instead of the solitary snow-white mountain lamb. The ewes were tame, coming when called for a feed of roots or a little hay, and no dog was needed to gather them. There was a concrete dip and foot-bath, and the year's routine was much the same as with our mountain flock except that everything happened earlier, tupping was in August, lambing in January and shearing in May, and there was no trouble from liver fluke on the dry healthy Cotswold land.

The soil of the farm was a light, stone brash. In spite of its shallowness heavy crops were grown in the traditional five-course Cotswold rotation. This was made possible by the heavy stocking of the land. The whole farm was fully and economically mechanized with a good workshop of servicing. Mr. Frank was the expert here and did the repairs to machinery and electrical equipment, also organized constructional work and did the farm accounts. Mr George kept a ubiquitous eye on the farm in general and the livestock in particular, and trained the pupils. Both brothers were brilliant in their different and complementary ways and were much discussed by the pupils after hours.

The farm was worked entirely by pupil labour; in their first year the pupils were paid a small wage, and afterwards on a profit-sharing basis. All were potential farmers themselves and were prepared to work harder and take a keener interest in what they did than most boys of their age. The staff usually consisted of two or three boys and a girl. Most were the sons and daughters of farmers or professional men; the Henderson brothers had found that these were generally best fitted for the work, and profited most by it.

Gradually I slipped into the farm routine. The early rising on those dark cold winter mornings was an effort, but warmth and sleep were unimportant beside the interest of the farm. I knew early rising was good for me and doggedly I jumped out of bed each morning at ten minutes to five. Our family considered that half-past seven was early enough for anybody and I had an ingrained habit to break. After the solitary life of the mountains, Oathill seemed very busy with its comings and goings, the arrival of important visitors and its high output of stock and produce. It was interesting, too, to be with new people after having lived only with my family before.

Then two of the pupils left to take farms of their own and work became heavier. The farmhouse was now to be enlarged and the farm run short-staffed till the alterations were finished, for some of the bedrooms would be uninhabitable for a while. Now there was only David to work full time, with part-time help from me. We set our alarm clocks back to half-past four in the morning and managed to be in the cowshed before Mr. George. After the early stock work was done we had breakfast, and then I helped Elizabeth in the house and garden until dinner-time at noon. Here was an education in itself. Elizabeth, with her delicate prettiness and phenomenal capacity for getting things done, was an excellent teacher. I learnt to operate the washing machine and whip the clothes out on to the line by seven o'clock in the morning. I learnt how to cook huge quantities of food at record speeds, dress and undress the children, wash their faces, bath them, answer questions and mediate in squabbles.

In mid-November Elizabeth disappeared into hospital in the middle of the night, and a little boy was born in the early hours of the morning. Now I was in sole charge of the family and was relieved from all farm work except rearing the baby chicks which I enjoyed doing. I popped out to visit these in between household tasks, and to hear the farm news from David. For a short time at any rate I was a key person in the running of the farm; Mr. George had no time to deal with domestic arrangements and the care of the three children was in my hands. With Elizabeth's instruction behind me, all went well. Previously undomesticated, I found I could now look after a house and children. Then Elizabeth's cousin came to help me and I began to do some of the farm work again. Finally Elizabeth returned from hospital with baby Michael. She and Mr. George asked me to be godmother. Indeed I felt honoured. After years of waiting I was not only a pupil but now more intimately connected with the Hendersons.

The days became colder and shorter, and the last shreds of autumn left the gently undulating countryside to be replaced by the bareness of winter. Farm work continued steadily and I began to learn, besides the technical skills of good farming, what was even more important—the attitude of mind which produced such amazing results; the work-first attitude, the it's-quite-simple attitude, the use-your-brains attitude, the supremely effective Henderson outlook which was quite unlike anything I had come across before. It was intensely stimulating, all the more so because it was focused directly on the subject which interested me most—farming. I had an

106

exhilarating consciousness that I was doing what I most wanted to do, although at times it was not always easy or comfortable. As the builders invaded the house, knocked down walls, removed plumbing and took off roofs, living conditions became more and more difficult. The Henderson family were cramped in the small bungalow. David and I slept in the half-demolished house and had to go upstairs in our gum boots, for in wet weather the stairs were now a waterfall and covered with plaster and builders' rubble. We had most of our meals at the bungalow but early breakfast we made ourselves in what was left of the farmhouse kitchen. Here the Aga cooker was still alight but one of the walls was only a tarpaulin which heaved in and out in the wind. Rain came in here and there. At six o'clock on a black winter's morning I was once dismayed to find our breakfast loaf, immensely swollen, floating about in a bread bin full of water. Usually I had prepared the food by the time David came in, his hands blue and frozen from the tractor ride round the laying houses in the frosty darkness.

In spite of the difference of age and outlook, a sort of companionship had sprung up between us. We would chat in the evenings about what we were going to do on our own farms later, or David would talk about the boarding school he had just left; I told him about farming in the mountains, or we would discuss endlessly the life and work at Oathill. Both of us had a very limited experience of the world, David through his youth and I through the seclusion of seven years on a remote hillside, and so we found it fascinating to dwell on the new vistas that our present life opened.

All this time I was again very homesick. Carneddi, now out of reach, seemed infinitely desirable, and everything I had done there was seen through a delightful haze of sentimental recollection. I propped large photographs of mountain peaks along the bedroom chimneypiece, recited mountain poetry to myself as I fed the chicks in the brooder house and dreamed of the hills, with all the disappointments, set-backs, irritations and loneliness forgotten. Oathill Farm lay in a saucer-shaped hollow and its horizons were the slopes of near-at-hand fields. At times the feeling of not being able to see where I was became almost unbearable. For seven years my eyes had become used to great chasms of space and sky-tipping peaks and now the urge to climb the tallest tree in the vicinity and have a look round itched at the back of my mind. I did not have a bicycle and there was little time for walking. I used the short space of evening left after work was done for correspondence and for filling in the claim forms for grants on the improvements at home under the Hill Farming Act. This had to be done without delay as money was urgently needed for the running of Carneddi, and with nodding head I would sort receipts from the stack of papers I had brought with me and add up figures, while all the time half-past four the next morning and the alarm clock's raucous voice was looming nearer and nearer. Mother wrote every day, her letters bringing news of the farm and comfort from home, and I would reply, when not too sleepy, suggesting farm policy and telling of the new things I had learnt.

Mr. Frank did not often work with the pupils but there was much to be learnt from him by watching. I noticed particularly how he did any odd jobs without delay. I had only to mention that one of the chicken pen doors was loose on its hinges or that a hover was not working properly and half an hour later it would be mended; he was too busy to have a number of trivial tasks making calls on his memory. Generally he did not suffer fools gladly but sometimes his reactions were surprising. Once he took me out ploughing. I balanced on the tractor mudguard while he took a turn or two up and down, demonstrating the use of the plough. Then it was my turn to take the driving seat, Mr. Frank climbed up on the mudguard and we were off. I had sometimes driven the tractor before but it still felt very strange after the jeep at home. There was something thrilling about the ploughshares driving through the soil, and earth and stones furling effortlessly back from the mould-board, and the almost sinister power of the tractor. I liked ploughing—this was good fun. I managed several fairly creditable furrows, but the sharp turns at the end were tricky with the plough to raise at the same time as making the turn. The hedge at one end of the field and the concrete post at the other were narrowly missed each time but Mr. Frank seemed encouraging. At the end of the next bout I found I was turning even closer to the post than before and hastily put out what I thought was the clutch. Unaccountably the tractor kept on veering towards the fence. I heard spluttering sounds from Mr. Frank and in my panic lowered the plough. There was a snap and a crunch. Two of the posts curtsied over sideways, but the tractor seemed undisturbed by what it had done and proceeded effortlessly to mow down two more. Suddenly I realized that I had depressed the independent foot brake instead of the clutch and, rectifying the mistake, we came to a horrified halt. I sat waiting for the storm to break as Mr. Frank descended from the tractor and examined the posts. But no storm came.

'There're only cracked,' he said casually, 'I can soon straighten them.'

And so passed my stupidest action at Oathill, with never a word of blame, and Mr. Frank let me plough a few more furrows before I returned to the house.

My first Christmas away from home came and went with many homesick longings. The alterations to the house were nearing completion, while the days were becoming a little lighter and the weather warmer. Baby Michael was growing fast and Elizabeth would soon be able to move the family into the modernized farmhouse. I could go home now when I wanted. Spring was coming to the mountains in the west and the March winds would soon be roaring round their rocky tops. The small sheep on the slopes were heavily pregnant and I felt it was time to go back. I had achieved my ambition and learnt much, and so I left Oathill, having gained a godson, a firm friend in Elizabeth, a wise adviser in Mr. George and a good deal more confidence in myself.

10 Deep-Litter House

At home again, I looked at Carneddi and the mountains in a new light, informed by what I had learnt at Oathill and inspired by being the farmer once more instead of a very dumb and junior pupil. My parents had managed well while I was away but now they were glad to resign the responsibility again and I was delighted to take it. I could drive where I wished in my own jeep instead of being merely a passenger; once more I was running the farm. Now I could write and ask Mr. George if there was anything I wanted to know and I always was quoting him to the family. But just as railway lines, diverging at the points, begin by running close together although their destinations are far apart, so my farming at Carneddi was not startlingly different after I came home. The rainfall was just as heavy, the ground as rocky and money as scarce as before. The Hill Farming Scheme improvements, however, were beginning to make the farm seem more business-like; the new gates and good fencing, as they replaced the old bedsteads and sagging barbed wire, diminished the air of forlornness and faint decay that had hung over the farm; the enlarged farmhouse made a better centre from which activities could begin.

The first thing was to expand the poultry unit, I decided. I had a useful market for hatching eggs and a stock of good birds, and the turnover on poultry was quick. In the years at Carneddi the advantages of solid buildings had become apparent. I had lain awake on many a stormy night, listening to the wind tearing at the farmhouse, bending the spruce trees almost double and driving the rain in horizontal torrents on to the roof, while I imagined the wooden hen cabins being torn to pieces and sodden hens whirled away into the night. Once, at midnight, with mackintosh and gum boots over pyjamas, I had crept out to look if the cabins were still there. The force of the wind was terrific but the glimmer of my torch, penetrating the mist and hurtling raindrops, showed them still in place, shuddering violently, nerve-racked hens clinging to the slats, but still held firmly by the anchor wires. Sleepless nights were undesirable and I determined that if we had more poultry they should be housed in a permanent building.

I planned a deep-litter house, twenty feet by thirty, sited near the cowshed and the road, containing its own food bins and housing two hundred birds or so. During the winter breeding season the birds could be let out to range and in summer, when hay stood thick in our front field and eggs were not used for hatching, they could be kept intensively and the ground outside rested. There would be an eight-foot sliding door in the gable nearest to the road to admit the jeep and trailer for a yearly clean-out, and a small door at the other. Steel hopper windows would run the length of both walls; nest-boxes would be on one side and perching slats and a droppings pit on the other.

It was a good plan on paper; my main concern was how to pay for it. The credit balance in my account was sufficient only for ordinary trading; I had no savings now. I wrote to the bank manager asking for an overdraft and he agreed to it if I made a statement of my assets. Prim, Daphne and Blackie were entered under the collective heading of 'Cows in Milk', £120. All my friends, the farm animals, appeared in the appropriate columns, their market values swelling the total to quite a respectable figure. The overdraft was in the bag, and, light-heartedly, I accepted a new millstone round my neck. The deep-litter house just had to pay for itself and quickly too.

The local builders were approached and agreed to do the work for an hourly wage. Our friend, the architect, promised to draw the plans and keep an eye on the proceedings. No Hill Farming grant could be obtained for a poultry house: hen-keeping was not considered to take a part in normal hill farming practice. This official view was annoying for no one

1. Butter-making. The author pours cream into the churn.

2a. Swimming Ashore. The sheep are pushed over
the brink from the pen, six feet above deep water, and swim
across the pool. This cleans the wool a few days
before shearing.

2b. Shearing at Tan Rhiw.

3. Moel Hebog in winter, from Carneddi sheep-walk.

4a. Carneddi Farmhouse, 1945.

4b. Carneddi Farmhouse, 1960.

5a. The Farm Buildings, 1960 from Clwt yr Wyn.
Left to right: Cowshed, silo, carriage shed, deep-litter house.

5b. Carneddi after an early spring snow-fall.

6a. Hoeing the strawberries in Gotal, June 1959,
after planting out in April.

6b. Paul and author loading hay in Cae tan Beudy, July 1959.
Mot, the sheepdog, looks on.

7a. Ty Mawr Cottage. Front view, showing the new roof.

7b. Ty Mawr Cottage. Back view of the new roof,
with a skylight open for Fluffy, the cat.

8a. Film Unit on Location.
The Chinese city that was built in a month
on the Welsh hillside.

8b. Filming the Bombing Scene. Ambulance stands by.

in his senses would attempt to perch a full-scale poultry farm on these precipitous slopes where watchful foxes were for ever on the prowl; cattle and sheep would always be the main stock. A few well-managed hens, however, benefited the land for sheep, and helped the farmer's pocket with a smaller regular income. Now, with no grant forthcoming, the hens and I would have to produce the capital by ourselves.

Originally I intended to help the builders as much as I could, perhaps speeding them up and saving a little money. I could mix concrete and carry bricks, and perhaps learn to lay them. The foundations were begun and I hovered anxiously round, trying to find a way to be helpful. The builders were cheerful and hard-working but obviously considered me a menace, unsuited to the lifting of heavy weights and incapable of learning the masculine mysteries of the building trade. Also a fault in the building caused by my meddling would have been their responsibility. Mentally I retreated. It was no good. With the road improved even the materials were carted up on the builders' own lorry and there was no chance to use the jeep for this as I had done for the house extension. I should just have to pay for everything.

In the evening after the men had gone I prowled round examining their work, feeling a mixture of pleasure as the walls rose higher and higher and apprehension at all the money it was costing. I studied the foundations and method of laying the bricks, and tested the horizontals and verticals and the consistency of the cement. Building seemed simple enough and I felt quite sure I could do it myself, given plenty of time and no one to stand by criticizing. Indeed it seemed as though it might be a pleasurable and fascinating occupation.

The walls rose, the windows were put in place and the springings were reached. Now it was time for the roof to go on and a joiner arrived to help. I continued evening scouting activities but, for one who could not saw down a straight line, the carpentry of a roof seemed daunting. However, I watched closely.

In the New Year of 1954 it was finished, a large cement-skimmed building perched on the main spur. Far down, from the main road, a glimpse of its white asbestos roof could be seen near our cowshed and the dark green tops of the Christmas trees. It seemed to give a hint of business-like activity, up there high on the rocky slopes.

I walked round the earth floor of the spacious cement-smelling interior, making plans. Two hundred pullets would be needed to fill it, but I could rear many more if the brooders were put inside and temporary pens of wire netting made. The ground had never had poultry on it before and, with peat moss over the earth, chicks would do well enough for one year. I could sell the surplus pullets as growers and the rest could continue in the deep-litter house where they would later lay. There were also nest-boxes and roosting slats to be considered and, since I had spent so much already, my father was persuaded to begin the task of making them. We bought lengths of new timber from the timber yard and, painstakingly, he began the construction of twenty-eight nest-boxes which were to fit under the windows on the south wall.

Meanwhile I moved the brooders out of the toolshed into their new quarters in the deep-litter house, and made some rough wire-netting pens. It was a relief to have plenty of space. In the past time had been wasted in clearing a corner of the old shed to accommodate the brooders, and temper expended in stepping round nailboxes and tins of paint to attend the chicks, while a bang on the head from an incautiously placed rake handle was not uncommon, or a cascade of odds and ends from an overloaded shelf. However often I tidied that shed it would jumble itself up again in no time, and it was pleasant to leave its clutter behind and have the chicks under the spacious roof of the new house.

The chicks were custom hatched from our own eggs by Mr. Ephraim and returned in lots of a hundred by train each Wednesday, until there were five hundred chirping and scratching in the new pens. An advertisement in the local newspaper produced buyers for two hundred and fifty and, selling at 10s. 6d. each at eight weeks old, they soon earned some money to reduce the overdraft. They reared well in their new quarters, and only three or four in every hundred died. In the afternoons the sliding door, the gap now fitted with a wire-netting frame, would be pushed open revealing the tremendous view of Moel Hebog and its foothills, while the sunshine slanted directly into the pens causing the chicks to bask and take delighted dust-baths.

Pullet-rearing was proving pleasant and profitable; it ought to be a permanent addition to Carneddi's economy. The only difficulty was that after the first year the new house would always contain adult laying birds. The thought of hole-in-the corner chick-rearing, back in the toolshed again, was not tempting but still it was only May; there was plenty of time to think of the problem in the autumn. I might have made some money by then.

The surplus pullets were sold, more than two hundred remaining, and my father began to fit up the beautifully made nest-boxes and perching slats. These we called Father's Fowl House Furniture and, when they were installed, they made the new house look very efficient. He also connected a water pipe and put a tap inside the door for filling the founts; I could not afford automatic ones at that time. Old chemical drums at 2s. 6d. each made useful bins when fitted with a lid, and held two and a half hundredweight each.

In July the first pullets began to lay. Soon I was sending a case of eggs to the packing station, and then two. Attending the birds under the new system took only a short time, and thirty minutes a day saw all the work done. With the shortening autumn evenings I hung two pressure lamps in the house and gave the birds an extra feed. Their working day was still twelve or thirteen hours and, instead of the usual autumn fall in egg production, the daily total continued to increase.

I was very pleased; the deep-litter house represented progress. With too little capital and a very great ignorance our early efforts at farming had been amateurish. There was nothing much to see but the wild country, the stone barns and a few grazing cattle—a beautiful scene but one touched with barrenness. There was no machinery and little tilled land. Even our sheep were not a particularly impressive sight; the flock of a hundred seemed a small bunch when gathered and had little of the grandeur of the great flocks of larger sheep farms. Yet Carneddi, with all its smallness and poverty, had a

115

tough compactness and a spiritual freedom which never failed to attract the attention of visitors. With its feet set in the billowing woods and its upper limits climbing towards the bare mountain, it clung to the hillside, land of thin springy turf, cold water, fresh air and isolation. Now the new deep-litter house added a touch of material prosperity to its rough slopes, prosperity to be produced from the farm's own increase, a token that the natural wildness was not always in conflict with our efforts and could be used to give us a liveli-hood without itself being spoiled.

In November we mated Brown Leghorn cockerels to the pullets and, at the beginning of December, began to send two cases of eggs to the hatchery each week. The better price for hatching eggs increased my egg money by a third and after the food bills were paid there was a small regular surplus to go into the bank. The overdraft was already shrinking.

Until Christmas the weather had been mild. Christmas morning came in dull and warm for December, with dead bracken still glowing on the hillside and coppery leaves still attached to the beech trees as though autumn were unwilling to depart. The animals were attended to and then we went to church. By afternoon the skies were slate grey and it was much colder. Inside the house fires burnt in every room and lamps were lighted against the early dusk of a winter's day. Berried holly from the little tree by our mountain wall decked the pictures and the clock, and all but essential work was put aside for the time being. The hens were to be fed early so that a long evening was free for leisure and celebration. About two o'clock I went outside to find the autumn colours fast fading out of the landscape and being replaced by greyness. Little drifts of ice particles were banking up into ruts and footmarks in the ground, and silvering the walls and buildings, while an east wind plunged across the chasm of the valley to buffet at our ridge. By the time the hens were fed, the milking done, the dogs fastened up and all the animals made comfortable for the night, it was nearly dark and the wind had developed a howling note and its gusts were fiercer than ever. The pres-sure lamps blew out as I was carrying them across to the deep-litter house and had to be lighted again, slowly and with numb fingers. Now almost the last job for the night was done; it was necessary only to put out the hen-house lights again at half-past eight.

Christmas evening, with its rejoicing and rituals, was all the more real and exciting for being spent in the mountains. Our own turkey was on the table and our own holly on the walls, while outside our cattle were snug in the barn and the spruce trees round the house whipped in the growing blizzard. Slacks and overalls were cast off for seldom-worn party clothes, the large feast cooked and eaten, a toast drunk to the absent Fred who had made so many past Christmasses happy for us, while the Christmas tree, pretty with candles and decorations, waited in the corner of the sitting-room with its load of presents. Now was the moment to slip out and extinguish the deep-litter house lights. The east wind had been strengthening all evening and had become a gale with savage gusts which tore at the house and dashed an almost horizontal stream of snowflakes past the lighted windows. Above the sound of the wind there had been an intermittent banging, hardly registered by the mind, but now, as I opened the front door, louder and more menacing. Something was going to blow away.

With mack, muffler and gum boots over best dress and nylons, I hurried the few yards to the deep-litter house through the wind with its needle-sharp cargo of ice. Already the east gable of the building was plastered with snow, and it was a fierce struggle to open the door against the gale which hurled a cascade of flakes in with me and slammed the door behind. The lamps had burned low and the pullets were perching stoically on the slats, ignoring the hurly-burly from outside, but I was alarmed to see a thin drift of snow over the floor and more eddying in through the ventilator and the cracks round the door. Here also was the seat of the ominous banging sound. It was a moment or two before I could trace it. Then I saw that three or four of the asbestos roof sheets were rising and falling in the teeth of the wind like the lid of a box flapping. Here was impending catastrophe. I expected to see the roof peeled off before my eyes and snatched away into the night, leaving two hundred cherished pullets exposed to the snow and bitter wind. The house would be half-filled with drifts by morning, the pullets frozen. It was an agonizing moment, standing there expecting to see one's hopes torn to bits in a few seconds. I could not bear the thought of the wreck of that roof. It must not blow away.

I ran to the house to get my father's help but he had gone out. My shouts were snatched away by the wind and there seemed no sign of him. By the light of a torch I scrabbled in the tool shed for hammer and large screwed nails for the asbestos sheeting and then, carrying a ladder, I struggled back through the blizzard to the deep-litter house. The roof was still on but lifting more than ever with each savage gust. I climbed up the ladder, torch held between my teeth, and found that the lower row of nails, smaller than those which I had in my pocket, had pulled out. Then the ladder and I were dashed to the ground with the next gust. Almost crying with rage and determination I climbed up again, clinging to the lifting sheets with a frenzy of despair. A slight lull allowed two of the big nails to be driven in and it was satisfactory to feel their greater length biting into the heavy purlin below. Then the next gust came with its fury of driven snow and I bowed helplessly over the edge of the roof until it had passed, and then began hammering again. I was gaining ground—the nails were holding and at last it was done. Limply I descended the ladder, laid it on the ground and made for shelter inside the deep-litter house. The roofing sheets, now firmly held, still provided a purchase for the wind and the purlins to which they were attached were now lifting ever so little in the frenzy of the gale. It was a sinister movement showing the fierceness of the forces of that wild night, but there was nothing more I could do. I returned to the house. My father had come in too. He had traced the banging sound to the silo roof which was also working loose, and had been weighting it down with heavy rocks. The wooden hen cabins were safe, he said, being on the leeward side of the spur. There was nothing else to do but hope for the gale to blow itself out. Mercifully it seemed to be dying down. The snow was stopping and the gusts were coming at greater intervals and less violently. Battered but thankful we resumed our Christmas party. By midnight the storm had spent itself.

Boxing Day came, calm and clear, with the driven snow lying white and peaceful on the hills. The deep-litter house still perched on its spur intact, and inside the pullets were busy going about the work of the day with a ceaseless hen-chattering and combs like two hundred little red blossoms, as they hopped in and out of nest-boxes, pecked in the troughs and sipped at the drinking founts. It was reassuring to see them all alive and well, but the four hundred pink feet were no longer scratching in dry litter but paddled through a sea of mud. The snow which had been driven in through every crack and cranny the night before had melted in the heat from the bird's bodies and soaked the ground.

'How are things in the deep-litter house?' Mother asked when I came in.

'Deep-litter?' I said sadly. 'It's the deep-mud house now.'

But the mud proved not to be very deep and after the top inch or so had been taken away in barrow-loads and more bracken and wood shavings spread about, the litter resumed its healthy state again. Later we strained heavy-gauge wire round the purlins and pegged it into the walls so that the roof was no longer held only by its own weight but was securely anchored down. If ever a worse gale came than the one we had on Christmas night, we should probably be blown away with it and past caring what happened to our buildings anyway.

11   Brooder House

The building of the deep-litter house was finished in the New Year of 1954 and the spring and summer of that year passed quickly. Then autumn came. I had drifted happily along all through the warm days, busy with shearing, hay-making and hoeing, and had given little thought to where the chickens were to be reared the following season. The new deep-litter house was no longer available; the toolshed was now inadequate; the problem was becoming urgent. A new building was needed, but it was depressing to think of spending more with an overdraft still at the bank. September came and October, and the pullets in the deep-litter house were paying their way and making a profit too. Perhaps I could afford a small cheap brooder house.

At the beginning of November I realized with a shock that chicks must be reared in less than three months' time. I must do something quickly. I consulted with Paul; his guest-house season was over and he was ready to begin farm work again. A home-made building seemed to be the answer and we sketched a plan of a shed made from corrugated iron, forestry poles, and lined with straw. It was the cheapest method we could devise but there were many disadvantages; it would be ugly and impermanent, and with iron roof and walls, even with a lining of straw, the temperature inside would be variable. We looked and looked at the sketch and assured each other that this was the cheapest method, but our hearts were not in the idea. I wanted a building comparable with the well-designed brooder house at Oathill; .Paul wanted to try something new; we were both tired of make-shifts and making do, of seeing flimsy and prefabricated work in the setting of the enduring hills. We wanted, we found, to try our hands at a new skill and make a tidy and lasting job of it; we wanted, in fact, to build a proper building. As on so many past occasions the decision was reached suddenly; the time became ripe and I launched myself on a scheme which a week ago I would not have seriously considered. We would build a brooder house of concrete blocks, and never mind the cost.

The next task was to decide where the site was to be. Flat ground on Carneddi is scarce and when we began to survey the land it was a puzzle to know where we could build. The deep-litter house and cowshed occupied a small plateau on top of the spur and on every side the ground sloped up or down in rocky undulations with hardly a couple of yards on the same level. The brooder house must be close to the farm for frequent visits, yet apart from adult hens to reduce the risk of disease. At last we decided on a sort of shelf, behind and above the farmhouse and divided from the deep-litter house by the garden. The proposed site was far from level but I hoped we could dig earth from the higher ground, use it to raise the lower and so make a fair-sized platform.

The next day Paul began the levelling. The weather had turned and a fine November drizzle set in, with the cloud line well down on the hills, earth sodden underfoot and the outcrops of slate shining with wet. Later in the day I went to inspect Paul's progress and found a great deal of earth and many rocks had been moved, making a raw gash in the slope behind the house. Paul was grimed and muddy to the elbows, his dungarees drenched and a gloomy expression on his face.

'We'll never be able to make a site big enough for the size of shed you want, if we have it here,' he said. 'There are tons of earth to be shifted and the difference in levels is over five feet. Have a look. We'll never get the work finished by February 1st.'

This was our deadline date.

His shaggy eyebrows, beaded over with a fine dew of rain drops, seemed to jut out more than ever. This news was disheartening. I examined the site again more carefully and found he was right. The fall was indeed more than five feet but a tangle of heather, bracken and ferns had at first masked the slope, making it appear more gentle than it really was. We sat down on two boulders in the drizzle to consider the situation and discussed all the other sites we had thought of before, but none seemed suitable. We had no more bright ideas.

'There is nothing for it,' I said at last. 'It will have to be here. All we can do is to make as big a level space as we can by, say, December 1st and then build the brooder house to fit it. I won't do any other farm work and, if we both concentrate on this, we ought to get results.'

Paul agreed to this plan since there seemed no other. We were at odds with the mountain terrain and the only course was to adapt our methods and accept the limits it imposed on us. The next morning we both set to work, aware now of the size of the task and very determined to complete it, aware also of the hurrying days and the shortness of the time left to us. I did the milking before dawn and after dusk; my father took over some of the stock work which was part of my usual routine, leaving me free to spend every minute of the shortening winter days on the building site. The weather was dull, damp and cold but we ignored it and with shovel, pick, crowbar and barrow we laboured in the mud. Paul found he had a knack with boulders and they slid into place for him with the same lack of obstinacy that they offer to a Welshman. He began to build a stout embankment with large stones from an old wall, some of them weighing two or three hundredweight apiece, slippery with mud and sharp with slaty splinters. I filled up behind the embankment with nobbly stones which were unsuitable for wall-building and had been rejected by Paul as having 'no shape in them', and also with load after load of earth. The earth first had to be loosened with a pick before I could shovel it into the barrow. After a while I reached roots from the big sycamore and ash trees which grew behind the site, and here Paul had to leave his wall and hack them through with an axe before I could go on digging. It was heavy work but, as we made progress, we began to enjoy ourselves. The prospect of having a real brooder house, and moreover one built by our own hands and at, we hoped, a moderate cost, was inspiring. Our bedraggled, mud-stained clothes and chapped, dirt-begrimed hands were of no importance.

We were complete amateurs; neither of us had attempted such a task before or knew enough to take the lead and our building project grew into a joint adventure. It stimulated hours of conversation, conjecture and a constant flow of bright ideas, and meanwhile the plan and method gradually matured. Nothing but the proposed brooder house was talked about at Carneddi's dinner table. During meals, Mother was overwhelmed by a conversational flow of bricks and mortar while my father, mind trotting briskly to keep up with the latest development, offered helpful suggestions. I was lucky to employ Paul for without him I could never have attempted the present brooder house scheme. He had worked on the farm for five winters now. At ordinary agricultural rates his wages did not amount to much but he was intelligent and clever with his hands. He approved, it seemed, our efforts to make a living from the mountains, he enjoyed farming and was willing to identify himself with our work for no great financial gain.

By November 30th the site was completed. It was as big as we could make it; the front was banked up with a sloping wall of boulders, the back squared out of the mountainside behind. We measured, and found that a building twenty-seven feet by thirteen feet six inches could be safely set on this platform, and thus the size of the brooder house was decided. Concrete blocks were the chosen material as they made an easily-built cavity wall and each was equal to twelve bricks. The next morning, December 1st, Paul arrived at the farm with our preliminary plans drawn on sheets of graph paper. Two large squares on the paper represented one 18 by 9 inch block. Now we could estimate the number of blocks and the amount and sizes of timber needed. I had already consulted our architect friend, the Colonel, and received a promise of help if required. On this scheme, however, I hoped that we should not trouble him. By combining the geometry and art of our school days with later-learned common sense, Paul and I found we could produce our own plans which later we used as working drawings.

The shed was to be twice as long as it was wide, to face due south and to have an entrance door in the west gable. Four large windows in the front reached almost to the ground. The lower half of the windows, covered by wire-netting and shutter doors, could be closed in bad weather, or opened to admit direct sunlight into the pens inside. The upper half would be filled by hopper-type glass windows. Three small windows would run the length of the back wall to give extra light. The roof was to be of asbestos sheeting and supported by purlins on two trusses. It was quite straightforward; we only had to do it.

First we dug a trench to receive the foundations of the north wall. We both knew how foundations should be laid but, with no experience behind us, we felt almost reluctant to begin mixing the concrete. We knew that the work must be accurate if the wall above were to be true, but did not know what margin of error—and there was sure to be some—we could afford to tolerate. However, two heavy planks were laid on edge in the trench a foot apart, carefully levelled with our new four-foot builder's levels, and the concrete and hardcore was packed between them. This took all day. Then in the dusk of evening we stood surveying our work. We felt like builders now, in our cement-smeared clothes; we termed foundations 'footings' and had a serious intention of producing a permanent building upon the spot on which we stood. True, the planks seemed to have moved a little during our operations and the surface of the concrete to have become slightly bumpy, but perhaps this was usual. We scraped our trowels and shovels and finished work for the day.

The next morning we were on the site again early and began to extend the length of the north footing. We were both a little apprehensive about the quality of the previous day's concreting but neither mentioned it. By and by the Colonel, interested in our activities, visited the site. He admired the size and strength of our platform. Then he examined the footing, the first real step towards our shed. There was a pause. Then, very tactfully, he pointed out that our work was not, in fact, accurate or strong enough and that the whole success of the building depended on our having really good footings. If we could use less hardcore, he said, and more concrete, take great pains with smoothing the surface and widen the footings a little, he thought we should get good results. His advice saved us hours of wasted work. We began again and made a new and superior footing on top of the old. It took two or three days but when the containing planks were pulled away the result was good. The bubble on the spirit level told us without a doubt that the work was accurate. I was very pleased.

The Colonel must have been responsible for the mania for accuracy which now possessed me and which was to govern all my labours until the work was finished. Everything had to be levelled, measured and lined up two or three times over before I was satisfied. I felt that the animals might have disturbed our vital markers. The sheepdogs in particular were a nuisance, wandering round the building and sprinkling each new bit as it was erected, and more than once we found a line of small cat footmarks imprinted for ever in our fresh cement. Time was short and Paul found my slowness irksome but after a few days, as confidence increased, I became quicker and there was no doubt that my fervid measurings had improved the quality of our building. The footings were well begun.

In the meantime three hundred and fifty-six concrete blocks had arrived, the number we had estimated from Paul's graph paper plans. They were unloaded at the end of the road but were still fifty yards from the brooder house site. Paul began to barrow them round to it. Each block weighed about seventy-two pounds when dry but these were very wet for it rained almost every day. I had bought a strong barrow with an inflated tyre, and it charged on its unending journeys along the uphill path, slippery with mud, with first Paul and then Daddy straining between its handles. Gradually the stack of blocks by the cowshed diminished as the pile on the site grew. Then it was time to begin laying them. We unrolled the strips of damp-course along the surface of the footings and the first blocks were laid. Again we were very slow. Any small mistakes on this lowest course would be magnified to an alarming degree by the time we had reached the height of six feet and again I indulged in an orgy of measuring, checking and rechecking.

When the first course of blocks was laid we were able to measure the diagonals. If both were equal our building was a rectangle, if unequal it was merely a four-sided figure and might be difficult to roof. We stretched the tape with care to get a uniform tautness for both measurements. There was one and a half inches difference between the two. Paul felt sure that on such a length the discrepancy was very small and so we built on. Gradually we became quicker and were laying twenty-four blocks an hour with an accuracy that delighted me. The weather continued cold and wet but we were now so fascinated by our work that we hardly noticed. Once there was a light snowfall in the night but by morning it was melting again and we could continue. Frost, which would cause the mortar to crumble, was the greatest danger but each evening, the skies were overcast and the temperature remained above freezing-point during the night. On Christmas Eve we set up the four front window-frames and began to build between them. By the last day of the old year we had reached the springings, eaves' height on the south wall. We had a month and three days before the first batch of chicks arrived from the hatchery.

During this time, between his rounds of the stock, Daddy came frequently to view the mushroom growth of the building and offer a suggestion here and there. I think he was surprised, as indeed I was, at its professional appearance and rate of progress, and in the evenings he could be seen pottering round, gazing with rapt attention and a proprietary air at the latest additions. Mother came too, often with mugs of hot coffee to put into dirty hands, and was very encouraging with her praises of our cleverness and the beauty of the building. Now the red tiles of the kitchen floor were always tracked over with cement-white footsteps, our clothes were filthy and difficult to wash, and our fingers cracked with lime burns. Now, also, the mountains seemed more lovely than ever with their bare winter trees and cloud-draped peaks. Building was a happy occupation.

On January 5th we set up the shallow north windows and

reached the springings on that wall. Then we finished the east gable and began on the west which had been left until last to allow us to get into the building easily with our heavy loads of mortar and blocks. Already our minds were running forward to the problems of the roof. For the sake of speed the roof trusses were made by a coach builder, and I fetched them home one day on the jeep with a trailer load of asbestos sheets. The last block was laid on January 10th; we were racing against time. Then we began to put up the roof. Here we were faced with new problems and the confident rhythm of block-laying was halted. We referred to the plans, consulted, and slowly the trusses went up, and the wall-plates and purlins after. Made wise by the gale which had so nearly wrecked the deep-litter house, we wired the purlins to the wall as we put them in position. Then, in spite of a stiff breeze, we slid the sheets of asbestos up on to the roof, and Paul, crawling on the timbers, hammered them into place with very large nails.

By Saturday, January 15th, the roof was finished. On Sunday the snow came, thick and heavy, whitening the hills as far as the eye could see and on Monday it was still snowing. Paul's motor-bicycle came chugging up the hill with difficulty and, as he dismounted, I knew what he was thinking: how fortunate we were to have beaten the weather by a bare twelve hours. We gazed exultantly at thick snow lying on the brand-new roof and at the dry comfortable interior of the shed. Nothing could have been more satisfactory than this sudden change in the weather, which underlined the wisdom of our haste.

Now we set to work to make the door, glaze the windows and line the roof with a thick layer of straw held in place by wire netting. There were still dozens of small jobs to be done before the brooder house was finished and so we did not slacken our pace. The frost came, gripping the hills in an ice-bound clasp but all the mortar was dry now and, in spite of cold and clumsy fingers, we did not care. The last big job was to lay a concrete floor. When stones were a nuisance the whole farm seemed to be scattered over with them, but now that we needed a layer of hardcore they seemed to have vanished away. Those in the vicinity of the brooder house were soon used up and there was still a great area of floor to be filled in. I took two buckets and went rooting about below the crag behind until I found, at last, a patch of shale, old ice-age debris with stones of about the right size. Paul set up planks to divide the concrete into sections and give a guide to the correct level while I filled in with shale. Vast amounts of concrete were required to cover the floor and we mixed great heaps of it on two old sheets of tin. Then I carried it inside in bucketfuls while Paul worked it to a level. It was difficult to exclude the cats at this point and there is a line of small disdainful footmarks still on record across the brooder house floor. About this time, too, there was a dearth of hen- and calf-feeding buckets. The stones and concrete had taken their toll of our building buckets and several bottomless wrecks lay amongst the bushes on the rubbish heap. Finally the main floor was laid.

It was now January 29th, just four days before the first lot of chicks would hatch. The planks between the floor sections had yet to be lifted and the cavities filled. There was no time for refinements now and, as soon as the floor would bear our weight, we decided to proceed. Paul grasped the end of the longest plank and lifted and, like the stirring of an elephant's back, the grey concrete on either side lifted with it. He dropped the plank hastily. If we weren't careful the floor would be ruined but we had to take the risk. I found some boards, laid them on the concrete on each side and stood on them while Paul again lifted the plank. This method worked quite well and, apart from a few small cracks, the edges of the still-damp cement remained intact. We removed the rest of the dividers and began to fill up the cavities. Dusk came before we had finished. It was essential to lay the last of the concrete now so that it would have a day or two to dry and so I lighted the pressure lamps and we worked on till ten o'clock that evening when the job was finished.

The next day Paul began to make the interior pens, and my father to paint the window-frames and door in opaline, a light greyish green, a shade which toned well with the grey building and fitted unobtrusively into the landscape. On

Wednesday, February 2nd, we made good the verges where the gable ends joined the roof, and I carried the brooders up from the toolshed, assembled them and lighted the paraffin lamps. The weather was cold and raw so I installed a blue-flame heater and soon the damp cement-smelling interior was beginning to take on a pleasant cosy warmth. The last job that night was to fit a draught strip round the door. The brooder house was now complete in every detail from the bright oat-straw lining of the roof down to the new green paint on the door—neat, convenient, pleasing and permanent.

On Thursday, February 3rd, the chicks arrived.

Building the brooder house was by far the most satisfying task I had yet done. Later I worked out the cost. The materials and their haulage came to £106 12s. 6d. Besides that there had been Paul's wages for the ten weeks which the job had taken from the first shovelful of earth moved on the site to the final fixing of the draught strip round the door. All this I was able to find from the farm account.

Some four years later the Colonel was showing a friend of his round the farm. He happened to mention that such a shed as our brooder house could not now be built by contractors for less than £800. I was surprised and delighted. I had not realized that we had produced anything so valuable. It seemed that now we were richer, not only in experience and enjoyment, but in property too.

12   Fred's Furlough

The New Year of 1955 brought us good news; Fred was returning to England. A family wedding provided her with an important reason to take a holiday now and the vague plans for a visit crystallized into reality. Her passage was booked. During all those long five years we had kept in close touch by letter; I sent news of the farm, Fred told me of her adventures in Australia on her sheep farm. A terrible drought had been followed by a bush fire and her sister's house, where Fred and her husband lived at the time, had been burnt to the ground, and their lives had been saved only by their hiding in the green passion-fruit vines. All their sheep had been destroyed in the flames and their new fencing burnt. She told me how they had begun all over again and lived in a tent for a year until they could build a new house of their own. Her letters held all the qualities of Fred as I remembered her, were indeed like a voice from the past, and yet so much had happened in those years that I felt she must have changed. I longed to see her again before time had widened the gap in our close relationship too far.

Now that we knew Fred was coming, the months which must pass before her arrival suddenly seemed a long time to wait. But spring was coming. The quickening tempo of farm life kept the days hurrying past at their usual brisk speed and there was never time to be dull. During the spring I planned to erect a concrete tower silo of the type then used at Oathill. Silage-making in the little silo had been such a success that I wanted to be able to make more. It would give us an insurance against the wet Augusts that came regularly to the hills. In bad years some of our mowing grass had never been cut at all, while dishevelled little haycocks crouched, sometimes for days on end, in the driving rain, turning first yellow and then black and there was nothing we could do about it until the weather turned. It was the same on all the sheep farms; the mountains gathered rain and storm clouds even when, on the coast, the sun was shining. Now, whatever the weather, all the crop from one of our fields could go into the big silo and we should have a good start in the yearly battle for the cows' winter food.

A pit silo was out of the question at Carneddi for where we could excavate the ground was a bog; in the dry places it was solid rock. The chosen silo was a prefabricated structure, ten feet high, and on arrival appeared to be a fearsome-looking object. It had reinforced concrete uprights with slotted sides and slabs like paving-stones which fitted between them. The slabs weighed a hundredweight apiece and the uprights much more. Three steel bands were provided to hold it together. The erection of so heavy a structure was awkward. Each upright had a concrete 'shoe' into which it fitted to prevent movement at the base. We arranged these 'shoes' in a circle on the plinth which Paul and I had built in readiness and the first upright was lifted into place by my father and Paul. This was accomplished by much straining on their part and nerve-racked exclamations of 'Are you lifting?', 'This way now' and 'Look out!'. I hovered round anxiously, unable to find a way to help and expecting to see both crushed to death at any moment. At last it was in position and stood pointing ten feet skywards, swaying slightly and supported by two of us. Then three slabs were put in place. The first was easy, being at ground level; the next more difficult as it had to be put on top of the first, while the third had to be lifted almost to shoulder height. I was left to mind the upright on my own while the other two did this, but the slabs already in place gave it some stability. Three more slabs were added to the other side and now I was in charge of the post and six slabs while yet another post was put in position. The components fitted together loosely, held to some extent by their own weight, but we felt that a false move or a gust of wind might disturb their precarious equilibrium at any moment and send the whole lot toppling. It was like a house of cards. Mother was fetched from indoors to help support the most insecure sections and, as fast as possible, the rest of the silo went up, three slabs and an upright, three slabs and an upright, until the circle was complete. The final post had one flange missing and the last slabs were slipped in from outside and held in position by steel pegs. Then we fitted the bands. It was a relief to hear the slabs crunching into their sockets as the nuts were tightened, and know the whole structure had been drawn together and become stable.

There were another two courses of slabs to go on yet, but these would be put up later when the silo was partly filled. We could then stand on the packed grass inside and lower them into the post sockets from above. Our silo was now assembled. It certainly presented a queer appearance, with the uprights still poking four feet into the air above the level of the slabs now in place. It could be seen from the village, rising between the cowshed and deep-litter house roofs. There was no other tower silo in the district and we received some humorous inquiries about our rocket-launching base.

All this time Fred's ship was sailing nearer on its journey half-way round the world. Air-letters were posted to Fremantle, Colombo, Aden, Port Said and finally Gibraltar. Then there was no need to write again; the next time we exchanged news we should be face to face. The ship docked at Southampton in the middle of June and I longed to be there to meet her, waving and waving as she came in. But it was not possible. All the sheep farms were ready for washing and shearing and it was necessary that I should be at home to help with Carneddi's share of the work.

Fred was to spend a few days with her relatives before coming to us. The day of her arrival in Wales was a Sunday. Few buses ran on a Welsh Sunday and none at all between Beddgelert and Caernarvon, so I planned to drive to Caernarvon to meet her with the jeep. I looked forward to our reunion with great anticipation. During the ten years in the mountains, I had led a secluded life, meeting few people and spending long hours with no company but my own and with only the animals to talk to. The people I knew well had become especially important, and Fred was among the most important of them all. Her affirming presence was almost a necessity and even her failings provided material for cheerful teasing.

We prepared her room and cleaned and polished the house. I made a huge celebration cake and iced it with a map of Australia. The only shadow over her homecoming was that Zenda, my white Alsatian, would not be there. Fred had always been devoted to the family dogs. After Waggles, my childhood pet, had come Zenda—big, aristocratic and beautiful. There were, of course, the sheepdogs—Mot, my father's dog, and Dash who was Mot's daughter and belonged to me, but neither were very good with sheep; our farming experience was not then really equal to the skilled job of training and working sheepdogs, and we still relied much on Tom. Fred was fond of all the dogs but Zenda was her especial pet. He did not take much notice of her if I were there, but if not he would follow her affectionately until I returned again. When Fred went away I think he missed her. The pleasure of seeing him again was one of the joys she anticipated, but in the previous year a stiffness had crept into his hind legs and he became partly paralysed. The vet could do nothing for him. He was only ten years old and seemed to feel no pain, and yet the appeal in those sad eyes could not be ignored. It became clear that he found life was not worth living if he could not be my constant companion. He hated to see his place usurped by the active carefree sheepdogs and be helpless himself. One day in April of that year the vet came and the life that had grown so burdensome was put to an end. There would be one less to welcome Fred when she came home.

On the day before her return the jeep broke down. The cheerful chug-chug of its engine changed to an irregular popping gasp and no amount of trying would put it right. It would have to go to the garage but the week-end was a bad time for repairs, and it could not be mended for the next day. Mrs. Staunton, Bill's mother, instantly offered the use of her car. It was a large and elderly Rover whose thoroughbred qualities were still apparent in spite of the inroads of rust on the bodywork and the bits of hay and sheep manure on the back seat. I was not used to driving a vehicle with the steering on the right, or indeed an ordinary car of any sort, but I accepted the offer eagerly. Fred could still be fetched in style.

Sunday came, fine and warm, and I set out on the journey to Caernarvon. After the open jeep, the Rover felt like a small bus as I drove along the narrow winding roads. By and by I became more confident and was soon enjoying the comfort of a saloon car. After the hard springs of the jeep and the gales which usually blew round one's unprotected head, it seemed the height of luxury. On either side of the road the fields were thick with mowing grass and here and there, on the better farms, some had already been cut and its sweet scent wafted in for an instant through the open windows as I passed. The Castle Square in Caernarvon had the air of subdued activity characteristic of a fine Sunday afternoon in Wales. There were few buses and cars but a throng of people in their Sunday best sauntered in the Square, while seagulls wheeled above the castle walls and behind were the bright waters of the Straits. A little late, I parked the car and jumped out to scan the crowds, looking among the summer dresses and dark Sunday suits for the figure I had come to find. A black hat caught my eye, a white blouse and a black skirt, a figure also searching the crowds. Dark eyes under the hat were turning in my direction, were lighting with recognition and joy, a figure was taking urgent steps towards me. It was Fred, unaccustomedly smart; Fred hurrying forward now, suddenly blind and deaf to the people, the seagulls and the castle walls; Fred hugging me with her face ablaze with happiness while I hugged her. People paused, looked a little, passed on. Our happiness was no concern of theirs although some faces were smiling too.

There was so much to say that it was almost impossible to begin, but beaming silences filled any pause as we drove home. The years and Australia had not changed Fred. She was just as I remembered her. There was another joyful reunion with the rest of the family when we reached Carneddi. We had intended to have the old red stair-carpet rolled down the garden path in Fred's honour but she and I returned so quickly that it was not done. However such touches might have passed unnoticed in the excitement of the greetings.

And so, happily, that long hot summer of 1955 began. May and June had been mainly fine but in July every day was set fair with cloudless skies and shimmering heat over the hills. Shearing was accomplished without the usual delays of waiting for good weather. Fred left us again for a short while to attend her niece's wedding and make a round of visits to friends and relatives. We prepared for the silage-making. If there was one year when we did not need to make silage, this appeared to be the one but we decided to go ahead. We had no means of knowing what deluges the year might yet have in store and the handsome new silo was a great incentive. Gwilym Dolfriog came with his tractor and mowed, while my father and I carted the freshly-cut grass up to the silo with jeep and trailer as fast as we could. After an hour in that burning sunshine the swaths began to assume the blue-grey tone of partly-made hay and it was essential that the grass for the silo was green. It was packed in and allowed to heat. The heating was helped by the addition of molasses and water when necessary. We had a rough gauge of the temperature by plunging a crowbar into the silage overnight and feeling the end of it in the morning. If it were comfortably warm to the touch the temperature was right, if too hot to hold more grass must be loaded in quickly to exclude air from the lower layers and arrest the process of heating. Each layer had to be consolidated evenly and this we did by marching round on the grass as the silo was being filled, with good treading sessions between loads. Hikers walking up the road were surprised to see heads and later, as the level rose, shoulders and bodies revolving round inside the tower as the stamping was done. That hot season it was difficult to keep the temperature down and each day there was the constant request of: 'Can you come and stampede?' to all members of the family. Even Mother, with her bad head for heights, was conducted up the ladder.

The level of the silage rose quickly and soon it was time to put up the last two courses of slabs. It was a high lift to get them up but my father, Paul and I with the assistance of a friend, Jim, raised the first course into position. The next day we were ready for the final course and Jim was not available to help us. The heavy slabs must now be lifted eight feet and we wondered how it was to be done. Paul said he had an idea and disappeared into the toolshed. After a while he returned with a hastily-constructed trolley on two wooden rollers. He extended the aluminium ladder to its full length at a gentle angle against the silo and placed the trolley at its foot. Then we put a slab on the trolley, tied a nylon climbing rope round it and, with Paul hauling from above and me pushing and steering from below, it sailed to the top. It was an operation fraught with anxieties. The ladder sagged, the trolley rollers screamed complainingly and the whole thing threatened to pitch sideways, but it worked and one by one the slabs went up. The trolley, doing the work of an extra man for us, was named 'Jim'.

Now the silo was almost full and from its ten-foot vantage point the silage-stampers had a fine view of the valley stretching to the sea under the July heat-haze. We could see the tiny figures of Tom and Daniel Dinas in their hayfields far below and, farther away still, the squares of brilliant citrus green which marked the growing aftermath of fields already carried. On either hand were the mountains, flat now like cardboard scenery in the unbroken sunshine, with the white specks of newly-sheared sheep flecking their upper limits.

When the silo was filled we topped it with two loads of green bracken to prevent wastage in the upper layer of grass. Then, with the aid of 'Jim', we trundled large rocks up to the top to weight the whole mass down and arrest any further heating. Then we began the hay-making. In spite of the drought the crop was good after a heavy manuring, but the fierce rays of the sun penetrated the swaths and dried them before our eyes. Morning after morning dawned with uninterrupted heat, and by evening, load after load of good hay had been carried into our two barns. We ourselves became burnt brown in the sunshine and bathing suits took the place of clothes. Mud and gum-boots were forgotten and we wore sandals or went about barefoot. Fred was now home with us again, Mary was on holiday and on August 1st we carried our last load of hay. We had never known such a good summer. Every field had been mown and every corner cut with the scythe. Both barns were filled to their roofs and there was even a small stack of hay by the cowshed.

I took to sleeping out on Bryn Nithio, a rocky eminence in front of the farmhouse. Here, in past generations, the farmers of Carneddi had threshed their oats with flails, as the name of the hill bore witness, and I spread my ground-sheet where long ago the silver husks had been. The nights were almost too beautiful for sleep and I would lie awake, watching the moon ride over the mountains, the silver glint of moonlight in the river and the moonglade on the sea. I heard the owls calling from the woods below and the far-off trickle of water, and smelt the waft of hay from the night-time fields and the curious smell of earth cooling after the day's heat. I woke in the mornings to see milky vapours filling the valley, and to find the grass all lush with dew and often one of the tabby cats seated, tea-cosy fashion, on the corner of the ground-sheet to keep me company.

The days of August followed one another in a succession of swooning heat. We often went to the river and sometimes to the sea to wash away the grime of farm work. The streams were drying up now, their beds empty with once-green moss turning to parched flakes. The desiccated earth cracked and shrank away from the rock outcrops and the little moisture-loving bog plants shrivelled. The water supply at Beudy Newydd ran out and Mary Alice could be seen crossing two fields with her washing. There, by a shallow pool, she lighted a stick fire, boiled her clothes in a bucket and spread them on the bushes to dry in the blistering heat. Our own spring was failing and each morning we looked anxiously to see if the tank had filled again in the night. The garden plants wilted and Mother and Mary collected washing water in buckets from the waste pipes to pour on their thirsty roots. We left the plugs in our hand basins and used the same water over and over again. The hens and cattle were thirstier than ever and crowded round buckets and water founts more eagerly each day, while the trickle from our spring diminished. It was the only water left on the farm. The fields took on a tawny colour and autumn tints appeared prematurely in the woods. There was a hint of anxiety now in every cloudless morning. For six weeks no rain at all had fallen and there had been very little during the spring.

Then at the end of August the skies clouded. For two days no rain fell and then, at last, the first shower came. It spattered lightly on the husky ground and did little more than lay the dust, but it was the beginning of a change. It was several weeks before the spring ran at its normal rate again but the long drought was over. Between showers we had sunny days, cooler now with a breath of autumn in the air. Brian came to stay, and he and I gave a climbing demonstration for Fred and Mary. Neither had seen a rockface climbed and so we showed them how it was done on Canyon Rib in the Aberglaslyn Pass. They stood in the road below while a few cars also stopped and their occupants joined the watchers and passed remarks on the rashness of the figures on the precipice above. Mary said afterwards that there was one thrilling moment when my foot was to be seen trying to take futile steps on to nothingness as I attempted to climb round a sharp edge of rock. They came away, having found the demonstration enjoyable and enlightening.

The summer was ending and days were shortening. Fred's holiday, which in the spring had seemed to stretch ahead indefinitely, was suddenly nearly over. We wondered if she could cancel her passage and stay till Christmas—it was hard to believe that the pleasure of Fred's presence, the good times and jokes were almost at an end—but reluctantly it was decided that she must return as planned. She left Wales to pay a final visit to relatives while I went up to London to stay with Mary. I would say good-bye to her there.

It was a long time since I had been to Town. I knew London a little from day trips as a child but, since our move to Wales, there had been few outings. I had paid occasional visits to Paula and Anne but there had never seemed the time or money for a conventional yearly holiday. New schemes on the farm seemed to absorb all my surplus of both. Nor did I feel the need for holidays. There was neither tiredness nor boredom to escape, and the longing to travel and see new places could conveniently be put aside until the fascinating developments of the farm were further advanced. Also the mountains were so lovely that I was reluctant to leave them and the life on their slopes was a healthy one; there was little to tempt me away. At the same time I had no intention of becoming a recluse. With Fred's departure nearly here, I decided to spend the three weeks until her ship sailed with Mary. William Owen promised to help my father with the milking, and I took the train to London.

During the years in the mountains I seemed to have lost touch with city life. The cars, the people, the shops, the streets and the miles and miles of smoking chimneys were subject to my fascinated stare. In five minutes' walk I saw more new faces than in a whole year at home. I got lost in the Tube and nearly run over by the traffic, but it was pleasant to walk the crowded streets in my smartest clothes, with clean finger-nails and no ever-demanding animals to attend.

I took a part-time job as maid in a nurses' home. This sprang chiefly from a desire to mingle with the natives and see again how the other half of the world lived. It also helped to pass the time while Mary was teaching and provided a few shillings towards fares and meals. The mornings I spent sight-seeing, the afternoons at the nurses' home and the evenings were free to be with my sister.

About noon I took the Tube to work, had lunch at the nurses' home and then donned my blue overall for the after-noon's activities. It was a new and interesting experience to go to work. I could never quite regard what I did at home as coming into that category; it was, after all, exactly what I wanted to do; I issued my orders and then carried them out myself; there never seemed much of a dividing line between work and pleasure to me. Certainly the results did not always earn money but necessity and the months at Oathill had improved my powers. Here I had only to do what I was told, I earned 2s. $4\frac{1}{2}$d. for every hour and there was no respon-sibility at all.

One of my colleagues was Pat, a beautiful Irish girl. She was Getting Engaged, she told me, and we had whispered conversations in the Matron's bathroom about the delights of this state. Then we would separate, I to polish my floors and brush my five flights of stairs, Pat to clean the kitchens. Later we would meet again in the School where the student nurses were instructed by Sister Tutor. It was Pat's job to clean this but usually I helped her as she hated to be alone there. The School was in the basement. It had echoing cement floors and was dimly lighted by windows below ground level. Even electric light did not give it a more cheerful atmosphere, and after the flock of student nurses had swept up the stairs with clattering feet, it seemed strangely silent and eerie.

'Sure and I hate the place,' said Pat. 'It gives me the creeps.'

Jimmy, the skeleton in the lecture-room, was a source of fearful interest to her as he hung in the shadows, and she would set his bones a-rattle with a nervous touch as she passed, exclaiming: 'Who was he when he was alive, God rest his soul!' More sinister to me were the two dummies in the next room, a life-size man and a baby, who lay for ever between the clean sheets of their beds with a half-human presence and the still faces of corpses. Yet there was a feeling in the air that if you looked up quickly enough you would catch their eyes following you round the room.

Time passed slowly in the nurses' home but when five o'clock came, Pat and I would let ourselves out of the back door and run down the steps into the warm city-smelling afternoon. Now Pat's thoughts were turning towards her boy friend and the evening's dancing ahead, her lovely face still pale with the fatigue of other late nights. Now was the time I tasted the savour of city life and imagined myself into the shoes of all those people tapping along the pavement, all those people behind steering-wheels and all those people in houses where the lights were flicking on. We passed quickly along the streets—everyone was going quickly, geared to the activity of so many other human beings—and our way was beginning to be illuminated by the artificial sunlight of shop windows and the sky flashed with constellations of neon lights. The moon, in fact, was dimmed and passed almost unnoticed over the chimney-tops.

Then, towards the end of my three weeks' stay in London, Fred's last day came. Her ship sailed from Tilbury the following afternoon but I had elected to go to my stair-sweeping at the nurses' home. I felt that a final parting at the quayside was more than I could bear. I felt it would be far better for Fred to be busy with the bustle of embarkation and the company of her sister who was going too, and with thoughts of her waiting husband and memories of an unshadowed summer in the mountains. My sad face then could only remind her of the pains of parting. And so we met on the evening before she sailed. With sadness and happiness mixed, we walked the streets together. From the throng of Trafalgar Square we were drawn to the quietness under Admiralty Arch, along the Mall with its string of lights and so to sit on a seat with the peaceful bulk of Buckingham Palace behind. We said all the necessary things in bright and cheerful voices but our eyes were sad and our footsteps slow and reluctant as we retraced our steps down the Mall. The moment was prolonged with a cup of coffee in a late-night restaurant but the atmosphere became so full of the weight of impending departure, of mute good-byes and unwilling separation, that we were thankful to leave its deserted brightness, where one waitress wiped cups and saucers behind a chromium bar, yawning to go home, and escape into the impersonal, hurrying street. There was nothing to be gained by lingering now. Our brief good-bye was said in the scurrying rush of the Underground, with the rattle and roar of the trains drowning our voices; a hug and a kiss, and then the herds of people were between us, more and more of them as we went in our opposite directions and I felt, sadly, that it would be a long time before I saw Fred again.

13   The Festive Season

Summer and autumn would have been a slack time at Mr. Ephraim's hatchery if he had not kept turkeys. Anglesey and Caernarvonshire have not a great tradition for poultry-keeping; it is mainly cattle and sheep country and a farm's supply of day-old chickens is taken in the spring for laying in the following autumn. Mr. Ephraim, therefore, used his labour and equipment from June until December for the production of Christmas turkeys.

My brooder house was to be occupied by replacements for the laying flock and a number of growers for sale from February to June. Then the birds would be put outside in folds and it seemed that the handsome new shed would be standing idle for half the year. This fact suddenly came to mind in about May of the first year. Earlier my satisfaction in the building had dazzled foresight out of view. Now I realized that, with £150 invested in it, the brooder house should be kept productive all the time. Here I could learn from Mr. Ephraim. I had a high respect for his judgment and if turkeys were a paying proposition for him they might be so for me too. They could be kept without alteration to the pattern of our farming or any additional expense apart from the cost of day-old poults. On deep-litter in the brooder house they would be easy to manage and safe from foxes.

I wrote to various turkey breeders but I was too late; all the poults had been booked months ago. It was disappointing to find that the bright idea of turkey-keeping was to be frustrated from the start. In despair I wrote to Mr. George. I had kept in touch with Oathill since I left, and Elizabeth and the children came for holidays quite often. Mr. George, although too busy to stay long himself, would arrive to deliver or collect his family, stay the night and have a look round the farm. On the whole he seemed to approve my efforts, and himself had a great love of the mountains. He would stroll round the holding in his quiet way, saying very little but, at the end of the tour, he might drop a few very pertinent remarks to which I listened attentively. I had found from past experience that it was well worth while to take note of Mr. George's pronouncements. Occasionally he would deliver such a saying as: 'Ruth doesn't mind doing without a few necessities so long as she can have her luxuries.' This remark, I think, was directed at the pale blue portable typewriter I had just bought, or it may have been another of my exuberant purchases; anyway I took note. Now he replied to my letter, saying that if I tried a certain farm in Oxfordshire I might get what I wanted. The charm worked. There would be poults available on the date I specified.

By the end of June the last of the pullets were outside in their aluminium folds. Paul had designed and made these specially to meet our requirements, and I found them a very useful complement to the early intensive rearing of the chicks. Each was made of one curved sheet of aluminium with semi-circular wooden ends, and was light and small enough to be lifted into the back of the jeep when the time came to move them from the hay-fields. The runs were in two sections, also for easy movement, and they articulated well over the slopes and confined the birds safely from marauding carrion crows.

Now the brooder house was empty and I was ready for the turkeys which arrived at the beginning of July, seventy-five balls of chocolate, sepia and gold fluff, worth half a guinea apiece. At Mr. Ephraim's suggestion I had installed a dozen day-old cockerel chicks in the brooder a week earlier. These were now the same size as the newly-hatched poults and had found their way round the layout of their home; they knew where it was warm and dark to take a snooze and knew also that food and drink were to be found at the cooler, lighter perimeter of their quarters. This information they passed on to the turkey poults, which were slower and dreamier by nature, and none were lost through a failure to master their surroundings, for at this tender age hunger or a chill could kill them quickly. Soon they were as perky as the cock chicks and I let them out into the great world of a peat moss run. Here they became conscious of their turkey-hood and the future gobblers pranced on tiny toes in the motions of display, attempting to drag their down-covered wings and fan their non-existent tails. I grew very fond of them. Soon their feathers began to sprout into a glory of white-flecked bronze and there was a trace of wistfulness and trust about their lustrous eyes. They would gather round at feeding-time with dignity and hopeful expressions and without the rude manners of a hen. But they could be fierce too. As they grew older I was fascinated to watch how, on occasions of turkey emotion, the red of their faces drained away leaving a shade of turquoise blue, and then as quickly flooded back again when their feelings changed once more. The sunlight would slant in through the wire mesh of the windows, the glass all removed now to give the airy condition that they like, and the gobblers, crops full, would become aware of it and of their pretty hens and one after another they uttered the word 'chut', wings were dragged with an ecstatic shivering of quills and forty tails blossomed into spreading fans. Now, too, was the time to try out the voice and the first resonant gobble was followed by thirty-nine other gobbles, rapid facial colour changes and the lengthening and shortening of little above-beak tassels. Then suddenly they would all think of something else, return to normal shape, size and colour and go pecking round the troughs for an overlooked pellet or two. It would be some little time before the thought of 'chut', gobble and fanned tails came to mind again and they would begin the procedure anew.

Kale-time was one of their exciting moments and, as I shook the freshly-cut leaves out of a sack on to the floor, they would rush forward with cries of delight, seize sprays of greenery in their beaks and rush off again with a spearhead of other turkeys in pursuit. When they realized that there was enough for all, the panic would die down to contented twitterings and peckings. As night came they would retire to roost at the highest possible points. As many as were able to find room would flap up on to the brace beams of the roof trusses and after preliminary shufflings and tiltings backwards and forwards would settle down in the peaceful attitude of large birds roosting for the night, with only the occasional plop of a falling dropping to break the silence. The brooder house was directly behind and above my bedroom and sometimes in the night I could hear the sudden flap of big wings and a solitary startled gobble, and I would wonder if a turkey nightmare, connected with the Christmas season, had cast its shadow over one member of the roost.

About October I began to think of marketing my flock. A local farmer who also kept turkeys gave the address of a Manchester trader to me, and I wrote to make inquiries for a possible sale. This was a new venture, I had no local contacts and, in such a thinly populated county, the demand for Christmas turkeys did not appear to be great. I was pleasantly surprised when Mr. B. arrived promptly from Manchester in person. Turkeys were evidently a worthwhile commodity. Used now to dealing with the shrewd, soft-spoken Welsh farmers, Mr. B. presented a new type. Thickset to the point of heaviness, he still had a wiry alertness which smacked of a knowledge of the wicked world and long expertness in business deals. I doubted if I would be a match for him. Without previous experience or the quick brain of a Mr. Frank, I was rather hazy about how much I ought to ask to cover expenses and make a profit. I knew the amount I had spent on food but had little idea of how heavy the birds would weigh. To my advantage was the fact that I wanted no more than a fair price and that the turkeys were undoubtedly of prime quality. So Mr. B. and I bargained round the kitchen table. My first condition was that he must kill and pluck the birds. The thought of doing this ourselves was unbearable, although I didn't tell him so. He agreed to it for the reduction of a few pence per pound. He suggested a low figure, I a high one, but finally it was agreed, after numerous compromises on both sides, that the price was to be 4s. 6d. a pound for both stags and hens, that our premises were to be used for plucking but the feathers should be mine. Mr. B. gave me £50 deposit as a token of his good faith and extracted a signed agreement of our terms from me. He had been let down in the past, he said, by producers selling their stock to someone else if prices suddenly rose, and I was aware of his glance searching my face to detect any shady characteristics which might lurk beneath a naïve exterior. Then he departed with promises to telephone me at a later date.

The last of the leaves fell flaming from the trees. Christmas parcels were despatched on their way to Fred, now back in Australia. The cattle were brought down from their high grazing grounds and the rams loosed to roam among the flock. Days were colder and nights longer now, and in the mornings the low-lying land of Gors Goch was white with frost. Winter was taking a grip on the mountains and the highest peaks had a dusting of snow. People's thoughts began to turn towards Christmas and cheerful cards multiplied on our chimney piece. About this time I was searching the newspapers for mention of turkey prices and each time I found one my heart sánk. Six or seven shillings a pound was quoted as being expected and although I was well aware that producers' profits were much reduced by the middlemen's cut, I began to feel I had bargained away my birds too cheaply and wondered if I should make any profit at all. The turkeys were eating enormously now and Bibby's lorry came grinding up the hill almost every other week with a ton of turkey, hen and cattle food on board. Albert, the driver, was our frequent visitor and although he symbolized great expense—it cost nearly £40 every time the lorry came—I was always pleased to see him; he was indefatigable in carrying sacks along the slippery path to the brooder house, and nothing was too much trouble for him.

Now Christmas cakes and puddings were made, and brown-paper parcels began to arrive, while an outward-going stream from us was carried down the hill by Matty Postman, who was always kind in executing commissions. Christmas was nearly upon us and one evening there was a telephone call from Mr. B. in Manchester. He would come on the Friday evening before Christmas, he said, pluck the turkeys through the night and depart with them on Saturday morning. He asked me not to feed the birds on the previous day.

Suddenly the holiday season seemed rather gruesome. Normally all our animals were sold for breeding and reached the slaughter house only after long and useful lives, and at several removes from us. Now, instead of complacency as a producer

147

of useful food, I felt I was betraying my turkeys to their deaths. I was filled with scruples but, for economic reasons, it was too late to change my mind. I determined to make as good a job as possible of this distasteful undertaking, and this we did, but the painful ethics of life and death in the animal world remained unsolved.

The final Friday came. I herded the turkeys into half the brooder house, leaving the other half empty for plucking operations, and cleaned and swept the floor. Then I hung sacks round the pens to screen the live turkeys from what was going on next door. This, as it turned out, was an unnecessary precaution for later a few birds were to poke a head round the sacking curtain and watch the demise of their fellows with complete indifference. The birds were so tame that they were not in the least disturbed, and what worried me so much failed entirely to make an impression on them. Finally, I suspended horizontal rails for hanging the birds when they were plucked.

About five o'clock Mr. B. arrived with a friend, in what I sensed was a clandestinely-borrowed sausage van. The famous firm that owned it might have been surprised to see it winding up the narrow mountain road in a strange detour from its normal route. After they had had tea in the farmhouse, Mr. B. and Alf retired to the turkey shed where I had hung two pressure lanterns and provided everything I thought they might need. Shortly afterwards they were back at the door again. I had settled down to farm accounts and was closing my mind to any thought of turkeys. Now Mr. B. and Alf were having difficulty with the killing, it seemed, and would like help. They were traders in poultry and not accustomed to the present task. I had to go with them; the first consideration was that the job be done properly, however little I might like it, and so I went, taking a short length of rope. I knew just how a neck should be dislocated and had taught both my father and Paul the way without ever having killed a bird myself. Now I explained to Mr. B. and Alf, as light-heartedly and nonchalantly as possible, that if the turkey were suspended by the feet with its head about level with the operator's knee, great force could be brought to bear and the neck dislocated instantly. They found the method worked well and I left them as soon as I was sure they had mastered it.

148

About ten o'clock I took tea out to the brooder house. Now a pile of feathers lay on the floor and a row of birds, neatly plucked, hung from the rail, looking suitably processed, Christmassy and quite unlike the pretty creatures I had tended for so long. My spirits rose; the obnoxious task was being carried out neatly and humanely, and the finished product would undoubtedly please both poulterers and housewives. I felt we had done well and began to have hopes of a sizable cheque the next day.

We went to bed while Alf and Mr. B. worked on. The large cream-coloured sausage van was parked in the gloom by the deep-litter house, an alien visitor to our hillside. It was strange to lie in bed and think of the activity in the lighted brooder house, and all those Christmas dinners, originating in the mountains, to be eaten from Manchester dining-tables; stranger still to think it all began from an idea or two I had had a few months ago. Now I was nearly asleep. It was almost as though the turkey venture were only a daydream like many others and in the morning there would be no turkeys and no sausage van.

Suddenly I was wide awake and sitting up in bed. There might well be no turkeys and no sausage van in the morning. We had all heard tales of floodlights and Alsatian dogs, barbed wire and all-night patrols to protect the big Norfolk turkey farms from theft. It would be easy for Alf and Mr. B.—and now I saw them in the role of crooks—to finish their plucking in the early hours of the morning and steal away in their sausage van while we were all asleep. The £50 deposit cheque represented only a part of the value of the birds. It was clear now why they had chosen the unusual course of working through the night. I slipped out of bed, pushed my feet into rubber-soled shoes and took a peep out of the back door. The windows of the brooder house glowed with light and I could hear the men talking inside. Collecting torch, pencil and paper, and slipping a duffle coat over my pyjamas, I let myself softly out of the front door and tip-toed over to the sausage van. By the cautiously-shaded glow of the torch I wrote down its registration number. This would be an extra safeguard but I would lie awake all night and listen for the sound of its engine. Then I tiptoed back to bed, pleased with my own alertness. For five minutes I lay awake with ears attuned to every sound and then, in the usual way, fell into a deep and dreamless sleep.

. The first light of morning was at the window when I woke. I looked out. Reassuringly the pale elephant shape of the sausage van by the deep-litter house showed in the dawn light. The turkeys were not, after all, speeding unpaid for on their way to the city and the suspicions of the previous night caused a twinge of remorse. On the way out to the cowshed, I met Alf and Mr. B. descending stiffly from the sausage van, grey-faced, cold and bad tempered. Apparently they had given up at three o'clock in the morning with half the turkeys still unplucked and had dozed in the back of the van. It had been cold and hard inside. They were disgruntled and bore all the signs of an uncomfortable night, red eyes and stubby chins. It was essential that I cheer them up; they were not crooks after all; their plans were going astray and, as my customers, I must have them pleased and satisfied and the business of the farm going efficiently. I took them into the warm kitchen, Mother cooked breakfast and they began to revive visibly. Then for the rest of the day I helped with the plucking. It was not what I had planned but now the foremost idea was to finish and be done. The men were now in good spirits again as the work speeded up. I plucked away steadily in a sea of feathers while the rows of finished birds multiplied on the hooks. At last the final suit of feathers was removed from the final bird and it was time to weigh the carcasses. Mr. B. produced his spring balance and I, still a little wary, produced mine. We checked the two against each other and when it was found that Mr. B.s balance registered less than mine, he thought mine was the better of the two. I was quite agreeable to using it; it was tested for weighing milk and I knew it was accurate.

The birds made a fine show. They were big and broad breasted, with small plump legs and pearly skins. They were also heavy and the scales ducked and danced with the weight of them. There were going to be a lot of 4s. 6d.s even if it was not a high price. The largest of all weighed twenty-five pounds and Mr. B. pulled a long face at this. He complained that it was too big for anybody's oven and so I withdrew it for our own Christmas dinner. Then Alf journeyed backwards and forwards to the sausage van with loads and bunches of turkeys on his back, while Mr. B. and I retired to the house for the reckoning. That turkey venture ended with the biggest cheque I had ever had and at five o'clock, just twenty-four hours after it had arrived, the sausage van trundled away down the hill, with all the turkeys and a satisfied Alf and Mr. B. inside.

There was just one more thing I had to do. I made a sum and found that, after the cost of the food had been deducted and a modest amount charged for the few hours a week I had given in labour, I had made a net profit of £100. I did not know whether to be more surprised or pleased. Outside, the brooder house was strangely silent, with nothing there but a big pile of feathers and the faint odour of poultry manure.

The turkeys had been successful and I planned to keep them again. After the chick-rearing season was over, poults from Christmas 1956 were installed in the brooder house, the number now increased to eighty. As before they did well and this time I had the added confidence of experience. I joined the cost accounting scheme of the Agricultural Economics Department at Aberystwyth and carefully entered all my figures in the book that was provided. At the end of the season I would get a profit and loss account and be able to see comparable figures from other producers.

It was not until September that I became aware of the first hint of trouble. There was a sentence or two in the newspaper about the increased turkey population of the country; because of the good prices of previous years so many more million turkeys were being kept, and many farmers were rearing them for the first time. From then onwards I followed these press announcements with increasing anxiety; there was even mention of flooded markets and the current prices quoted were very low. I wrote immediately to Mr. B. but, when after a week or two no reply had arrived from him, my fears were confirmed. I wrote to numerous other wholesalers but they showed very little interest, offered infinitesimal prices per pound, and not even one would consider killing and plucking the birds himself. The landslide had begun. Other producers, like myself, were now haunted by the nightmare of having hundreds of birds on their hands. They knew that after

Christmas there would be no market for their turkeys and yet the stock would be occupying buildings needed for other purposes and consuming increasingly uneconomic quantities of food. Panic selling began. Many producers preferred to suffer a small immediate loss rather than face the prospect of a much bigger one later. More and more turkeys flooded into the market, while prices plummeted lower. Housewives, wholesalers and butchers were pleased and every deep-freeze in the country groaned with frozen birds. Finally, as the price continued to drop, only the housewives were likely to benefit; everyone else in the turkey trade faced disaster.

The farmers who, like ourselves, kept turkeys only as a sideline, were luckier than many. The disastrous season served to demonstrate with bitter emphasis the importance of that old saying about eggs and baskets. I had already found that if one branch of our farming was hit by falling prices or rising costs there was always another that was making money. Although we were not in a position to make so much in a good year, neither would we have to go out of business in a bad one and, with a nucleus of stock as a starting point, we could quickly expand any branch of the farm which appeared to be booming, without making major changes of policy. I had, however, counted on making money from the turkeys and had already spent it in my mind. After the financial glories of last year, it was wretchedly disappointing to think of losing those profits again this season. The only hope of salvaging anything from the wreck appeared to be a bid for the consumer market. In this way I could collect the middleman's profit to help make good my loss as a producer. The disadvantage was that we should have to kill and pluck all the birds ourselves and probably truss quite a few of them. Paul said he would do the killing and this, at least, was one problem solved.

Then came the task of trying to sell our despised birds to the consumers. I looked up the numbers of a few hotels in the district and seated myself grimly by the telephone. I was not good at this sort of thing.

'Is that the Mountain Hotel?' I asked in confident, saleswoman's tones. 'I wonder if you are interested in buying some

152

good quality turkeys. The manager is out? Thank you, I will ring again.'

'. . . some good quality turkeys. Yes, we will pluck them. Yes, we will dress them. Yes, we will deliver them. Two on the 23rd? Thank you.'

'. . . quality turkeys. 3s. 9d. a pound? 3s. 6d. a pound? Well perhaps 3s. 3d. a pound. Only small ones. Thank you.'

'. . . turkeys. You are already supplied? Thank you.'

'. . . turkeys?'

'. . . turkeys?'

I could endure only a short spell of this, the unloading of an unwanted commodity on a dead market. I had to break off now and again for a cup of coffee or a look at the mountains in their bleak winter loveliness. The telephone bill mounted, the list of local hotels was exhausted and so was I, but about twenty birds had a destination for Christmas and would show a tiny profit. Only sixty more to go. I racked my brains for the sort of institutions that would need large numbers of turkeys. Hospitals, perhaps. But after another session on the telephone I found that hospitals had their own regular suppliers and were not interested in cut-price jumped-up newcomers like myself. I was now getting a slow trickle of orders from local housewives, tempted by the low prices, but this did not do much to reduce the number still unsold. The turkey-eating population of North Wales seemed very meagre. We would have to go farther from home where more people might eat more turkeys. Here Paul, seeing my haunted expression, came to the rescue. He had a 1930 Austin 7 with a canvas hood and celluloid windows. The engine sounded like the noise of an old sewing machine much amplified or, as my father described it, one felt as though one were driving in an alarm clock, but it ground along valiantly and did thirty-five miles to the gallon, which was much more economical than the jeep's fifteen. It also had the added luxury of the hood. Paul now offered to drive me round the countryside until all the turkeys were sold.

One day at the end of November we set out. We dressed in our best clothes to counteract the eccentric appearance of the Austin; it was essential that we seemed poised and prosperous with a valuable commodity to sell. I thought the Army might be one possible customer and believed that Christmas Dinners for the Troops were an important part of army life. Our sixty turkeys would be a mere nothing among so many. And so we set off for Chester, this being the nearest large town and the Headquarters of Western Command.

The trip developed into a jaunt in spite of the grim issues at stake. Wrapped in blankets against the cold and the penetrating draughts of the Austin 7, we enjoyed the drive over the hills and through the pleasant landscape of Cheshire, noting the state of farming in the wintery countryside as we passed. Here a flock of sheep, there a field of kale caught our attention. At Chester we visited N.A.A.F.I. Headquarters with the kind help of a chaplain whom we knew. N.A.A.F.I. was most obliging but it appeared to think in terms of frozen turkeys from such places as Yugoslavia rather than prime quality home-bred birds. It might, however, be able to assist us in a small way, and would let us know later. With this we had to be content.

Now came the task of touring the hotels. It might have been depressing but we felt singularly carefree that day. The anxiety of the past few weeks seemed to have worn itself out and we could see the funny side of our situation. Paul was to canvass half the hotels, I the other half and we arranged to meet later for a cup of tea and to review our progress. Two shillings a pound was the minimum we could charge and barely covered the cost of production. I was thankful, as I advanced across thick pile carpets in search of catering managers, that we had discarded the idea of approaching possible customers in the guise of poor farmers in gum-boots and slacks. At least my lambs-lined winter coat looked expensive and gave me confidence to tackle those sleek catering managers and their formidable chefs. In the end I retired defeated and arrived at the tea rendezvous without a single word written in my order book. Paul had had no luck either. We might have known that all those hotels were much too efficient to depend on the chance visits of turkey hawkers for the feeding of their guests. We laughed about our experiences; there was nothing else we could do. After tea we tried three hospitals and a mental home, with no results from any of them.

Chester had not proved very fruitful and we decided to turn towards home again and canvass the North Wales holiday coast on the way. In spite of all the setbacks we were still enjoying ourselves and above the roar of the little engine Paul was singing Scottish airs, while I considered our whirlwind tour and began to feel very, very experienced. We had one last resort, the ice-cream factory in Llandudno. If everything else failed we could park the birds in the deep-freeze and cash in on them little by little, at cut prices, to the hotels during the summer.

'We shall be laughing at this in a year's time,' said Paul, but oddly enough we were laughing then.

At the first of the holiday towns we stopped in search of butchers, hotels or hospitals. I asked Paul to wait, descended from the Austin 7 and, on an impulse, walked briskly into the first butcher's shop, trying to assume the air of a prudent housewife.

'Are you taking orders for Christmas turkeys?'

This was a new impromptu technique.

'Yes, madam. Can I help you?'

'I was wondering how much they are likely to cost this year.'

The butcher's expression was kindly and helpful.

'They should be cheaper than usual. I haven't bought any yet, but say, about 4s. 6d. to 5s. a pound.'

'Thank you so much. I will call again later.'

I hurried out of the shop. Paul was waiting a few yards farther down the road.

'Now's your chance. He hasn't bought any yet.'

It was Paul's turn to go in while I waited expectantly. He came out a few minutes later with a pleased expression.

'Fifteen for 3s. 9d. a pound!'

This was the best price we had yet received and brought the total number of ordered turkeys up to nearly fifty. We felt a little guilty at having used a stool-pigeon technique but it added to the amusement of the day. I was very pleased when, the following year, this same butcher placed an order with us again. He said he had been well pleased before.

We visited a few more hotels as we followed the coast road home and managed to get two or three more orders for single birds. Most places, however, were shut and boarded up for the winter, while the promenades, the marine drives, the boating lakes, shelters and swimming pools were deserted except for seagulls, and washed clean by winter rains. Our final call was at the ice-cream factory. We discovered the cost of freezing and also that there was plenty of room in the cold-store. One of the storemen took us to see the little arctic rooms, where white rime sparkled in the electric light and where turkeys were already stored, neatly packed in polythene bags, hard as rocks and glittering with a seasonal glaze of frost. He told us that cold-store work was very healthy and the storemen had the same freedom from colds as polar explorers. He wore thick leather gloves to protect his hands from frost burns. Outside again, the cold air of the November afternoon struck us with the seeming heat of a summer's day, so great was the difference in temperature. Feeling quite warm we climbed back into the car and rattled off on the final stretch of the journey home.

I felt satisfied with the results of our tour. It was unlikely that we should ever experience a worse season than this and I felt we should now manage to cover the costs of production. We had been able to enjoy the comical side of the situation and should be rich in experience if not in cash.

A few days later the voice of N.A.A.F.I. came on the telephone. A camp in mid-Wales would require some turkeys early in December. The price was low but at least it would mean a few less birds for the deep-freeze and I was glad to diminish our numbers before the last great slaughter in the week preceding Christmas. We delivered the N.A.A.F.I. birds in the Austin 7, the springs sagging with the weight of twenty pounders on the back seat. We might not be making much money but the delivery jaunts made a pleasant break from farm routine. The canteen man was complimentary about the quality of our birds, pinching their fat breasts and nodding his head delightedly. We left in a glow of approbation, glad to know that our work was appreciated. That troublesome season had its few satisfactions.

Now we had only to draw up a tactical plan co-ordinating work and deliveries to save as much time and petrol as possible. Then we began on the killing and plucking, weighing and labelling as we went along, and checking with our order list. Mother retired to the dairy with sharp knives, buckets, a pile of newspapers and a revolted expression, and set to work on trussing such birds as had to be ready for the table. We always knew when she was engaged in this task by the five cats disposed outside and facing towards the dairy door. Helpers with the drawing of leg sinews—and this required some force —had to dodge craftily through the door if all five were not to go streaking in and dive head first into the buckets of offal.

At last the work was finished. The brooder house was silent now after the frantic activity of the past few days, and filled with nude figures depending from their hooks. I spent the evening before the big delivery in making out the customers' bills. There were some fifty turkeys to go, weighing nearly seven hundredweight, and it would be necessary to use the jeep and trailer for the journey. Before going to bed I looked out at the cold starlit sky and hoped it would be fine.

The next morning we were up before dawn. There were no rear lights on the trailer and the journey must be made in the short span of the December day. The trailer was lined with a tarpaulin, and my father and I, in the half-light, trudged back and forth from the brooder house with bunches of turkeys. Arranged head to tail in layers they filled the trailer to the brim and we covered them over with the loose ends of the tarpaulin and tied it down. The trussed birds in their plastic bags were packed into the back of the jeep itself and, collecting invoices, thermos of hot coffee and sandwiches, I was ready to set out. Paul accompanied me to help with the driving and unloading and he waited for me in the village. It was almost light now, the sky overcast with mist low on the mountains and a wintery chill in the air. The journey proved something of an ordeal. Half-way to our farthest point of delivery it began to rain, steady cold rain that fell on our unprotected heads, found a gap between necks and mackintosh collars and trickled down our flinching bodies to make a puddle where we sat. Wearing rain-coat, duffle coat, jacket, sweater, and sou'wester over unfurled balaclava cap, I was still wretched. Paul, who appeared impervious to discomfort, did most of the small deliveries, and by the time we had reached our farthest point the rain had stopped and I began to revive a little with the help of hot coffee. The careful packing had kept the turkeys dry and undamaged. Our final call was to be the ice-cream factory, but before this we made a lucky chance sale to a fishmonger and only nineteen birds had to go into deep-freeze. After weighing and the collection of a receipt, these birds were borne away into the polar regions and we climbed stiffly back into the jeep, feeling that the chill that was to be in their bones could be no greater than the one at present in ours.

As the sun was setting in a fiery winter's glory and the last of the daylight draining out of the sky, we came winding up the hill to Carneddi, where lighted windows held promise of a hot bath and hot meal inside. The last of our troubles were almost over.

The final local deliveries were carried out quickly and in a festive spirit two or three days before Christmas. There was nothing more to worry about. We had done our best to counter the disastrous season. Allowing for the sale of the deep-freeze turkeys in the summer at similar prices, I thought we had made about £10 profit. Later, when the Agricultural Economics Department cost accounts were circulated, I found we had been very lucky indeed. Among twenty-five producers listed I was one of the only six who had made any profit while some of the big turkey farmers had lost several thousand pounds. It was annoying to hear afterwards how, in spite of the glut, there was finally a shortage in some parts of the country and how prices had risen there to 6s. a pound or more.

And so Christmas passed and the New Year came and that was the end of a most extraordinary season.

14   Strawberry Mountain

Nineteen fifty-seven was the year of rock 'n' roll, sputniks and strawberries. Of these, strawberries were most to occupy my mind. My interest in them began in the autumn of 1956 when the Ministry of Agriculture inquired if I would be willing to propagate virus-tested strawberry plants for the Nuclear Stock Association. I was much surprised and said that I knew nothing about the propagation of strawberry plants. It was possible to learn, however, and the Horticultural Advisory Officer arranged to visit me to discuss the matter.

Mr. E. G. Williams arrived a few days later and explained the position. It seemed that virus diseases seriously affected the strawberry-growing industry and much reduced production and profits. East Malling Research Station had recently evolved a technique for combating this scourge. Certain selected strawberry plants were grown in cabinets in which the temperature was above normal. The viruses in the sap were killed, while most of the plants survived. These precious virus-free plants were then propagated in an insect-proof glass house, where they could not be reinfected, and later the runners were sent to special, isolated areas or closed gauze houses for further propagation as Foundation Stocks. Aphides, the ubiquitous greenfly, were the chief means of spreading a virus from one plant to the next. If the aphides could be controlled, the plants continued to grow and multiply in a disease-free state, and provided a source of healthy stock for fruit producers. The Nuclear Stock Association had been formed to promote this work and were now looking for further suitable areas for the production of Foundation Stocks, which would be grown under contract. The Stocks had to be a mile from any other strawberry plant and at least ten miles from any main fruit-growing district. Mr. Williams thought that Carneddi met these needs.

Here seemed to be an opportunity to turn the farm's natural disadvantages to profit. The altitude, high rainfall and austere vegetation appeared all to be favourable to the production of disease-free plants, while the small patches of ground where a plough could be used would be adequate for the crop. The terms of the contract were simple enough; the propagated plants belonged to the Nuclear Stock Association and must be cultivated according to approved methods; in return I would receive, at the end of the season's work, what seemed to me a princely sum and any surplus plants could be sold privately. The work, in fact, seemed to suit the farm and the farmer and I agreed to become a Foundation Stock grower.

The next task was to take soil samples, and Mr. Williams and I went out with soil auger and little bags. The half acre already under the plough, where I had grown enough potatoes, carrots and swedes to last the family through the winter and a small patch of kale for the cows, was considered suitable for the 1957 strawberry bed, and we filled a bag with soil. Then we moved on to look at other possible sites. Foundation strawberries could not be grown on the same ground more often than once in four years—a precaution against pests and diseases—and it would be as well to look for sites for future years. Walking over the humpy little fields and drilling here and there, we found several half-acre pieces where the soil was deep enough for strawberries. Later I had the results of the soil tests with a recommendation for fertilizers, and was pleased to find that our ground was perfectly clean and healthy.

Next we were visited by Mr. Gardner, the Regional Horticultural Advisory Officer for Wales, and he seemed equally pleased with our situation. Carneddi's new enterprise had begun. I opened a file labelled STRAWBERRIES, and in it placed the cultural notes and information I had received from Mr. Williams and Mr. Gardner. We should need a cold-frame to house the potted plants through the winter and I sent an urgent message to Paul to come at once. He arrived and together we constructed a six foot by four foot frame from two old windows, with off-cuts of corrugated asbestos for the sides. It cost us nothing except time. The Nuclear Stock Association had kindly advanced £40 of the contract money, at my request, to cover the initial outlay of launching me as a Foundation Grower, but we wanted to economize where possible. The toolshed was tidied again and more of its old relics hurried to the rubbish heap, leaving a large area of the concrete floor exposed. Here I mixed the John Innes Potting Compost No. 2 from a recipe given to me by Mr. Williams. Then I purchased five-inch flower pots from Bangor Market and fetched them home in the jeep.

The strawberry plants arrived from East Malling early in November and we potted them in the manner prescribed by Mr. Williams. We had six different varieties and it was of the greatest importance that we did not mix them. At that time, a Cambridge Vigour plant appeared much the same as a Royal Sovereign and it was only later that we became aware of the differences, the waxiness or downy appearance of a leaf, the size and number of the leaf serrations, the shade of green or the direction of growth of hairs on the leaf stem, so that each variety looked then as different from the other as faces in a crowd. We potted each sort separately and marked the edges of the pots with different coloured paints, two blue spots were Talisman, a blue and a white Huxley's Giant, one silver Cambridge Prizewinner and so on. It was tedious but worthwhile until our experience increased. Then we carried them all out and put them in the frame.

During the winter I often went into the garden to admire them and open the frame, water them or sometimes to brush the snow off the glass. This was work that I liked and it was pleasant to think it was useful and would benefit people in other places, far away from our small hill farm. Mother, a keen gardener, would come and hunt slugs. My father who claimed, misleadingly I believe, that he did not know an oak tree from an ash, took little interest in the plants, but when February came, with hard and frosty ground, he and I carted twenty trailer loads of poultry manure from the deep-litter house and spread it on the arable land. After the plough had been, he set to work to fence it round with rabbit netting. I ordered a knapsack sprayer and a quantity of insecticide. We were all ready for the season's propagation.

In March Mr. Gardner called again to inspect the strawberries before they were planted out. One had damped off during the winter but the rest were growing fast; new white roots filled the pots and new green leaves were unfurling. I was rather proud of them. It was the new green leaves that held Mr. Gardner's attention. Carefully he opened their folds, peered closer and then removed a tiny green speck on his finger-tip. It was an aphis. Foundation strawberries, I knew, must be free from aphides, and here was one whose champing invisible jaws had probably injected a deadly virus into those soft green leaves. I felt alarmed, but Mr. Gardner explained that so long as it was not a strawberry aphis all might be well. They were the ones which transmitted the virus. It was quite easy, he said, to tell a strawberry aphis from the other kinds; its tummy touched the leaf when sitting down and there were knobs at the ends of its body hairs. I took another anxious look at the aphis on his finger-tip; I could hardly see the creature at all and it was impossible to tell whether its hairs were knobbed or not. Apparently one had to view it through a microscope to find this out and, with one or two more which he discovered, Mr. Gardner imprisoned it in a match-box together with a piece of strawberry leaf.

'I suppose you never have aphides in your garden.'

'On the contrary,' said the Regional Horticultural Advisory Officer, 'they delight in cocking a snook at me.'

He recommended that I spray the plants immediately with Metasystox. This was a systemic insecticide which I had bought for the purpose and which was absorbed through the surface of the leaf, circulated round with the plant's sap and which brought instant death to any greenfly which might take a bite. The knapsack sprayer had not yet arrived—partly the reason for my not having sprayed earlier—but that afternoon I took a fine-rose watering-can and applied the Metasystox liberally. Later I heard with relief that my aphides had no knobs and all was well.

It was dry that spring. The lambing had begun well and the first small white figures were skipping after their mothers over our greening fields. The first tracery of buds, too, was touching the trees with a hint of yellow and pale green, and here and there a larch tree, already fully clothed, burned in the forest like an emerald flame. Early in April, after an application of compound fertilizer and after the ploughed land had been disced, we planted out the strawberries. The rows were ten feet apart and the plants at six-foot intervals in the row. Paul painted name posts for the different varieties and, when the job was done, the field looked immaculate and impressive in the warm spring sunshine. The dry weather, which had made our work and cultivations easy, was now a disadvantage to the newly-set plants and each evening for a week, as the sun was dipping behind the mountains and shadows lengthening, we lugged buckets of water out to the field and soaked the roots. There were one hundred and ninety-five plants. Then showery weather came and, firmly established now, they grew into dark green pyramids of glossy leaves. As a crop they looked odd in that mountain landscape in the widely-spaced geometrical rows. Everywhere else the bracken, heather and gorse swept up past jumbled outcrops to the skyline in a maze of spring colours, while on the lower land stone walls looped the contours in a jigsaw of small fields. The layout presented a puzzling picture to people walking up our road, a strange variation to the traditional pattern of farming in the locality, and many inquired curiously what crop we were growing.

Soon a hint of paler green was flushing the ground between the strawberry rows; the weeds were coming up. With no suitable machinery of our own for cultivations, I had bought a small aluminium push-hoe for £4, and with this I trotted up and down the field, leaving behind me a foot-wide swath of devastation among the seedling weeds. The hoe was light and worked very well so long as it was used often, the soil was friable and the weeds small. Another job was to put two or three slug pellets by each plant. Some of the Welsh slugs are as large as mice and can eat a young plant at a single sitting if not repelled. They come in two colours, a sparkling black, or sepia with vivid orange edges, both very voracious and repulsive. We were not much troubled by them that year on account of the dry weather and later, when the rain came, the plants had made so much growth that the loss of a leaf or two did not matter.

We were now spraying every four weeks to make quite certain that stray aphides did not found a colony on our strawberries. The Metasystox was poisonous and needed handling with care. I wore mackintosh, gum-boots and rubber gloves for this job, and washed them well in the sheep dip afterwards. A mask over nose and mouth was also recommended but, after a trial, I discarded it and took care to keep the spray jet near ground level. In spite of the peculiarly nauseous smell, it was more than I could bear to have my face covered in that warm weather while being bundled up in waterproof clothing and with the hard edges of the tank digging into my hips. Still, windless weather was the best for spraying and as the breeze usually dropped at sunset, this was the time I often chose to do it. Lengthening shadows, sun setting over the hills, the springing life of the farm around me, it would have been pleasant work but for the sickly reek of chemicals, and above all the midges. As the shadows fell, these appeared in their millions to dance in the twilight and feed on me. It was almost as though they knew that, with gloves damp with poisonous spray, I could not scratch them off. The smell of Metasystox did not seem to deter them in the least. In spite of liberal applications of anti-midge cream, they swarmed into my hair to drive red-hot needles into my scalp and it became a test of endurance to bear the irritation until the spray tank was empty and I could snatch off the gloves and, puffy-faced and furious, squash them.

Now the runners were creeping out between the rows and a green web of small plants extended round every parent. The ceaseless task of hoeing became more difficult as the runners rooted and could not be disturbed. We gave a top-dressing of poultry manure to stimulate mid-season growth and added Karathane to the Metasystox when a hint of mildew discoloured the leaves of the Royal Sovereign. Mr. Gardner, on his monthly visits of inspection, seemed very pleased with the plants, but he spent some time holding a leaf of Huxley's Giant up to the light. There was some doubt, he said, whether, in this variety, Virus IV had been killed by the heat treatment at East Malling. I also looked at the suspicious light spots in the leaf but was thankful that, if virus were there, it was not due to any neglect on our part.

Paul was now helping me regularly on the strawberry patch. He had closed his guest house and worked for me half-time, or sometimes more if I neeeded him. The hoeing had to be done constantly, the stolons layered to prevent their blowing in the wind and the roots of the new plants being bruised; the blossoms must be removed—we were the only people for miles around with posies of strawberry flowers on the dinner-table—and the varieties prevented from running into one another. All this, with my share of the regular farm work as well, was more than I could do alone. Paul seemed to enjoy the work as much as I did, and between us we kept the runner bed looking very tidy.

Then came hay-making time. After shearing the weather had settled down to another wet Welsh summer, with showers nearly every day and sometimes hours of driving rain. I was now in a dilemma. The silo was full and we needed to use every fine moment to collect the last of the mowing grass for hay. Yet it was useless to attempt hoeing in wet weather; the weeds were simply moved from one spot to another and, with damp soil adhering to their roots, flourished as healthily as before. I did not want to neglect the hay harvest for the strawberries, or the strawberries for the hay and began to be in danger of neglecting them both. The old arable was dirty with weed seeds from many previous years and, with the constant rain and the stirring of the soil, fresh crops of seedlings kept germinating as fast as the old ones were hoed out. Redshank, may-weed, fat-hen, groundsel, chickweed and, most difficult of all to eradicate, meadow grass and creeping buttercup, they were all there in our arable land. And hanging over our heads, like the sword of Damocles, was Miss Butfield.

Miss Butfield, strawberry expert from the Ministry of Agriculture, was to inspect our plants at the end of the season, early October perhaps, and on her verdict would rest the issue of our Foundation Certificate. If the runners were smothered in weeds, she would not be able to see them; might not even be inclined to look. I decided on a twofold offensive; Robin Hughes, now thirteen years old and on holiday from school, was engaged to weed each day; the rest of the family, Paul and I would work in the hay whenever the weather was fit; when mist and drizzle descended, Paul and I would weed, pulling them up and barrowing them off to the headlands where it did not matter if they took root again. Somehow the hay was carried to the barns between showers, some of it poor musty stuff, some quite good, but just enough to last the cattle through the winter. And the tide of weeds began to recede on the strawberry patch.

Miss Butfield was much in our thoughts at that time, indeed became almost a legendary figure.

'Miss Butfield won't like to see all these weeds,' we would say.

'Miss Butfield hates to see meadow grass in Foundation strawberries.'

'Miss Butfield does not approve of people who stand on a perfectly good runner while they are talking.'

Those damp days of weeding developed an atmosphere of their own; lush cushions of chickweed tangled up with the stolons, creeping tide of new little redshank seedlings, muddy hands and black finger-nails, slugs and earth-level insect life, and mist shrouding the mountains.

Paul said: 'I shall appeal to Miss Butfield. I shall say: "It is very important that we earn some money. This is Ruth's living and her 'bread and but' field. Please give her a Foundation Certificate." '

And so it was, drizzle and jokes, aching backs and mud, and the green expanse of weeds being pushed back along the strawberry rows, but every day a little more luxuriant and difficult to root out. Sometimes, at night, I lay awake listening to the patter of rain on the roof and thinking of all those weeds growing away madly in the darkness outside. It was unlucky that our first strawberry season should be so wet, and that the arable had been so dirty. I resolved that, if only we could succeed this year and were given a contract for the following season, I would make sure that the weeds were never allowed to flourish again.

By the end of August the weeding was done; that tide of intrusive unwanted vegetation had been rooted out, had given up its last hopes of producing yet another crop of seedlings, and strawberry plants again predominated on the strawberry field. True, there were signs that a battle had been waged there; large piles of weed corpses lay on the headlands and the runners had a slightly battered appearance, but I hoped that before Miss Butfield's inspection they would revive further. I was still uncertain of the outcome of that inspection. I had never seen anyone else's runner beds and could not tell how our work would compare with other standards. Meanwhile we waited.

The morning of the inspection dawned like so many others that year, grey with low cloud blotting out the hills, and falling rain. We called this type of downpour 'string' rain as it appeared to fall in continuous spouts with no intervals between the drops. Outside the cattle stood miserably, behinds to the weather, heads down, while the hens, damp and annoyed, sheltered under their cabins. It was a poor welcome for Miss Butfield.

Inside, Mother was making coffee and telling me the rain was sure to stop, when we heard the car drive up. Feet scrunched on the stones, the dogs barked and Miss Butfield and Mr. Gardner were at the door. It seemed too wet to go down to the strawberry field but meanwhile there was coffee and shortbread, and we discussed the wet season. The rain continued to fall steadily, scraps of mist floated by on a level with the woods below and we had second cups of coffee. After the third cup Miss Butfield stood up for it was clearly useless to wait for the rain to stop. We all put on raincoats again and Mr. Gardner partially shrouded his tall figure in a lady's plastic mac which he happened to have with him, and pulled the pale blue hood over his ears. Then we went out and down to the strawberry field. The rain was, perhaps, a little lighter now, but it still pattered down steadily from grey skies. Paul came out from the barn to join us and wait for the verdict, with the water dripping off his old Burma campaign bush hat. We bunched together miserably, resenting such weather on such a day. Miss Butfield seemed not to notice it now and proceeded down the rows with her attention fixed on the plants. Huxley's Giant was the first variety to be inspected, and here she paused by one of them which seemed a little different from the rest. It had a slight reddening of the leaf stems and a suggestion of dwarfing in the youngest leaves. We had noticed it a few days earlier but, in our inexperience, the signs meant nothing and previously it had been as healthy as its neighbours. This, said Miss Butfield, was a plant in the first stages of breakdown due to green petal virus and must be rooted up with all its runners. Paul and I looked at one another, long-faced and sober; we had never heard of green petal virus before. It was a virus, we learnt, carried by leaf hoppers from affected clover in the surrounding fields, and though ubiquitous and tiresome, was not so serious as the other viruses since it was easily recognizable and quickly caused complete collapse of the diseased plant. The leaf hoppers were not killed by systemic insecticides and the method of control was a D.D.T. dusting on the headlands. The hoppers hopped from the field to the headland and there died before they could reach the strawberry plants beyond.

Miss Butfield then confirmed the presence of a lurking Virus IV in the Huxleys. Paul and I became, if possible, more dejected. Now the weeping skies seemed to fit the feeling in our hearts, our hopes to be laid alongside the heaps of weeds on the headlands. But Mr. Gardner was studying the mountains, glimpsed through the mist, with an air of pleased serenity; now Miss Butfield was proceeding on her course through the rain, along the rows of Talisman, the rows of Cambridge Vigour, the Early Cambridge, the Royal Sovereign, the Prizewinner, without stop or pause. At last she straightened.

'Very nice,' she said. 'You've got some very good plants here, and a good crop of them.'

Our spirits lightened. We knew then that the sun was shining behind and above the rain clouds although we could not see it. We should get a Foundation Certificate.

Later on the Nuclear Stock Association report on the

Foundation and Elite Stock runner beds was circulated. This was our first opportunity to compare our work with that of others and to see the names and addresses of the N.S.A. growers. Most were situated in the south-east of England, one in Wales, but nobody else right in the mountains as we were. I was the only woman grower. Our Huxleys had been rejected, but all the other varieties had a Foundation Certificate and the reports read something like this:

NAME OF GROWER.	Miss R. J. Ruck.
VARIETY.	Talisman.
NO. OF PARENT PLANTS.	38.
TOTAL CROP.	3,000.
REMARKS.	Growth good, no aphis, no visible virus symptoms.
CERTIFICATE.	Foundation.

Our results compared quite well with those of more experienced growers. Other stocks besides ours had been rejected, some had crinkle virus, some yellow edge, one bed was affected with *Aphelenchoides Ritzema-Bosi*—the chrysanthemum eel-worm. We read of fascinating ills whose names now held significance for us. We were becoming experienced too.

The N.S.A. now asked me to propagate plants again the following season, the number to be increased to two hundred and thirty-eight. I was glad to accept the offer of a further contract; I had enjoyed the summer's work and strawberry propagation added point and zest to the isolated hill life, and brought interesting contacts with other people. The work was also in line with my ideal aim for Carneddi, high quality production that needed the sort of care and attention I could give. The nature of the farm did not allow for spectacular achievement, nor indeed was I capable of it, but I liked to feel I was making some small gains along the road to independence, self-sufficiency and usefulness. Referring to tasks properly done but seemingly small and unimportant in themselves, Mr. George had once remarked: 'The cumulative effect 'is striking.' I remembered this—indeed often

169

murmured it to myself as an encouragement while doing everyday chores—and now I found that our various enterprises were adding up to one small hill farm that was paying its way, and one interesting and healthy life.

Now was the time to lift, pack and despatch the end product of the season's work, our thousands of strawberry runners. A Caernarvon greengrocer had promised me a load of orange and onion boxes for packing the plants to go by rail and these had yet to be collected. Then, suddenly, there was an outbreak of foot-and-mouth disease in the county. The very name of it has a sinister ring to a farmer's ear and we listened soberly to the Welsh News on the wireless. The restrictions on the movement of livestock would affect us immediately and complicate our farming plans. Our draft ewes and wether lambs were sold but the ewe lambs had not yet been sent to the wintering farm and new rams were still to be bought. Also I hesitated to drive into the infected area to fetch the orange boxes.

We waited to see what would happen. During the next few days the disease spread from the first infected smallholding to two or three more, and then spread farther. It was years since there had been foot-and-mouth disease in Caernarvonshire. Being a stock-breeding area, the main movement of animals was away to the lowlands and its natural isolation had kept the district safe. Now the disease struck with extra virulence at farms which had never before been menaced by it, where vets and Ministry officials were unacquainted at first hand with the symptoms, and at a time of year when farmers were preparing for winter, sending hundreds of cattle and sheep away to the autumn sales and moving stock from the hills down to the lower land. The position was becoming serious. At the outbreak of the disease most of the flocks were still on their summer grazing grounds high on the mountains, and here was an added danger. Tens of thousands of sheep wandered in vast unfenced areas, kept to their *cynefin* only by hereditary instinct and with no boundaries between them. Once the disease had a footing here, the work of generations would be lost with the complete slaughter of the mountain flocks. It was said that more than a man's lifetime would be

170

needed to acclimatize new sheep to the hills.

Further outbreaks were reported almost every day, now appearing haphazard in farms over a wide area. Carneddi itself was just outside the restricted zone, with the nearest infection eight or ten miles away, but it was spreading so quickly that we had a feeling of dread. There was a good deal of coming and going up the Carneddi road now, but at such a time visitors were unwelcome, unnecessary journeys were not made and strangers regarded with suspicion, for infection might be carried on a dirty boot or tyre. Jones Williams spread straw across the road and I soaked it with a strong solution of disinfectant. Higher, at the gate leading on to our land, I put a bucket of Jeyes and a churn brush. Paul painted a large sign and fastened it on to the gate, where it hung forebodingly.

FOOT-AND-MOUTH DISEASE PRECAUTIONS
Please disinfect feet and tyres.

Perhaps it was no more than a gesture, but we felt we had at least done something to protect our stock.

We waited anxiously for news that the disease was being brought under control. More and more stringent precautions were taken, but to no avail. An outbreak was confirmed at Nant Peris, where the last small farms adjoined the Snowdon massif, and now everyone expected the final disastrous news that the mountain flocks were affected. Climbers and walkers were asked to keep clear of the hills. Ministry of Agriculture door-mats were wetted with Jeyes. A wide strip of sawdust soaked in germicide guarded the Menai Bridge and the island of Anglesey. Ugly rumours and suspicions were abroad. Now forty-eight farms were affected, and a macabre air of pestilence hung over the mountains.

It was impossible to delay the fetching of my orange boxes any longer; a whole list of plants was waiting to be despatched and I must pack them and send them away. Reluctantly I prepared to run the gauntlet of the Caernarvon road into the heart of the infected area. It was a miserable drive, with the nagging anxiety at the back of my mind that I might bring

171

infection home to Carneddi along with the orange boxes. The countryside lay in all the beauty of late November, with the last fiery glow of autumn fading from the woods and melting into washed-out yellows and decaying browns under the vapours of winter. The healthy stock on a hundred small-holdings had been slaughtered to make a safety belt round infected farms, and for several miles along the road, not an animal was to be seen, not a sheep or cow or pig, where before they had grazed in dozens, and there was a feeling of mourning and desolation.

Nearer to Caernarvon the sky was darkened by a smoky pall, and I realized with a slight shock that it was coal smoke coming from the pyres of diseased animals; here a solitary smoking heap, there a whole row of them a few fields away, with the sooty fumes rising lazily and a faint, sickening smell of charring. The forlornness and menace of the scene were almost unbearable; there the guarding policemen, the locked gates and KEEP OUT signs, the work and hopes of small farmers destroyed.

I loaded up the boxes as quickly as possible and drove home, glad to leave that pestilent area behind and be once more where the life of the farms was normal, and sheep and cattle grazed the fields. Jeep tyres, gum-boots and the thirty boxes received a meticulous disinfecting on the boundary of our land and then I drove on, hoping with all my heart that I was bringing no infection with me.

But, although we did not know it, the last outbreak of foot-and-mouth disease had occurred. We waited, dreading more bad news, but none came; miraculously the mountain flocks escaped infection. The death toll was high; some thousands of sheep, and hundreds of cattle and pigs had been slaughtered. Those of us whose farms had been spared were profoundly thankful. Many were very generous with cash and stock for the sufferers, and all were sympathetic. Gradually the normal life of the mountains was now resumed and restrictions lifted. It would be six months before the empty farms could be restocked, but elsewhere business was as usual. Belatedly our lambs went away to wintering but it was too late to change our rams, the ewes were already pregnant.

About this time we all had Asian 'flu simultaneously. Farming is rather like the theatre—whatever happens the show must go on. The least afflicted one staggered round the hens, milked the cows and nursed the others until his or her temperature soared too high. Then someone with a lower temperature took over, and the sufferer crept off to bed to recover in the minimum length of time. Finally, we were all up again and the business of strawberry lifting began in earnest.

Paul and I forked up the runners round each parent plant, shook the soil from the roots and piled them into orange boxes. Then we carried them into Capel Anwes barn for dressing, bundling and packing. An old door was set up on boxes to serve as a table, and the kitchen stool taken to sit upon. Here we snipped off the joining stolons with nail-scissors, removed dead leaves and counted the plants into bundles of twenty-five. The bundles were secured with rubber bands and packed in sphagnum moss in the orange boxes which were then nailed down and labelled. The weather was mercifully fine but the days were short. Applications for plants rolled in from Elite Stock strawberry growers, and we lifted, snipped and bundled endlessly, twenty-five plants to a bundle, twenty bundles to five hundred plants, forty bundles to a thousand. Still we were not getting through the orders quickly enough and we began to work after dark by lantern light, and sometimes had Ted, the part-time postman from Beddgelert, to help us. We worked mostly in silence for usually one of us was counting, and the only sound was the gentle hissing of the pressure lamps or the stamping of a heifer outside in the darkness. Our lamplight scarcely reached the cavern of the roof above, where the beams, cobweb-hung and lodged with now-deserted swallows' nests, sheltered us as it had sheltered our predecessors and their animals for five centuries and maybe more. Only our virus-tested, twentieth-century strawberry runners were something new in its history. It was cold in the barn and, as we rustled through the piles of plants, we gradually became numb, shifting from one frozen foot to the other, until we had finished the heap and it was time for bed.

Some nights, for the days were so short, we forked up

runners in the field with a lantern perched on the kitchen stool; it was eccentric but efficient. It amused us to think what the recipients of the plants would say if they could see them being lifted thus, in a little circle of yellow light with the great night sky of stars above. We laughed over this topic when raising plants for an export order to New Zealand. Paul suggested that we tell the imaginary inquirer that we were trying to accustom our runners to the idea that it was now daytime over there. Also we wondered how the plants would fare, having completed their summer's growth in Wales, to find themselves precipitated into an Antipodean spring without any intervening winter.

We took to star-gazing when we paused to straighten our backs. There was the beautiful constellation of the Plough tilted across the night sky behind Carneddi house, for ever pointing to the North Star. Sometimes we saw the November moon rising redly over the mountains like a spectral image of the sun, tinting its attendant froth of clouds to a pinky gold. There, we picked out Castor and Pollux, there Cassiopeia, there the Swan. I had learnt to tell the time by the stars while at Oathill, and this we did to amuse ourselves, but when we saw the three bright stars of Orion's Belt appearing over the mountain's rim, we knew that it was getting really late and time to go in. Sometimes, after dark, it was necessary to gather a last bit of sphagnum moss to finish the packing of a box. With pocket torch and sack, I would go down to one of the ditches, where now there was cause to be pleased that it had not lately been cleared out. There were rich beds of sphagnum in its overgrown length. Long green strands choked its course and these were developing into ever more luxuriant cushions which, if left undisturbed, would eventually form the basis of a new peat bog. This moss was ideal for our purpose; it was naturally sterile and so could be used for packing the export orders without fear of its carrying disease into the importing countries. It was cleaner and made a tidier job of the packing than the granulated peat generally used by plant growers. I fished it from the ditch in dripping handfuls, dark green and brown and eight or nine inches in length, and wrung it out like a dishcloth before stowing it in the sack. There were drier tufts of moss growing up the bank and this I took also, lighter green here, shading down to yellow and a bleached white at the roots. It would be bitterly cold, grubbing in the ditch under the starlit sky with pocket torch clenched between my teeth, but at last I would have enough and return to the lights of the barn to finish packing the box.

Now the consignments of plants were being sent off at a great rate to destinations all over England. Twice a week we took the finished cases to the station for despatch, and ticked them off our list.

'That's Sir Dymoke White's order done,' said Paul, hammering in the last nails of the box. 'Now for Darby Bros.'

Besides New Zealand we sent plants to America. These export orders were very stimulating. It was amazing to think that the product of our barren mountain acres should be required in other parts of the world, and we packed them with extreme care. Now our farming could no longer even be considered as a cranky aberration of ex-town folk; we were doing a real job. When the airmail postage on one of our parcels to New Zealand amounted to £19, the village post office was somewhat surprised; there weren't enough stamps in stock.

It was with a feeling of relief that, in the middle of December, we finished lifting the last plant and packing the last box. There had been a small surplus of plants in some varieties, and a few hundred of these we had lifted and sold privately. The weather was now cold and inclement. Late autumn and early winter, which previously had been our quietest time, had changed to a hurly-burly of activity with long hours of work and no opportunity for holidays or quiet evening pastimes. Fingers were chapped and cracked with the cold weather and constant contact with soil. Christmas was almost upon us and with it turkey-plucking time. It was a satisfaction to have all that work behind us, while new virus-tested plants from East Malling were ranged in the garden frame in their pots, undemanding till the spring. It had been hard work but intensely interesting, and when my cheque from the Nuclear Stock Association arrived in the New Year, I felt it had been more than worth while.

15   Ty Mawr

The small farm of Ty Mawr borders Carneddi land to the south. Its thirty acres of small fields and rough grazing lie on the spur away from roads or other buildings, and are fringed with oak woods and precipitous rocky shelves. There is a very old, very small cottage, and the farm buildings consist of two lean-to sheds, a squat pigsty and half the Capel Anwes barn. When we moved to Carneddi in 1945, it was some years since anyone had lived at Ty Mawr. Nettles grew tall in the sheep pen, a slate or two was sliding off the barn roof, rushes were springing up in the ditches and yet there was an air of secret life about the place, an aura of the old people and the old times which was only intensified by its desertion. There were legends attached to the farm and it was said that the cottage was once occupied by a witch who roamed the hills around Nantmor in the guise of a hare. John Williams acted as bailiff for the landlord, shepherded the small flock and cared for the few heifers and store cattle which grazed there. The cottage was empty, its roof sagging a little more year by year under the load of hand-hewn slates, and the only life was the screaming jackdaws in the chimney stack.

Before we had enlarged the house, the bedrooms at Carneddi were very cramped. It was difficult to accommodate visiting friends, and we thought of renting Ty Mawr cottage as an extra sleeping place for the summertime. The landlord agreed to let it to us for £10 a year. He had a few repairs done; the flagged kitchen floor was made up, parts of the walls replastered and gutters put on the eaves. Then we furnished the downstairs rooms with a few chairs, mats, a table and two divan beds. The two rooms above were little more than a loft

177

lighted by diminutive skylights and here, in the gloom, plaster was falling between the rafters, spiders worked incessantly at their black webs and woodlice trotted across the floor. The roof was low, and rags of rotted sacking hung from the beams and brushed one's forehead unexpectedly. After one look up there, we firmly closed the door on the stairs and left the spiders and woodlice to their own occupations.

The fireplace of the living-room was set in a huge oak-beamed inglenook with a bread-oven at one side. The flue had been partly bricked up above the grate but by peering, one could see up the width of the chimney, and the corbelling and odd ledges inside were faintly visible in the light from the square of sky above. The chimney looked as though it would never need sweeping for there was enough room for a man inside it. The gate was meant for burning logs, and we had some roaring fires there. It smoked a little when cold, and odd wisps of smoke would appear through cracks in the loft wall, and sometimes downstairs too, in places surprisingly far removed from the fire. The plaster lining of the flue had perished, but we did not mind; the lingering smell of woodsmoke was quite pleasant and seemed characteristic of the older Welsh cottages. The smoke was troublesome only when it syphoned down the parlour flue and billowed out into the room. We cured this by stuffing up the small grate with some sacks and a mouldering cushion. The parlour had been divided from the main room by a matchboard partition, but this we had taken down to give one large room and we used the old dairy as a kitchen.

The witch of Ty Mawr must have been a kindly old lady, singular more for wisdom than black magic, since she left behind her—or at least later occupants of the cottage did—an aura of cheer and friendliness. There was none of the bleakness sometimes to be found in an old, deserted house or cottage. No past deeds of horror can have been committed there, for the ghosts of Ty Mawr were benign spirits. I was quite content to sleep alone under its old roof, out of sight or sound of any other dwelling, and the owl calls in the wood and the creak and whisper of the ancient timbers did not make me afraid. The only time I was disturbed was when a bat took to coming inside and flitting round the low kitchen celling. Bats are charming enough in their proper place but I did not like this one indoors, and its visits used to necessitate a hasty, pyjamaed trip to the farmhouse to fetch Mother to get it out again. Finally I outwitted it by hanging a piece of lace curtain over the open window.

Ty Mawr proved a source of delight to some of our friends. Here longings for the Simple Life and Back to Nature could be thoroughly satisfied. Others, however, had to be accommodated at Carneddi. After one peep at the upstairs loft or a view of the water supply—a trickle which emerged from oozy marsh land—a peculiar expression became fixed on their faces, the cries of: 'Delightful,' 'Charming', took on a hollow ring, and we felt that those sorts of country pleasures were not for them. Paula and Anne were among those who appreciated Ty Mawr's austere simplicity, the charm of its bulging walls and its great age. Even those last necessary trips out into the field at night, the puffs of wood-smoke down the chimney, or even the descent of a jackdaw down the same way had the savour of novelty for them.

One night Paula and I were preparing for bed. I explained about the bat and put the piece of lace curtain across the open window. Then we blew out the light and settled down, with the soft whisper of the fire's flickering the only sound in the silence. I was almost asleep when a small voice said:

'Do you think you could take that bit of curtain down?'

'I can if you like, but the bat may come in again.'

There was a pause in the darkness; then Paula, very sleepy but anxious-sounding, said she had a feeling that it might try to get in anyway, and the sight of it flying round wearing a lace curtain would be very upsetting. I had not thought of this possibility. We solved the problem by shutting the window firmly.

For a few years Ty Mawr was inhabited intermittently by us and our friends. Impromptu parties were held there and wood-smoke trickled out of its crooked chimney into the evening sky; laughter and talk floated through the windows. Then the Carneddi farmhouse was enlarged and there was less need to use Ty Mawr. Its roof was gradually deteriorating as one rafter after another sagged with rot, shifting the slates above it, while the little leaks grew bigger. The buckets and basins catching the drips in the loft increased in number, and occasionally overflowed through the living-room ceiling. On wet nights, a faltering tune of plink, splash, plop, plunk could be heard playing away eerily upstairs. Woodworm punched their holes unceasingly through the old roof timbers and the fine dust of their activities mingled with the bits of plaster on the loft floor. Ty Mawr had become almost untenable and, reluctantly, we gave it up.

A new roof for the cottage would have been expensive, and the old one was past repair. It would have been unreasonable to expect the landlord to do much for our meagre rent. I made a half-hearted offer to buy the farm but I had not much money to spare and he was unwilling to sell. Nothing happened and the cottage was once more left to the jackdaws. Occasionally I prowled round it in the evenings after feeding the cattle in our half of the barn. Little swirls of dead leaves, blown under the door, now lay in the hallway; more chinks showed through the roof, and the old box tree grew up over the window, shutting out the light. Year by year the laburnum in the garden flowered unseen and spread its carpet of gold on the grass. Sometimes in the autumn we came to pick the tart black plums from the plum trees or, in the spring, to gather daffodils. Mostly the place was deserted. The porch fell down; a window got broken, and a snarled tangle of blackberry briars sprang round the walls. In a few years it would be a roofless derelict, like so many more hidden away in the inaccessible folds of the hills.

In 1955 I had the promise of a legacy of £50. The idea of spending it on a grand holiday or some new clothes was appealing, but I decided to try again to buy Ty Mawr. Perhaps the landlord would be willing to sell the cottage by itself. Luck was with me. He said he was sorry to see the place falling into disrepair but he had no real use for it now. He was willing to sell it to me for the £50, and also include the half acre garden field in at the price. I was delighted. Ty Mawr, even with a collapsing roof, was to me a very desirable possession. I had no ready cash for repairs and a use for the cottage was not immediately apparent, but it was old, beautiful and right on the borders of our land, and I loved it.

In autumn I became the owner. Besides the cottage, there was the pigsty, a small stone hut, the laburnum and plum trees and, in the spring, a carpet of early-flowering daffodils. The first job was fencing the garden field to exclude the Ty Mawr flock and give our own sheep the benefit of the grazing there. Paul had now given up his guest house and was living in Beddgelert with his mother, doing part-time work and various contracting jobs, and he was readily available at the busiest times of year. He came to help with the fencing and, while we strained the wire and hammered in the staples, we discussed the problem of the cottage roof. A new roof was needed, and suddenly the course of action became clear; we would do the job ourselves and I would borrow from the bank the money to pay Paul and buy the materials. We should save a good deal in this way, and the good boards and ceiling joists would be salvaged before it was too late. How this new over-draft was to be paid off was left conveniently obscure; I could think of this later and perhaps it might be possible to let the cottage.

I told the family that I planned to reroof Ty Mawr. As usual Mother, when confronted with one of my projects, assumed as a matter of course that it was practical. My father's attitude was more complex. He received the news with a hint of aston-ishment and dismay—I was used to this—and a suggestion that inevitably the new roof, when put on, would collapse. At the same time he seemed to have faith, was very willing to help, and so perhaps his dire predictions were offered simply as an antidote for my own optimism.

In bleak January weather we set to work. The brambles and the box tree were cut back, and suddenly Ty Mawr became the centre of great activity. We pushed off the old roof in a morning, standing in the loft and striking upwards from inside with shovel handles. The thin oak laths, nailed on so many years ago, shivered into rotten splinters and, with their load of slates, cascaded down the remaining part of the roof and landed with a crump on the ground below. Showers of ancient plaster pattered down on our heads, and clouds of dust rose. Spiders and webs vanished in the landslide and woodlice dashed for shelter as their universe disintegrated. With the gusto of juvenile delinquents we worked at destruction, and daylight flooded into the attic for the first time in centuries. There was nothing worth salvaging from the wreck except the two tiny skylights and the ridge tiles. The slates were heavy, hand-made ones, with a hole at the top for the oak peg which had held them in position: many were cracked and all were spoiled with successive layers of plaster and cement which had been used for patching. Most of the rafters and the ridge pole were rotted away and collapsed at a touch. Only the oak purlins and the truss, made from whole trees, were still sound. An outer layer had been powdered to dust by woodworm but the core of the trees remained iron hard. Now we saw the fine workmanship of the old carpenters, the oak shaped and fitted with their axes, augers and draw-knives and pegged with dowel pins, the whole fitting snugly together, following the natural curves of the wood's growth. These we took down, and then Ty Mawr was roofless and exposed under the winter skies.

We made one discovery under the roof. Two little tins were tucked in a cranny. The paper labels, discoloured with age and damp, were inscribed, 'Sleep in Peace,' above a picture of two Victorian children in frilled nightdresses, sitting up in a double bed. Below this the labels proclaimed: 'Death to Bedbugs, Lice, Ticks and Fleas.' The tops of the tins were punched with holes. We deposited them on the rubbish heap, and I was glad I had not known about them in earlier years.

The cottage was to be roofed in traditional style. I had bought a book called *Teach Yourself Roofing* and this was our main guide throughout; indeed we often crawled down from the roof to consult it when our confidence wavered. We also studied other people's verges, eaves, gulleys and hips with deep interest. Mrs. Staunton allowed us into the loft of her new house and, at some peril to the bedroom ceilings, we crept round examining the construction from underneath. This solved one problem. Here there were unsupported purlins twenty-five feet long, and the span of Ty Mawr was only twenty-three feet. We could safely do away with the truss which before had cut across our attic at shoulder height and made it necessary to duck when crossing the room.

I ordered all the materials for the roof. The price of small slates for the area to be covered was half that of large ones. They could be cut from poorer deposits of slate; also they were unpopular because of the extra labour required, but since our own labour was of the sweated variety this was unimportant to us. I chose slates ten inches by eight inches and saved £50. It began to snow on the day they arrived. We unloaded them carefully from the lorry and stacked them by the side of the road. I had intended to carry them across the sloping field of Buarth Ty Mawr in the jeep but, even in four-wheel drive, the tyres spun helplessly in the mud and slush, and the vehicle slewed sideways on the rising ground. In the end my father painstakingly wheeled them across in the barrow; they weighed three tons. When the timber arrived, we had to carry that too. Now rain was alternating with sleet and snow, and still the jeep could not traverse the field. The purlins, twenty-six feet in length, were so heavy that they seemed to crush us into the ground and our footmarks dug deep into the mud, but at last it was all carried to the cottage.

More for speed than because we doubted our capabilities, we asked John Price, the joiner from Portmadoc, and his mate to help us get the timber in position. For two days they worked with us, the cottage ringing with the rasp of saws and the sound of six-inch nails being banged home, and at the end of that time the skeleton of our roof was in place.

It was now the beginning of the second week in February and we were eager to finish before lambing in five weeks' time. Days were still short and the normal farm work had to be done as usual; the cattle were all inside and the brooder house was full of chicks. I tried to do as much routine work as I could before dawn in the mornings and after dark at night, as I had done when we were building the brooder house. I devoted the daylight hours to work on Ty Mawr, taking sandwiches down for lunch to save the short walk up to the house in the middle of the day. Paul and I brewed tea on a stick fire lighted in the old grate, and drank it seated on a tree stump we had dragged inside and a dilapidated basket chair. The shelter of the deep inglenook was the only dry place in the roofless cottage. Heavy showers fell intermittently every day and water poured through the bedroom floor into the living-room below. The flagged floor was awash in places, and grimed with ash from the fire, old plaster and new cement. Our tools leant up against the walls in the driest places, and the bags of Portland cement and firewood shared the inglenook with us. The dinner half-hour was spent in study of *Teach Yourself Roofing* and discussions of our technical problems.

The new roof timbers, having been laid on wall plates, were about four inches higher than the old. This, with the fact that they did not sag, increased the headroom considerably. With plenty of light coming in through new skylights and no skull-cracking tie beam, the attic would be a pleasant room and very different from the old, dark bogey-hole of the past.

Roofing felt must now be laid on the rafters before the battens and slates could go on. It was windy on the day we did this, but we were grieved to have the cottage naked to the February skies and an ideal day might be long in coming. Paul perched on one gable end, I on the other; between us was a seven-yard strip of loose felt that rose and fell with every gust and hit the rafters with a sickening slap. It was frail stuff and we were anxious not to tear it. We sighed with relief when each strip was safely nailed down, and at last the whole roof was covered, but I hoped it would not blow hard that night. The next morning came, the roofing felt was still intact and we began to nail on the battens. These were only three inches apart from centre to centre and some hundreds were needed to reach from eaves to ridge. Here great accuracy was required, as a slight miscalculation at the eaves might result in a wide error by the time the ridge was reached and the lap of the slates would be wrong. Now we checked and rechecked and resorted often to the pages of *Teach Yourself Roofing* for reassurance. We wondered constantly whether we might have made some mistake that would not be apparent until the work was finished. While using materials that were costing £150 of loaned money, we could not afford to be careless. But as each stage was reached and passed, and the work looked more and more like a job done by real builders, our spirits rose and confidence increased.

The first slates went on, looking incredibly professional, and their small size adding to the charm of the roof. We had one curving verge, as in the original, with each slate shaped separately, and this gave a touch of craftsmanship to the work. Through the last weeks of February we hammered in nails, five thousand slates to cover the roof, two nails to each slate, ten thousand nails in all. We became proficient in cutting slates with the zax, a chopper-like tool which also had a spike on the upper side for making holes. The slates had been holed at the quarry but here and there, round the skylight and along the verges, specially shaped ones were needed, and these we made ourselves. It was bitterly cold, crouched on the roof with merely a toe-hold on the battens; bones became chilled by the icy wind from the mountains, and fingers so numb that it was difficult to hold the nails, but the old sense of creative urgency spurred us on and the physical rigours seemed unimportant. It was a happy spring, and happy work for me, with the feeling that, with our own hands, we were reversing the process of neglect and decay in one wild corner of the hills. For Paul the days were overshadowed by his mother's ill-health and, when the slating was only half-finished, he asked me if he could camp at Ty Mawr to lighten the burden of her housekeeping. This seemed a good arrangement and would also save the time spent in journeying to and from Beddgelert. Now he made himself a corner under the finished part of the roof, and lived there uncomplainingly in Spartan conditions. Fluffy, the half-Siamese cat, moved in too to keep him company. He said his bedclothes blew about in the wind at night, but he seemed quite contented. Mother sent down hot meals, and he was no longer a visiting worker but part of the farm.

In the first week in March we hammered on the last slate and replaced the old ridge tiles; the roof was finished. It was a triumphant moment and we gazed in pleasure at our handiwork. Ty Mawr was now rescued from ruin, and was once more trim and neat with an air of simple prosperity about it.

The slates fitted snugly, like small grey scales, proof against the winds and driving rains of winter, and we were glad to find that no raw look of newness spoiled its appearance. As before, the cottage was part of the wild, lovely country from which its structure came, the Welsh slate, stone and oak, with the low, plain design of a hill farmer's home.

Now my thoughts turned to summer letting, for the rent could be used to reduce the loan. Furnished lets would be the most profitable and, with this in mind, we set to work. The pace of life on the farm was quickening with the spring weather. Every day lambs were arriving; manure waited to be carted to the fields; ploughing, harrowing and planting must be done, but in every spare moment I cleaned, painted and distempered, while Paul pointed the south gable of the cottage. I borrowed a few bits of furniture from Mother; a cousin gave cushions, plates and blankets, and Paul produced some furniture left from his guest house. I bought a tea set, curtain materials, two Welsh honeycomb bedspreads and a chemical closet. The closet was housed in a sentry box on the north gable. Paul made this out of an old hen shed and it gave a beautiful view of Moel Hebog if the door were left open. Gradually the necessities for a cottage existence were assembled. With two beds in the bedroom and two divans downstairs, four people could be accommodated. With new paint, new curtains and well-polished furniture, Ty Mawr now looked attractive, comfortable and welcoming. At Easter I put an advertisement in a Beddgelert shop window and awaited results.

Quite soon there were telephone calls and postcards asking for further particulars. People came walking up the road to see for themselves. Though the conveniences were primitive by town standards, few inquirers seemed discouraged by the lack of plumbing, electricity or a road to the cottage. Indeed they seemed eager to draw water, chop wood, light oil lamps and make use of the hen-house closet. They liked Ty Mawr, for here the wild land came to their doorstep and red squirrels played in the trees; a fox might take its path close by and there was no other building in sight but the five-centuries-old barn. There were many townspeople, we found, who had longings for the lonely places of the hills. The cottage was soon booked for the three summer months.

Early in June of that year, Paul's mother died. I was very sorry that she never saw her son's handiwork at Ty Mawr. She would have liked it.

Before Ty Mawr was let, I had been warned that holiday tenants would be destructive. I heard they were absolutely diabolical in the way they smashed crockery, used table linen to wipe the floor, stubbed out cigarettes on the walls and left circles on the polished furniture during their wild drinking parties. They would also set the place on fire. I found this difficult to reconcile with the pleasant folk I had interviewed, but was assured that people did not treat furnished accommodation as they did their own homes. Perhaps hatchet-faced landladies were not fierce by nature, I thought, and were made so only by circumstances. It would be necessary, it seemed, to strike terror into the hearts of tenants at the first sign of any bad behaviour.

At the end of June Paul returned to his house in Beddgelert, and the first tenants, two quiet young men, arrived at Ty Mawr. I waited throughout their week's stay, ready to intervene but there seemed no need. The young men arrived daily for their milk and in the evenings smoke could be seen ascending from the cottage chimney. Their lights were extinguished early, and their presence on the farm was hardly noticeable. On the last day they paid their bill and quietly departed. I hurried down to the cottage. The familiar smell of wood smoke and new distemper met me at the door. The passage was tidy with the flagstones still damp from the mop. In the sitting-room cushions were well plumped in the chairs and the grate was cleaned out and filled by a freshly-crumpled newspaper. The bedroom was equally immaculate. There was no sign of breakages or damage anywhere. I said a silent apology to all tenants of furnished cottages, and hoped that those two young men had really enjoyed their stay.

This pattern of civilized behaviour was followed by all the subsequent tenants. They bought butter, milk, eggs, vegetables and roasting chickens from us, and seemed as grateful as if all they bought had been a gift. Some, on leaving, gave a

187

present to the cottage—another saucepan or perhaps a flower vase—in token that they had enjoyed the holiday.

The cottage was much photographed that summer and the holiday-makers liked to pose before the old doorway, with their water buckets on a yoke across their shoulders. I was often invited inside for a cup of tea. I enjoyed meeting these new people, and was pleased at the interest they showed in life on a hill farm. The cat, Fluffy, continued to live at the cottage and took the tenants much for granted. She slept on their beds but they did not seem to mind as she was a clean and attractive cat. They liked it less when she left half-eaten pairs of rabbits' trousers on the bedroom floor.

In September Mr. Knox and Mr. Dalrymple, the last tenants of the season, came to Ty Mawr. They brought their families with them and nine people—four adults and five children—now stayed there. Ty Mawr means Big House. The name perhaps arose from its association with the ancient barn Capel Anwes, once a medieval hall, but the cottage itself is very small. John Williams told me that, in the past, thirteen children were born and brought up there, but it is difficult to imagine how they managed. However, these two families fitted themselves into Ty Mawr with apparent comfort and, when I called, there never seemed to be too many children about, too many feet and legs to trip over, or too many coats and shoes in the hall. The children loved the farm. They fed the pet lamb, took turns at milking, collected the eggs and helped with many tasks. Mr. Knox and Mr. Dalrymple were also interested in our activities and made the suggestion of putting a private telephone between the farmhouse and the cottage. Mr. Knox was a telephone engineer and said it would be quite easy to arrange. This idea had never occurred to me and I was very pleased with it. With a telephone installed, many journeys would be saved, tenants could 'phone for milk and I could communicate easily with Paul if he moved into the cottage again in the winter.

And so it was arranged. They would put a private line to Ty Mawr in return for a holiday there in the spring, and I would buy the telephones and wire. They left with promises to return at Easter, bringing the equipment with them.

Now it was autumn and there was a touch of gold in the woods below the house. The throngs of tourists diminished and there were fewer cars and charabancs on the road. The holiday season was nearly over, the crowds were migrating back to town and soon the mountains would resume their winter solitude. Paul moved into Ty Mawr to help with the strawberry lifting and slowly the year slipped into winter. The leaves fell; the mountains changed through their successive garbs; dull rain-sodden vegetation changed to a mantle of hailstones, to snow, to frost and the weird wind-wrought, wedding-cake glaze of ice. The tempo of farm life slowed to the quiescent pace of winter.

Then the days lengthened into March. The last patches of snow in the mountain gullies shrank and disappeared, and all of a sudden it was spring. The Knoxes and Dalrymples arrived, their cars sagging with children, luggage and telephone wire. We spent the first evening in discussing the positioning of the instruments. It was decided that one was to go in the main living-room at Ty Mawr and the other in my room at the farmhouse. Mr. Knox had brought a third telephone which could be put at some other useful point if I wanted it.

The telephones were sound-power, ex-naval instruments, operated by magnets and needing no batteries. They were in iron casings with safe grips to hold the receivers during rough weather at sea. They intrigued me, and I felt that the mountainous wilds of Carneddi provided a suitable situation for their use, if they were not to be on board a battleship. Though originally very expensive, Mr. Knox had bought them, second hand, for 25s. each, and the whole scheme, including government-surplus telephone wire, would not cost me more than five or six pounds.

We decided to have the third telephone by the upper sheep-pen where the flock was gathered from the open mountain several times a year. This was about half a mile from the farm on our highest land, and I imagined with pleasure being able to call the farmhouse and say I would soon be down for lunch. The phone would also be an advantage at lambing time when we walked the high ground looking for

189

trouble and perhaps help was needed at a difficult birth. A naval telephone, too, would add an interesting touch of modern incongruity to that lonely stretch of heather and bog, and to the age-old occupation of shepherding.

Early next morning Mr. Dalrymple and Mr. Knox were busy in their role of linemen. The children kept arriving at the farmhouse with excited progress reports. Now the first instrument was fitted in the sitting-room of Ty Mawr. Now there were successful trial telephonings going on, with the second instrument in the field outside the cottage. Paul was cutting oak standards to carry the line. Although the G.P.O. telephone poles ran close to Ty Mawr, we did not dare to attach the wires to them and had to make our own route. Part of the distance to be covered followed walling fenced with two strands of barbed wire, and it was easy to run the telephone cables along these posts. Where there were no posts, Paul put them in. Now the linemen were proceeding towards the house, fastening insulators to the posts. Children stood along the route, relaying directions and guiding the snake of wire over the rough ground. Suddenly, to everyone's surprise, the wire came up very fast and free and it was found that one of the heifers had chewed through the trailing length of cable. The break, however, was quickly mended and the work went on. From the wall, the wire took a curve up to an insulator on the deep-litter house roof, and then joined the farmhouse at a high level to clear the only gateway in its path. It was then tacked across the front of the house and disappeared under the eaves into my room. The cable was scarcely noticeable at any point. It showed only a little where it crossed from the deep-litter house to the copse of fir trees in the garden, and I was pleased that its presence did not mar our hillside.

At last I could try the telephone, and I turned the handle briskly to call Ty Mawr. The calling noise was made by a howler instead of the usual bell—perhaps to avoid confusion with other bells on a ship—and a small orange light flashed to attract attention. Mrs. Dalrymple answered. The wire threading the hillside carried our voices clearly across the third of a mile between farmhouse and cottage. The telephone was a complete success.

When the first return call was made, I was startled. The orange light winked and the instrument uttered an agonized hoot which lengthened into a fluctuating wail. I had not realized that the call sound was as loud or as weird as this. Later we found out how to give a discreet toot or two by turning the handle slowly, since a full-throated howl was too nerve-destroying for anyone within earshot.

On the next day the third telephone was fitted. The wire took an aerial loop from the bathroom window at the back of the house to the crag behind, and then followed the fencing standards up to the gathering pen. The distance was a good half-mile and we made many journeys up and down through the bogs and over the rough ground. While we were working the ewes snorted in alarm at this invasion and trotted away with their lambs hustling by their sides. The small 'phone box fitted inconspicuously into the sheep-pen wall and we were ready to try the extended line. It worked perfectly. The howlers sounded both at Carneddi and Ty Mawr and interesting three-point conversations could be held on the new system. The three telephones were always linked and a howl from farmhouse to cottage would also wail from the box on the mountain, unheeded in the loneliness while signals passed below. We hoped that no passing climber would be startled by its banshee shrieks issuing from the wall. The sheep-pen receiver was on a plug and could be removed and carried down at times when it was not likely to be needed, otherwise anyone could listen in. Unlike the ordinary telephone, our system was always live and we preferred to be able to disconnect the mountain box for this reason.

After the Easter holidays the two families went home, but I remembered them every time I said to Paul or other occupants of the cottage: 'If you want something, just give me a howl.'

16 Welsh Blacks

For three generations and ten years none of our cattle have met the male side of the family; instead a man with a tin box arrives by car. We find this method very satisfactory and the cows also seem content. With so small a herd a bull of our own would not be economic to keep, and before there was an Artificial Insemination Centre in the country we had to take our cows to visit other people's bulls. Jones Williams usually had a young one at his second farm two miles down the road. When the occasion arose, my father and I would set off, one of us in front of the beast to warn oncoming cars, and one behind to check any tendency to bolt for home. Although these were good little bulls they were not pedigree, and so, when later we heard of a well-bred premium bull at stud we used to visit him instead. The premium bull lived on a farm four miles away, and now our cows' outings became a lengthy business as progress was slow on roads crowded with summer traffic. It was annoying, too, on occasions when the service did not hold and the eight-mile plod had to be repeated three weeks later. Our shuffling progress along the road was sometimes interrupted by friends sweeping by in cars and then pulling up with exclamation of: 'And where are you going?'

When the Milk Marketing Board's A.I. Centre opened we made use of its amenities gratefully. The service fee was now £1 instead of the 2s. 6d. we had paid for local bulls, but we considered it well worth while. Free repeat services were provided and the A.I. bulls were pedigree, selected for performance and worth a good deal more than most farmers could afford to pay for an animal of their own. Our cattle were hardy, home-bred Welsh Blacks and, when mated to these superior bulls, they produced some good-looking calves.

My aim was a pedigree herd and with the assistance of A.I. I hoped to have one. We had no money to spare to buy pedigree females; we should have to breed them, and so I joined the Welsh Black Cattle Society and registered the herd prefix name of 'Carneddi'. The Society had a Grading-Up Register in which any cow of a good Welsh Black type could be entered as a Foundation Dam. In three generations full pedigree could be reached by the use of pedigree males. The original Betty, Brute and Grandma had been sold leaving us with no female issue, but Prim, the little heifer we bought with the farm, gave us two daughters, Blackie and Daphne, which we registered together with Seren, the daughter of Jane. Thus Jane and Prim were the founders of our herd and all our cattle are descended from them.

Grading-up is a slow process when the herd consists of only three or four cows and their followers. Heifers are two and a half years old before they calve to produce the next generation, and half the number of calves are male and destined for beef. Nine years passed before our first full pedigree heifer calf was born.

In 1951 the Welsh Black Cattle Society standardized their system of ear-marking and allotted a letter to each year. This was tattooed in the calves' ears together with the breeder's mark. We decided to name the calves according to the letter of the year in which they were born. Nineteen fifty-two produced Blackberry, Betty and Blodwen but 1953 gave us only a crop of Charlies. Nineteen fifty-four was not much better with Dilly as the solitary heifer, and 1955 gave us no females again. Then my cousin, a doctor, mentioned that some medical research seemed to indicate that fertilization early in the heat period tended to favour the conception of male offspring, while late fertilization favoured the conception of females. I wondered if this might apply to the bovine world and accordingly summoned the A.I. man only at the last moment. The result, if it is possible to draw conclusions from so few calvings, has been satisfactory. For the next two years three calves out of four were heifers; Golly, Gert and Gwen appeared in 1957, and Heather, Honey and Holly in 1958. After this I did not pay so much attention to late insemination; we had reached the stage where all new heifer calves would be pedigree. At this time also the subsidy on steer calves was raised to encourage beef production, and I found that male calves were as profitable as females, so I was pleased with whatever calf was born.

We sold one or two milkers a year and they were replaced by home-bred heifers. I used to enjoy bidding at sales, but the appraising eyes of farmers and dealers focused on the ring were more than I could face when one of our own animals was to be sold. Instead my father would drive our cow before prospective buyers while I was content to wedge myself into the crowd and watch. He had a technique of his own in the sale ring and was never panicked into selling at the wrong price as I might have been. He would enter the ring, prodding the cow onwards, with a mournful expression on his face and his hat at half-mast down his forehead. The bidding would begin at a low figure but since the cow was undoubtedly good, the bids would come quickly. My father continued his circular perambulations of the ring, turning the cow to show her good points to the customers, while the auctioneer rattled off his patter and the crowd shuffled and stared. If the price rose above the highest figure we had hoped to get, my father showed no sign and, if his expression changed at all, it was to one of more settled gloom.

'Fifty, fifty, fifty. Who'll give me one? Thank you. Fifty-one, fifty-one, fifty-one. Fifty-two anywhere? Fifty-two. Perfectly right and straight in the bag. Fifty-three, fifty-three.'

And so it went on. Presently the bidding would hesitate and stop. The auctioneer, feeling he had extracted the last pound from the watching faces, would call: 'Is she a seller, Mr. Ruck?' But Mr. Ruck seemed deaf and continued to mooch round the ring with never a sign that he had heard. The buyers seemed more responsive than he was and in desperation the auctioneer turned to them and the price crept higher in ten-shilling bids. Finally my father's attention was attracted when it seemed that no one would venture a shilling more. There was a whispered confabulation and resigned head-shakings, but the auctioneer seemed to have won for he exclaimed: 'She's in the market for sixty.' By then people must have had time for second thoughts or else feelings of sympathy for the sad figure in the ring for a few more bids were placed before the auctioneer's stick rapped on the rostrum and our cow was knocked down for a good sum. The proceedings had taken twice as long as usual, and my father left the ring looking as though he expected the bailiffs, but on the way home he had a pleased smile and we agreed that the price was not at all bad.

After our second year at Carneddi we never bought cattle but always bred our own. Beasts not acclimatized to hill land, we found, were subject to many perils which those born at home seemed to avoid. There was poisoning from bracken, rhododendrons and acorns, all of which were abundant on our land. There was liver fluke and the tick-borne killer disease of red water which, if unnoticed while cattle were on their high summer grazing, would cause death in forty-eight hours. There were also the dangers of the terrain itself, the broken cliffs and scree slopes, and the deep ditches draining peat marshes. Home-bred cattle appeared to develop a tolerance of these troubles, and a native caution. Of the six animals which we bought in those first two years, one bullock died of a septic wound caused by a fall; a heifer from acorn poisoning; a cow snapped off her horn in a tumble from a ledge; there was a case of severe fluke, and for weeks afterwards the sufferer was fed half a dozen eggs a day until its strength returned, and all the animals had to be treated for red water. It was a sorry crop of trouble and we learnt our lesson. Among the dozens of home-bred cattle which we have since kept, there have been only minor ailments and calvings have been accomplished without difficulty.

Besides being a dolorous task, digging a grave for a cow is hard work. Gors Goch is our graveyard, the only land on the farm where it is possible to dig deep enough. Here, consigned to the deep peat soil of that hanging valley, lie our losses, a few rough mounds along the perimeter where the beech leaves fall and the rushes whisper. Here almost certainly the farmers of Carneddi, long since dead themselves, buried their animals. For many years now only a few sheep or a hen or two have gone on their last journey to that hidden valley. Here my father, with long-handled spade and depressed expression, performs their last rites with a black sheepdog as mourner, interestedly seated on the graveside. And it was here too, just over the wall where the valley extends to Corlwyni's land, that a more spectacular funeral took place.

It happened a few years ago at the end of a particularly long bleak winter, a winter that had followed a wet cold summer, and whose legacy was to be seen in the scarcity of hay in our barns and the mustiness of its quality. We were all looking forward to the spring when the growth of grass would outstrip the flock's ceaselessly grazing jaws and our rakish cattle could lose the hollow-ribbed look of that winter. As yet there was little sign of spring except in the fluffing out of catkins, and the herbage still had its winter bleakness and the wind was still cold. Paul and I were making fencing stakes in the oak woods above the house when we heard the first sounds of trouble. Below, where William Owen's cowshed was screened by the fall of the land and a tracery of bare twigs, we could hear a cow calling with a strange, painful urgency. Earlier we had seen William Owen going down the path in the direction of his shed. We continued with our work for a while. Then the cow's bellows rose above the sound of the saw again. The note of agony in it was unmistakable and we stopped to listen. The calling had now taken on a pitch which seemed almost beyond the powers of a bovine throat, an irregular howl expressing the ultimate in despair and torment. It echoed back from the sides of the valley till the air was racked with the sound.

'I'm going down to see what's happening,' I said. I felt I could not go on sawing.

Just then we saw the figure of Mrs. Owen appear through the gate of Corlwyni's upper field, a little black figure in bad trouble hurrying down the path to Carneddi. Far below us we saw her scurrying with the speed of despair. The cow's bellowings had for the moment ceased and the sorrowful wailing of the woman below now floated up to us. Then she disappeared from sight behind the shoulder of the land. I set

197

off for the house, shocked by what I had heard, hurrying through the trees, sliding down the rockfalls, crunching over the old, dead bracken. When I reached home Mrs. Owen had already left. She had asked Mother to telephone the vet as their cow was very ill. There was nothing else we could do to help, she said.

After a while, mercifully, the bellowing ended, and later I saw the vet's assistant park his car by our cowshed and pass down the footpath to Corlwyni. On his return I asked him what had happened. The cow, he said, had died before he arrived. He could not ascertain the cause of death. This was bad news and a serious loss for the Owens. On small upland farms, it is hard to make a living and a cow is an important source of income. Besides this, for a while each animal is a member of those lonely farmsteads, born and reared there, tended by all the family, with its own name, place and part in the hill life. The Owens had always been very good to us and it was impossible not to feel their loss almost as if it had been our own. There were many nights when William Owen had risen from his bed to help us with a calving, coming with as much alacrity and interest as he would have done for his own beast. His resources were ours for the asking. He was our good neighbour and his troubles also affected us.

The next day a mournful February mist had descended over the land, hiding the mountains and bringing a light, cold rain. Moisture collected on the branches of the trees and spotted down in big drops on the leaf mould beneath. The sheep were grey shapes in the grey mist, their backs dewed with water. There was no wind. I heard a car grinding up the hill in low gear, and the vet arrived. He was not satisfied with his assistant's report on William Owen's cow and wanted to know what had caused its death. The mist enveloped him as he disappeared down the path.

Presently he returned with a prepared slide of the dead cow's blood and set up his microscope in our kitchen. After a long scrutiny he invited me to look and I saw a light, luminous, violet circle with a cluster of darker violet rods gathered in the centre.

'They're anthrax bacilli,' said the vet.

His words summoned a covey of sinister shades into our kitchen, recollections that anthrax was usually fatal and could affect human beings. They recalled half-forgotten tales of awful agonies, of turning black, and of imported hides and shaving brushes. Anthrax was a notifiable disease and the police must be informed. The situation was serious.

Later in the day I walked round to Corlwyni to deliver the message that policemen would be coming to fence in the corpse. I found Mrs. Owen alone. She seemed over-wrought and her English had deserted her. My news troubled her even further. Their cow had been ill and had died, but she felt there was nothing criminal in that and nothing to warrant the arrival of the Law.

'Not want the police,' she said. 'The cow, it dead. What for police?'

I tried to comfort her a little but had no Welsh words to make her understand, and so I left. I walked thoughtfully down the field, feeling sorry that this trouble should have happened. Then the floating vapours revealed the figures of five policemen coming up to meet me in single file. They were enveloped in rain-capes and puffed a little on the rising ground, their boots sliding on the wet earth. We exchanged the time of day and they passed on into the mist towards Corlwyni. Poor Mrs. Owen.

The next day activity began early. Twm, Mary Alice's husband, went by with two policemen and digging implements. Sergeant Owen arrived and installed himself in Carneddi's kitchen to be conveniently placed for the receiving of telephone calls. He seated himself on the sofa, upturned helmet beside him, and we gave him coffee and listened to the latest 'who-done-it'.

The procedure for disposing of the dead cow was formidable. The corpse was now enclosed by the fence erected on the previous day, and two policemen would stand guard to ward off straying animals and people. A special burning pit was to be dug with air vents in the direction of the prevailing winds, and a quantity of coal, paraffin and straw was allotted for the funeral pyre. The orifices of the carcase must be plugged before it was dragged to the pit to prevent any matter from leaking out. The trail along which it was moved must be soaked in disinfectant afterwards. Once burning was begun the body was not to be left until it was completely consumed by the fire.

Later we heard that a veterinary surgeon from the Ministry of Agriculture was coming to inspect the corpse and take further blood samples.

'I'll just slip down and tell the others,' said Sergeant Owen, retrieving his helmet.

Its unexpected weight made him look down in surprise. Neatly fitted inside in a circular ball was a sleeping Siamese cat. During the next twenty-four hours many helmets were to be incautiously discarded on the sofa by visiting constables, to be filled almost instantly by cats in need of a lawful bed.

Then a tractor brought ten sacks of coal, two bales of straw, logs, five gallons of paraffin and five gallons of Jeyes Fluid. The Ministry vet arrived and followed the route of the other sombre pilgrims, down the hill to the scene of death. William Owen appeared briefly, the tragedy of his lost cow swamped in the harassment of arrangements for its disposal, his secluded world invaded, his quiet life suddenly caught up in the strangeness of enforced proceedings which he was powerless to halt.

'What for all the bloody fuss?' he said bitterly.

No one knew how the cow could possibly have contracted anthrax. It had been born and reared at Corlwyni and had never left the farm. It seemed that cattle-cake or purchased hay could be the only source of infection. I went down to Nantmor in the afternoon and found the news had spread round the district. Everyone wondered if the infection would spread, and we were considered the second most likely candidates for death. All were sorry for the Owens, but for centuries hardship and difficulty had been part of the life of those hill people and they took misfortune very calmly. Many, like old John Williams, who had experienced his share of it, received the news with a twinkle in the eye. I saw him that afternoon.

'The people in Beddgelert do be keeping away from us in Nantmor now,' he said.

I walked home in the fine drizzle. Twm Gravedigger was returning down the hill with mud-covered mattock and spade, and I asked him how the burning pit had progressed. He told me that it was finished after much difficulty as the hole had been filling with water all day. Tomorrow the cow would be cremated and everyone would be thankful to see the last of it. He walked away homewards and was followed soon after by the police car. It was getting dark.

The fourth day after the cow died dawned like its predecessors with low cloud and light rain. At nine o'clock in the morning Sergeant Owen and four constables were to be seen tramping purposefully past Carneddi farmhouse and down the hill to their last distasteful task. Presently a trickle of smoke ascended lazily above the treetops. The funeral pyre was alight.

Paul and I were back at work on the fencing stakes. It chanced that, from our high perch on the wooded fringe of the Allt, we could look down through the shifting veil of mist to where the cremation was in progress a little way along Corlwyni's Gors Goch field below. We could see five dark figures moving round the spot from where the smoke rose in a straight column. Now and again extra activity increased the volume of the smoke, which towered upwards for a while and then dwindled away and diffused among the natural mists. The constables seemed to be provided with long poles or sticks with which they advanced for a poke at the mass and then retreated to the perimeter of the field. Occasionally a licking red flame could be seen, rising and then flickering out. Paul and I sawed and chopped, carried the stakes to the place where they would be used, and then piled up the brushwood. Below, the figures continued to revolve round the smoking heap, macabre and sinister as witches round a cauldron in that winter-bleak landscape. Soon the rain came on heavily and we retired to the house and our dinner.

Later, Sergeant Owen returned lamenting. He needed further supplies of paraffin. The rain and the windless atmosphere caused the fire to burn only reluctantly and indeed it had gone out several times. To make matters worse the pit was again filling with water. The policemen had brought no food with them and, understandably enough, Mrs. Owen, who disapproved of the whole affair, had not been near. Duty bound them to the spot until the last vestige of cow turned to ashes, but a corpse of such dimensions was not an inflammable thing and they were finding it difficult work.

More paraffin was brought and Mother carried cocoa and sandwiches to the miserable policemen. The smell, she said, was ghastly and they were cold and wet and looking very pale. At tea-time she went down again with further supplies. Now at last they were making some progress. Another five gallons of paraffin had produced helpful results and the fire was properly alight. However, it was not until ten o'clock that evening, thirteen hours after the pyre had first been lighted, that we heard the sergeant and his four constables trooping wearily up the hill. My father called out to ask if all was well and a voice replied: 'Yes, but indeed we have not had such a job before in all our lives.'

The sequel to this story is, in view of all that happened, rather strange. The next day word came from the Ministry of Agriculture that William Owen's cow had not died of anthrax after all. The tests of their veterinary surgeon proved that it had not had the disease. To the end our vet was convinced that the Ministry had made a mistake and that the cow had indeed died of anthrax. I had seen those curious rods under the microscope, but we never knew who was right.

17   Chinese Interlude

My father said it was a hoax. I had been out for the evening and returned late to find that Twentieth Century Fox Productions Limited wanted the use of our jeep on the following day to transport film directors up mountain roads. Beddgelert is a long way from Hollywood and it seemed hard to believe that such people were among us, but I went to the telephone. There was no doubt about it. When I came back I was hired at five pounds for the day. I was to pay for my own petrol and start work at half-past seven the next morning.

That night I tossed restlessly in bed. I was not used to film tycoons and wondered if I should be able to do what was required. The jeep was very old, with a variety of foibles which had to be coaxed and humoured and a breakdown would be humiliating. Also the weather might be bad and the jeep had no hood. I had explained this breathlessly on the telephone and, when the Production Manager had inquired what happened when it rained, I could only say that one got wet. I wondered if, after all, it would not have been better to stay at home.

The next morning I was up at five, milked, separated the cream and fed the hens. Then I backed the jeep out of the cart shed which served as its garage. In the raw light of morning and in the knowledge of its task for the day, it looked pathetically ancient and shabby. With dustpan and brush I swept out the layer of mud, dried manure and toffee papers which had accumulated in the bottom, and fetched an armful of sofa cushions which I arranged on the hard iron seats. This was the best I could do to prepare for those august posteriors which undoubtedly were used to every comfort. It was only for a day; they could bear it for a day, I thought, and then the jeep and I could retire into the obscurity of the hills again. Mercifully the weather appeared to be fine. Moel Hebog's summit had a dusting of snow and hailstones, but the sun glinted through the clouds. It was early in February 1958.

I had breakfast, changed into warm clothes that I hoped looked both business-like and becoming, and then bounced away down the hill with my father waving farewell from the corner by the cowshed. The time was ten mintues past seven.

In Beddgelert village there was the quiet of early morning with the smoke from newly-lighted fires pluming upwards, and Will Bryn Felin going from door to door with the morning milk. The only unaccustomed sight for those quiet off-season days of early February was a vast glistening car drawn up outside the Royal Goat Hotel with a uniformed chauffeur at its wheel. I was about to go into the hotel when a rattle of toe-nails on the road and a flying black figure proclaimed the arrival of Mit, my father's sheepdog. Here was an extra anxiety. Mit was a fanatically keen motorist and took every opportunity of following the jeep. He would appear when it was too late to send him home and so assured himself of a ride. He jumped into the jeep and on to a cushion intended for a film magnate, and sat up very straight, smirking with pleasure. There was nothing I could do about it now; he would have to come too.

A knot of people had gathered in the hotel porch. One was the Production Manager who told me that we were going to look for possible locations for a film. John Box, the Art Director, would accompany me, thus having a better view of the countryside from the open jeep. The rest would travel in the car, disembarking only when the roads became too rough or narrow for it. As John Box climbed in beside me he received a wet kiss from Mit. The others disappeared into the interior of the limousine and, with the laconic direction of: 'Follow that car,' we started off. It was, however, no easy matter to keep up with the Austin Princess which could travel at any number of miles an hour with seeming languor and comfort. At forty the jeep bounded about on the road, if it were unladen, with every part of its steel body vibrating fiercely. We had a grim

204

chase. Each time we started up the straight, the expensive black and chromium tail of the Austin was disappearing round the next bend. Mit was enjoying himself, with ears streaming back in the wind and eyes protruding. John Box sat silent, but whether he was occupied with the beauties of valley and mountain rushing past or merely trying to prevent his bones from being rattled to pieces, I did not know.

Round the next bend we came upon the stationary Austin. A narrow, muddy lane branched off uphill and the film people wanted to go up it. They piled out of their car, Mark Robson, the Director; Jim Newcome, another Director; the Production Manager, the Camera Man and the Construction Manager. All were dressed in deceptively casual clothes, in fisherman's-knit sweaters, light-coloured slacks, pom-pom hats and two-tone shoes. They were friendly and smiling, and exclaimed: 'Hi, Ruth' as they clambered on board, each to be rubber-stamped by Mit's nose. Their voices had a transatlantic twang, but later I was to discover that only Mark Robson and Jim Newcome were Americans. The intonation, however, was catching and I nearly acquired it myself.

'Gee, this is swell,' said Mark, settling himself on a sofa cushion. Far from regarding the jeep with surprise and disdain, the party seemed delighted with it, and indeed now it came into its own. In four-wheel drive I transported them up steep slopes, through mud and over rough ground where otherwise legs would have become weary and the two-tone shoes would have been ruined. Locations were examined, views were surveyed and finders were applied to the eye for a movie camera sight of the Welsh mountains.

'Gee, this is a wunnerful country,' Mark kept saying. The beautiful panorama of the mountains was making its impact on them; these lonely sheeplands, these wooded valleys with their cascading streams and stone cottages, this paradise of rock and sky and clouds, rich until now only in beauties for the eye and spirit, suddenly seemed as though they might have their value in dollars also.

We returned to the hotel for lunch. I might well have been consigned to a side table with the chauffeur of the Austin Princess—indeed expected to be—but Mark Robson courteously seated me at the head of his own table. There were more film people at the meal, perhaps a dozen in all, and the talk was mainly technical, but I began to learn more about the proposed picture. It was to be called *The Inn of the Sixth Happiness* and concerned the experiences of an English missionary in north China during the Sino-Japanese war of the late 1920s. It was based on a book called *The Small Woman* which recounted the life of Gladys Aylward and her trek over the mountains with a hundred refugee children. Mark Robson and his company had flown to Formosa, China and Hong Kong in search of locations for the picture, but political difficulties or unsuitable terrain had ruled them out. Then, by chance, photographs of North Wales had been seen. Strangely, these matched almost perfectly with similar photographs of the mountains of North China. The location was decided and China was to be brought to Wales. The picture was to star Ingrid Bergman, Curt Jurgens and Robert Donat. Now Beddgelert was to see things it had never seen before.

After lunch we went to Nantmor, and my friends in the village watched in surprise as the jeep passed by with its load of film personnel in their camel coats and pom-pom hats. I was able to park Mit here, where he could later be released when the jeep was out of earshot. Then we were off to the Ogwen valley, twenty miles away, with the jeep careering in the wake of the big car; then back to Pen-y-Pass and with everyone in the jeep we crawled up the old copper miners' track to look at some of the bleakest and loneliest country in Gwynedd. Then the light was fading from the sky and the little warmth of the day was gone, and so we turned homewards.

In the hotel after tea, I was about to leave with a new £5 note in my pocket when Mark Robson said: 'Say, we can use Ruth tomorrow, can't we boys?' The boys agreed that sure they would need Ruth tomorrow, and so I was engaged for the following day also.

At home the family were filled with interest and I gave them an account of my day's work. I had used perhaps 30s. worth of petrol but, even with this deducted from my £5, I had earned more in the day than I had ever done before. I had enjoyed the experience and the jeep had run well. Cold and tired but excited, I stumped off to the cowshed to milk.

The next day I felt more at ease in the company of my film tycoons. Now I was enjoying myself, the jeep continued to go and the weather was fine. This time we went to Portmeirion, the Italianesque village on a promontory of Tremadoc Bay. Mark wanted to find a location for the Yellow River and the sand flats of the estuary might have possibilities. He asked me where this type of scenery might be found and I helped him as much as I could.

'You see, boys,' Mark said, 'we want grass and scrub coming down to the water. This might be it, but the water's too low down.'

We were walking along the cliff path that runs from Portmeirion towards Portmadoc. Someone suggested that the Thames Estuary might be better.

'Sure, sure,' said Mark, 'we might use that too. Now this is how I see it. It's dark, see, but there's just a bit of light glinting on the water and there's this grass and scrub in the front. Then you see something come floating in.' He made floating movements with his hands. 'But you can't tell what it is. It's dark, see.'

All of a sudden we could see. The sparkling waters of the estuary had become inky, with only an oily glisten on their surface, and there was this sinister black mass floating into the bank.

'You know what it is?' said Mark. 'It's GUYS!' and his hands made them jump out at us. Almost, but not quite, there was the indrawn breath of a cinema audience at a celluloid climax. It was going to be a great picture, I could see. This scene, as imagined by Mark Robson, was in fact never shot, for a suitable location for it could not be found.

In the afternoon I was assigned to John Box who was planning the site of a walled Chinese city. The hill behind our own village of Nantmor was thought to be the best place for it, and we went there to take stills. We walked on to the slopes of Cwm Bychan for here the ground was too rough even for the jeep. Soon I was standing poised on the rocks, marking the site of a proposed pagoda and holding a light-coloured

Carneddi sofa cushion aloft, while John Box took pictures from below. It was strange to look up at Carneddi, permanent and peaceful, on the opposite ridge, while I was engaged, for the moment, in the glittering soap-bubble world of picture-making. I could see a small figure which must be my father proceeding along the skyline on the afternoon round, and the white dots of hens rushing to meet him. I wondered if he could see me, but John Box was calling and I must move farther along to stand where the gate of the imaginary city would be. Pegs were pushed into the ground, measurements taken and then it was time to stop work. I declined an invitation for tea at the hotel since I was so near home. My wages could be collected later. I said good-bye to John Box.

'See you in June when the shooting begins,' he answered.

For a short time I was the sole authority on the coming film. Nobody else had talked with the film-makers as I had done, but soon the feelers of Twentieth Century Fox were spreading through the district, a network of activity grew, and the rumours flying from mouth to mouth no longer had their genesis at Carneddi. Soon I was myself eagerly collecting gossip from the village. Strangers could be seen walking in Cwm Bychan. The taxi business in Beddgelert had its cars filled with film people hurrying from place to place. Bookings were made at the local hotels, guest houses and hostels for April, May and June when hundreds of people were to be accommodated during the construction of the sets and the shooting of the film. Even in the height of summer Beddgelert and never seen such activity.

The district welcomed the strangers wholeheartedly. Film-making was going to bring money and work into a country where both were scarce, and at a time of year when there were few tourists. Everyone was prepared to make the most of opportunity while it was with them. For nine months of the year the mountains were cloaked in solitude, and the inhabitants went about their traditional work of farming and forestry almost undisturbed by the hurry and bustle of modern life. The sudden influx of the film unit, to whom the ends of the earth were but a few hours' flying time away, brought colour and excitement to a customary way of life. But more than this, more than the attendant prosperity and interest, there was the feeling of secret pride that the mountain country was being recognized for its beauty and special qualities. Mark Robson, with the whole world at his finger-tips, had chosen the mountains of Eryri and its people were pleased. It was sweet to their ears to hear him say: 'Gee, this country has everything,' and enthusiastically they catered for his needs and identified themselves with his schemes.

Lambing-time had come again and, as we walked round the flock, we could see a network of steel scaffolding rising on the hill of Cwm Bychan. Daily we looked across the valley to mark its progress and gradually it took shape; the scaffold was covered with battens, and a city wall, with curly-eaved gatehouse and watch towers, grew where there had been nothing but slate and heather before. A steep road of railway sleepers wound up to the entrance. Then the stone walls began to arrive, great sheets of plaster casting from Boreham Wood Studios, on lorries so long that they could not turn over the Aberglaslyn Bridge and had to be unloaded in Beddgelert and transported on smaller lorries to Nantmor. The sheets were carried up the railway-sleeper road on Land Rovers and attached to the batten-covered scaffold in great sections. The painters came next with an alchemy of colours in fifty-gallon drums, and thousands of square feet of fake plaster stonework took on the weather-beaten look of ages, with green damp creeping up from the massive buttresses and flakes of golden lichen crusting the stones. The curly-eaved, dragon-topped roofs became an old rose red. From ten yards away the illusion was perfect. The people of Nantmor were impressed.

'It is just like Caernarvon Castle,' they said.

This walled Chinese city of Wangcheng was beautiful. It fitted perfectly into those wild surroundings and lent splendour to the great sweep of Moel Hebog behind it. Other sets were being built, too. A complete Chinese village appeared on the terraced workings of an old copper mine near Beddgelert, and there was a graveyard, with plaster monuments, in the village of Llanfrothen.

Local people were asked to sign on as extras for the crowd

scenes; they would be paid two guineas a day. Mary, Paul and I put our names down, for it would be exciting to be more than onlookers. Everyone else seemed to think the same and the list of signatures became immensely long. Names of people from miles away appeared, some with hopeful little notes about their dramatic and artistic ability. Mary and I looked about as un-Chinese as possible, with our blue eyes, fair hair and tallness, and our hopes of being extras faded now there were so many to choose from. Paul, we thought, might pass quite well as an Asian and, since there were fewer men on the list, might easily get a job.

Meanwhile the unfolding of spring kept us fully occupied. We were, after all, only interested spectators of the fabulous doings of Twentieth Century Fox. Farming seemed more important than film-making. The flock had given birth, and everywhere lambs skipped on the greening mountainside and every one must be injected against dysentery. The cuckoo had come and leaves were bursting. We must plough and plant and look after the teeming life of the farm.

Then, one Thursday at the end of May, the film's Transport Manager telephoned to ask me to drive the jeep throughout June for the unit. I had never for a moment considered that I might be offered a full-time job. The occasional day's work as a crowd scene extra would hardly have interfered with the farm routine, but a whole month was different. There was much to be considered. Shearing came in June; there were preparations to be made for silage and hay-making in July, and the never-ending task of hoeing the strawberry field. But my earnings would be good and there was still the last of the overdraft on Ty Mawr's roof to be cleared and, at the moment, no visible means of clearing it. Here was opportunity and I decided to take it. June's farm work would have to be squeezed into July, and extra help had from Paul. My main worry was the jeep and whether it would be able to do the work required of it.

I spent the last week-end in frantic activity. I trotted down the strawberry rows with the push-hoe. I moved as many pullets as possible from the brooder house into folds. I wrote business letters in the evenings and took the jeep to the garage for a last-minute check. At half past seven on Monday morning I was in my place outside the Royal Goat Hotel. Now the early morning quiet of Beddgelert was all dispelled. Five or six cars were pulled up nearby. A group of people were drawing on their after-breakfast cigarettes on the hotel steps, while others were walking rapidly past with typewritten sheets or folders. An occasional Chinese in skull cap, tunic and baggy pants was to be seen sauntering along the road, while farther down a huge maroon van marked 'The Location Caterers' was loading up food containers outside the Church Hall. Men were lifting heavy equipment into one of two camera cars. Across the bridge a sign had appeared on the Vestry Hall proclaiming 'Wardrobe', and every now and then figures issued from its door in twos and threes; a group of bandits in ragged jerkins and sheepskin caps, then a pair of Chinese talking rapidly in a strange language, then a few Japanese soldiers. Two buses roared through the village with youthful Asian faces pressed to the glass. The residents of Beddgelert were busy too. They were now completely film conscious. The subdued flutter caused by early rumours had been replaced by a sense of participation. They had assisted in the preparations for the film and knew just what was going on.

So my first day's work began. The location was in the Ogwen Valley and Dennis Elliot, one of the Assistant Directors, was to be my passenger. He was a tall young man whose crew-cut hair and drainpipe jeans were strangely at variance with his cultured accents. Here, at least, was one person who had not acquired a Transatlantic drawl. He told me that I was attached to the Second Unit which filmed the more distant shots, often using the stand-in for the star. The First Unit was concerned chiefly with the shooting of close-ups involving the principal actors, and this Mark Robson directed. There seemed to be a great number of Directors and Assistant Directors—'There's more bosses here than workmen,' one of the carpenters remarked. I never did quite work out the hierarchy, but Mark Robson was the one who had the last word. Today both units would be working together.

The vehicles of Twentieth Century Fox set off along the road to Llyn Ogwen. There were five or six furniture vans packed with an amazing variety of gear, from rifles and mule saddles to Chinese dolls and foot bindings. There were two canteens; several cars transporting the principal actors, actresses and important staff; caravans for Ingrid Bergman and Curt Jurgens, and cattle trucks containing the horses and mules. There were buses filled with Chinese children or technicians, the two camera cars and me. The whole, mighty caravan was on the move, a world in itself, which took its own life, jargon and strange tense atmosphere of unreality with it to any part of the globe.

Mists of early morning were clearing and shadows shortening as the June sun rose above the mountains. The parking grounds on both sides of the road by Idwal Cottage were alive with activity. Cars nosed in past ranks of restless horses and mules to cries of, 'Mind your backs, please.' The ramps of the furniture vans were down now, disclosing their amazing contents. From one, wooden saddles with high pommels were being unloaded; from another, rolled-up blankets, a vast iron cooking-pot, shabby baskets and bamboo poles; from a third, dozens and dozens of Lee-Enfield rifles, army canteens and water-bottles. The buses had disgorged their load of Chinese children, and now these milled round like a flock of excited little birds, a chattering of Liverpudlian dialect issuing from their Asian cherubs' lips. Dennis was trying to gather them together, and intoning through a loud-hailer: 'This way, children. Form up into a line. The little boy in the fur hat, come HERE! This way, children. Follow me, children.' Finally they straggled off down the track past the Youth Hostel in the direction of a pointing sign marked 'LOC' in red letters, which someone had attached to a tree.

The location for most of the shooting that day was along this track which skirted the wall of the Nantffrancon on the opposite side to the main road. It led down steeply, in places almost to the valley's floor, and then rose again. Its once tarred surface was deeply pitted, and finally the tar gave place to a rubble of stones, more like a river bed than a road. There was no space for vehicles to pass one another, and only a small area where the verge was dry enough and flat enough for them to turn. Only cars could use the road; it was too narrow and steep for the vans and lorries, and their contents would have to be carried down on smaller vehicles. The only small vehicle suitable for this was the jeep. A little crowd of property men and carpenters began to argue round its bonnet for priority. Soon I was trundling up and down the track with timber for the camera stands, with a heavy load of rifles and with a great pyramid of bedding rolls and the cooking-pot on top. These last were for the hundred children to carry on the scenes of their trek across the mountains. Then it was time for the tea and coffee urns to go down for the mid-morning break and, slowly and carefully, the jeep descended again, with dozens of cups a-tinkle, with folding tables balanced on top of slopping urns and trays of pastries balanced on top of them, and three white-overalled canteen men clinging on round the sides. Later I carried them up again, the empty urns, the dirty cups and despoiled pastry trays. Now and again a runaway horse came rocketing by with a Chinese bandit fighting for control, while a voice exclaimed through the loud-hailer: 'Don't gallop the horses, please. Please don't gallop the horses.' Some of the Chinese were superb riders but others, lured by the extra pay for horsemen, appeared never to have been mounted before, and a few of them landed on the turf with a harder bump than they expected.

The jeep was also in demand to carry passengers up and down. In four-wheel drive I could skirt round on the mud at the side of the road if we met an oncoming car, and so save endless delays, long stretches of backing and traffic jams. All day I piled up and down the road. I thought regretfully of the amount of petrol I must be using—to be paid for from my earnings—with so much uphill work often in four-wheel drive and booster gears. But I saw my new boss, Arthur Anderson, the Transport Manager, was noticing, and felt he was satisfied that I was doing important work. I was pleased for I wanted to be part of the hurly-burly of film-making, now I was here, and a useful cog in the great machine of Twentieth Century Fox. The jeep might be decrepit but I wanted to show that I could do the job for which I was paid as well as a man could. Later four or five Land Rovers and another jeep were also employed, when it was found how essential they were in the mountain country, but I still had a good share of the work, in fact was almost preferred and, while Jack or Ron were standing idle, there would be shouts of: 'Hi, where's Ruth?'

Throughout that month I drove the jeep as though it were made of cut glass and humoured its whims as discreetly as I could. One of its peculiarities was a failure to start again if it were stopped with the engine sloping uphill or tilting down from left to right. It required quick thinking sometimes to manœuvre into a desirable stopping position on those switchback slopes, without seeming to do so too obviously. Another worry was the absence of certain parts which the law required a motor vehicle to possess. The three or four policemen, who were always on point duty near the location, were my frequent passengers and at first a source of apprehension. But they never seemed to notice or else turned a blind eye to what was missing, and I attempted to drive as serenely and confidently as if the jeep were efficient in every detail. The constables and the sergeant were friendly, and often I used to take tea and cakes along the road to any who were controlling traffic at some distance from the canteen. In the evenings the jeep was sometimes used to collect the string of blue NO PARKING signs which had been distributed down the road near the location. This was accomplished rather in the manner of horsemen tent-pegging and the signs were gathered up while we were moving and without need for the constables to climb out.

On that first day I had little opportunity to watch the shooting. There were only brief glimpses of that fabulous, hundreds-of-pounds-a-minute procedure which was the final fruit of all other activity here. I heard the voice of Mark Robson, now a little tense, saying: 'O.K. Roll it.' and the honk-honk of the klaxon on the camera car to indicate that shooting for sound was in progress. Now all voices fell silent, all engines were stopped and animation was suspended, except for the pin-point activity in the eye of the camera. Then a voice cried: 'Cut' and everybody came to life again. The horsemen rode back up the hill ready for another take. Someone stretched a tape measure from the camera to the tip of Curt Jurgen's nose. Then: 'Roll it,' said Mark. The camera whirred again. The clapper-board boy jumped forward to thrust the number of the shot before it. 'One thirty-nine, take four.' The horsemen rode down the hill again towards that vital group round the camera. Second by second film was going in the can.

Later the Chinese children were filmed, trudging along the road carrying the bundles that earlier had come down in the jeep. Two carried the giant cooking-pot between them on a bamboo pole. Phyllis, Miss Bergman's double, walked with the throng with a baby on her back, for the shot was a distant one. Now sunlight and shadows chased across the hills, where sheep grazed on the higher slopes unmindful of the strange invaders below. Now the sun was slipping westwards, the shadows lengthening and the light becoming poor. Filming ceased and that nomad train collected its bags and baggage, stowed its props and gear into the cars, the vans and the lorries, and streamed back along the road to its hotels, while the mountains remained, as always, perfectly serene.

The Second Unit filmed at Ogwen all that week. Besides providing a suitable background for numerous trekking shots of the children, the bandits' camp was there. On a steep defile just off the track were ragged tents draped in skins, with charcoal fires smoking here and there between them. More skins and a litter of earthenware vessels and cooking-pots were visible inside the tents while stacks of rifles leant against the rocks outside, giving the place an air of primitive savagery appropriate to a mountain bandits' camp. A few horses and mules, tethered higher up, could be seen in the background. It was interesting to hear that those dirty rags and skins, chipped bowls and shabby baskets were among the prop men's most valued possessions. New ones could be obtained by the gross and were considered of little importance, but hundreds of pounds' worth of studio time had been spent in reducing the present props to so much junk—hours of soaking and drying, of being dragged round on dirty floors, kicked and trampled on, until all looked sufficiently old and battered to be the possessions of Chinese peasant folk.

On the day before the main shots of the bandits' camp were

to be taken, John Box came over to me. As Art Director, the camp was his creation.

'Know anything about sheep?' he asked.

I replied that I had a hundred of my own.

'Then come and have a look at this one,' he said.

It proved to be a dead wether lying in the bandits' camp. It was required as a prop to lend authenticity to the scene and had been bought locally for £10, and slaughtered the day before. Now, as might have been expected in the warm June weather, the stomach was distended with internal gases and a bad smell pervaded the camp. John Box was afraid that this might deter the cast and camera crews when shooting began on the next day.

'Do you think it would improve if it were gutted?' he asked.

I said I thought that once it had begun to smell it would go on smelling whatever was done. One of the workmen had already dug a grave, but this had filled with water. Everyone appeared disgusted and I was sorry not to be more helpful.

The next day I did not expect to see the sheep, but there it was in the middle distance of the camp, suspended upside down from a pole, with its insides removed, giving a grim reality to the scene. The scale of spending on the film had left me breathless, but it seemed that nothing must be wasted. All day the bandits and the camera crews were surrounded by the stealing odour of dead sheep. The directors made unkind remarks about the poor creature and from time to time walked away. Everyone was glad when shooting was finished and the sheep at last stamped down in the water-filled grave, its brief début in films over.

Hokka was the bandits' leader. He was dressed in shabby breeches, with cartridge belt encircling his hips and a torn sheepskin jerkin open to the waist. He had a curiously-shaped profile; the bullet head was cropped to leave nothing more than a stubble of hair, and the face grimed from the make-up man's paint pot. He looked villainous in the extreme. It was his sinister, hooded eyes which most held my fascinated stare.

'Looks good, doesn't he?' said the make-up man standing at my elbow.

'Yes, wonderful,' I said still gazing at that macabre face.

'It's the eyelids that do it,' said the make-up man. I was about to agree when he produced two little strips of plastic material from his pocket. They lay in his hand, greyish and skin-like.

'I just stick them over the corners of the eyes,' he said.

As the days passed, names attached themselves to faces which were becoming familiar, and I was on friendly terms with many of the hundreds of people engaged in making the film. The jeep was a favourite resting place for the Chinese. Between takes, eight or nine of them, bandits and peasants, would climb up and dispose themselves on its flaking khaki surface. Only the oldest ones talked Chinese among themselves. I attempted to learn a few words but there were so many different dialects that I made little progress. One of the bandits, who sat most often in the jeep was a Malay. He had handsome Asian features and had taken bit parts in many films, but the work was irregular.

'If I rely on film work,' he said with a shrug of the shoulders, 'I starve.'

He was studying to be a barrister and, after the examinations were passed, would return to Malaya. Everyone called everyone else by their Christian names and the atmosphere was very friendly and informal, but it was transitory. In a few weeks all the crowd of people, now working together so closely, would again be scattered to the ends of the earth.

I worked with properties, mostly, but also did every other job at times except for towing the caravans and the two enormous generators. No one ever asked me to do this and I was thankful as it might finally have stopped the jeep's ancient engine. The first trouble that developed was a fault in the steering. A sickening judder shook the whole vehicle at any speed greater than thirty miles an hour. The vibration was slight at first but increased daily until it was impossible to pretend that nothing was wrong. Even Dennis remarked on our pounding journeys to and from Ogwen: 'How soon do you expect this jeep to drop to pieces?' I telephoned to the garage and Mr. Roberts promised to do his best to improve matters, but it was difficult to find time for repairs. The jeep was a vital link in the transport system and could ill be spared, but I managed to get away one lunch hour. The garage man rose to the occasion magnificently, dropped everything and we dashed to the foundry where the steering column was welded in a few minutes. On the way home we found that the trouble was not completely cured. Back at the garage, Mr. Roberts noticed that one of the front wheels was but of alignment and this he changed with one from the rear. The judder was now almost absent; I should be all right until the welding broke. I was back with the Unit before anyone noticed I had gone.

The next trouble was more harrowing; the starter motor began to fail. In the past we had had periods with no self-starter and I was adept at using the handle, but a film location was no place to display this skill. The engine had a violent kick, the compression was great and care was needed to avoid a broken wrist. The film people were always in a hurry and every time I pressed the self-starter there was apprehension in my heart as I listened to the engine turning over haltingly, and a great thankfulness when at last it fired. I did not want to fail at my job now, just as I was beginning to enjoy myself, just as I was collecting bundles of fivers for which I had such good use. Spare parts for jeeps were difficult and slow to obtain but, by chance, Mr. Roberts had another jeep at his garage for repair. He was willing to take the starter from that. and hoped to get mine mended before this other jeep was wanted again. This was the last trouble I had, apart from the occasional oiling of the plugs which I was able to clean with the aid of box spanners borrowed from the canteen and emery paper from the property vans.

As I was a driver it was impossible for me to be an extra, but Mary and Paul had several day's work on the set. We found that only the residents of Nantmor and Beddgelert were needed, and the long string of casual visitors and people from far away never received a call. Those days with local extras had a special air of festivity. All our friends were there, unfamiliar in Chinese costume. The day's filming was like a vast fancy-dress party, with a two-guinea handout at the end, and a touch of the spice and glitter of Hollywood to add excitement. I found Mary in baggy blue pants and tunic, her blonde hair tucked inside a stocking cap, painting mud on the policeman's wife with a large whitewash brush. Paul was practically unrecognizable. His Chinese peasant costume became him so well that, with black skull cap on his head and at a few yards distance, I could hardly distinguish him from the genuine Chinese. He was smearing artificial blood on to a rag round his hand, in company with other wounded Welshmen. Later I saw them descending the steep path from Wangcheng in a file of refugees, Mary bearing a lighted torch and lugging a great basket, while Paul limped behind with two bundles swinging from a bamboo pole on his shoulder. Here also were the familiar faces of local sheep-farmers and village people with their wives, sons and daughters, yet strangely different now in their ragged clothing with blood- and mud-smeared faces, leading children by the hand, carrying others on their backs, pushing handcarts, lugging bundles, holding flaring torches and with here and there a goat jostling in the throng. The cameras were shooting with night-for-day filters. The scene, now under a cloudy June sky in mid-afternoon, would appear on the screen as a torch-light procession after dark.

On another day Paul was a Japanese soldier, and again he looked very suitable for the part. I saw him bearing a huge banner of the Rising Sun across a battlefield at the foot of Tryfan. The local lads had great sport firing blank cartridges at one another. The Labour Exchanges had been combed and every man on the dole that day was there in uniform. The loud-hailers, crackling slightly with annoyance, were used in an attempt to quell the exuberant firing which burst out here and there when filming was not in progress. 'That's enough, boys. Save your blanks. No more firing, PLEASE!' The temptation was great however, and desultory shots and puffs of smoke kept appearing all over the battlefield in spite of the authoritative tones of the loud-hailer. Paul said he saw one youth bending to tighten his puttees while another crept up and fired a blank just behind the bending boy's seat. The resultant yell was ideal for the battle scene.

Then one day my turn came. No extras had been engaged, but suddenly it was decided that soldiers were needed for shots of the capture of the Chinese city. Prop men, grooms, the boys from Special Effects, the electricians, the carpenters, bandits, make-up men and Bert the barber were collected for the Japanese Army, and straggled up the track to man the city walls. I was told to go too. I was very pleased for, besides getting two guineas on top of my usual pay, I had been yearning to be an extra. At the wardrobe van I was given my uniform and equipment. The steel helmet, while looking most realistic, seemed to be made of papiermâché with padding inside. It was very light and small and kept popping up so that it showed my hair. I hurried up the ramp to the city walls, toting my rifle and endeavouring to keep the tin hat well squashed down on my head.

'Blimey!' said Bert, the barber, when he saw me. 'No wonder the Japs lost the war.'

On the city walls, we were told to shout and wave our rifles triumphantly. With our backs to the sinking sun we should appear only as dark, exultant figures. Waving the eleven-pound Lee-Enfield was hard work and I used two hands, raising and lowering it rather in the manner of someone doing physical jerks, while my papiermâché helmet began again to pop up from my head. We all shouted as loudly as we could and I heard some rude words also yelled into the general din. After the sixth or seventh take my arms were aching. On the next ridge Carneddi lay golden and peaceful, catching the rays of the sinking sun, a scatter of hens dotting the grass round the fowl house, the hayfields a brilliant green. It was a different world from the fake Chinese city with its sham soldiers down below.

I had milking and feeding to do before and after work and eleven to thirteen hours of driving for the Unit, and I found I was beginning to get short of sleep. After the first few hectic days and when more Land Rovers were employed, the pressure eased and sometimes the jeep would stand idle for two or three hours. I used them to doze behind the steering wheel. The newness of filming had worn off and I was less eager to see everything that was happening. Someone lent me a paper-backed novel to read but I found the words running together on the page and my eyes closing, while the sound of voices, of engines revving and horses' hooves clattering faded farther and farther into the distance. Then 'DO you mind!' and I would open my eyes with a start and find I was wanted to fetch a load of rifles or Chinese children up the hill. 'DO you mind!' was one of the current catch-phrases on everyone's lips—'DO you mind!' if one was in a hurry and wanted attention, 'DO you mind!' in withering tones if people were obtuse or blundered. Now I came alive again; I was wide awake so long as I was working.

Sometimes I used the quiet periods to do farm correspondence, taking a folder of papers with me in the pocket of the jeep. There seemed little time for it at night and, during any daylight left after I reached home, I did some of the odd jobs which only I could do. The farm was my responsibility and it worried me to be away so much. I thoroughly enjoyed the excitement and glamour of my work for Twentieth Century Fox and my wages would pay the last of the money owing on Ty Mawr's roof, but I hated to feel I was neglecting the farm, even for a month, and so I did as much farm work as I could in the evenings and the early mornings.

Everyone who worked for Twentieth Century Fox was well looked after. When the weather turned showery, a hundred pale blue plastic macs with hoods arrived for the children, and a hundred pairs of gum-boots. There was also a van load of commando boots for the regular studio staff. They already had duffle coats, rain coats, and rubber boots with a stencilled M.G.M. or EALING or such cryptic words as FLOOR ELECT. upon them, but leather boots were also needed and so leather boots arrived. The Production Manager, who was responsible for all this, was very popular.

The canteen was good, too, and on days when extras were on the location perhaps six hundred excellent hot dinners would be passed over the canteen counter in a few minutes. Chicken, turkey and ice cream were usual and I began to put on weight. At ten o'clock break there was tea or coffee and meat pies, and at tea-time a bewildering variety of fancy cakes. Tea and chocolate biscuits were provided at 6 p.m. for drivers, technicians and staff who were still working. We were never hungry. At the end of every meal I watched choice morsels being tipped into the pig bin, which nobody ever seemed to collect, perhaps because of the sauce bottles, paper cartons and tea-leaves that went in as well. I thought of hungry beaks and jaws at home. The pig bin was too unsavoury to tackle, so the next day I brought a clean two-gallon can, with 'RUTH' lettered on the side in white paint, and gave it to Dave, the canteen man. Each day Dave filled it with morsels suitable for dogs, cats and hens, and in the evening I took it home. As the jeep wound up the hill, the four black figures of the sheepdogs were to be seen sitting on the skyline, drooling and quivering with anticipation. The jeep stopped and there followed a handout of mouth-watering extravagance. Hambones, beef-bones, mutton-bones, sausage rolls and large pieces of cheese were gulped down in the wolfish manner of Welsh sheepdogs or dragged away to be buried for a later feast. Mot, very old now, deaf and almost blind, could also detect when the film unit was on the Nantmor location. He would waddle down there at dinner-time, laboriously but enthusiastically, and quarter the ground round the canteen like a vacuum cleaner, in search of bread rolls and cream cakes which had been cast aside. He would then approach anyone who was still eating and offer to shake hands with them.

So the days passed in a crazy procession of wonders, excitements and lavish spending. I had never seen money spent on such a scale before. People jumped over precipices, galloped over rocks and crossed flooded rivers for an extra £5 or £10, and the more chances they had, the better they were pleased. The Unit soon collected a tenacious fringe of job-seekers, lured by the glitter and the cash. Local people already had their own niches in the film-making or were content to watch the spectacle from their own doorsteps, and these others were mostly strangers to the hills. They mingled with the throng, chatted with underlings and angled for an introduction to the assistant of an assistant director, but there was not enough work for all. The ancient jeep had been my open-sesame to this chimerical world and I was unable to help those of them who approached me.

I watched as Ingrid Bergman acted and spoke her part against the backcloth of the Welsh mountains. Sometimes she rode in the jeep. Her quiet, generous and modest personality made everybody like her, but I heard hair-raising stories of other film stars from the prop men. Between takes she would retire to a folding chair at a little distance from the crowd, roll up the legs of her Chinese pants and talk quietly to one of the directors, until Mark Robson said: 'Ready now, Ingrid,' when she would return obediently to the arc lights and cameras.

Some days were wet, and the Unit took shelter in its vans, buses, cars and caravans, watching the rain streaming down but poised for instant action the moment the clouds broke. They would hang on hopefully until four or five o'clock for the chance of a minute or two of precious shooting-time before nightfall. Then, if the skies remained leaden, the word went round 'We're wrapping up, boys' and van ramps were finally pushed up, engines revved and one by one the vehicles of the Unit pulled out through the mud and puddles and streamed off down the road towards Beddgelert.

When it was all over, a variety of odd recollections remained in my mind, themselves like flashes of film—Mark in his lemon-coloured jeans; somebody's wet socks agitating in the warm air from the generators; one little Chinese girl of perhaps three years old squatting unnoticed before several trays of fancy cakes on the ground, her boot-button eyes fixed unwaveringly on the infinity of treasure before her, while she removed and ate, with extreme concentration, the decoration from each. Then there was the day when three planes gave a display of aerobatics for a bombing scene of Wangcheng, when Special Effects had a happy time with black smoke, loud bangs and sheets of flame, when a fire engine and ambulance stood by on the location and, by chance, the Vicar arrived to add a final touch to the accident precautions.

The month was nearly over and I began to wonder if I should feel unsettled and dull with only farm work to do. It seemed hard to imagine the countryside with no cars and people blocking the roads, no curly-eaved pagodas on the hills and no sampan floating on the quiet waters of Llyn Dinas. The end of June came. The children left first. The vans, the lorries and the buses went home. The casual good-byes of constant travellers were said and the film-makers slipped away, out of our lives. A few men were left to demolish the sets, but in an incredibly short time these too had finished, had loaded their last truck and departed. There was not a fragment of pagoda, not a bamboo pole, not a rice bowl left to tell us that China had ever been to Wales. The turf was replaced, the rubbish gathered up, the hills were restored to the sheep and the mountaineers, and the grey stone villages in the valley were quiet again.

And I found I did not regret the going. I had enjoyed the spectacular mirage while it lasted, but it was not connected with reality and, with a feeling almost of relief, I turned again to work which was governed by the sun and moon and the slow revolution of the seasons. We picked up the threads of our normal lives. There were now many farms, cottages and small businesses which, all of a sudden, had a little extra capital to buy some of the things which they lacked. My overdraft had been cleared and my father had a new wireless. The jeep had a broken spring but it was still running.

18 'We must be at School all our Days'

The last good weather of the summer went away with the film unit and cuckoo, and the wettest summer I ever remember began. The shearing was performed in the early days of July. Everyone had left their sheep until filming was over, and I was able to go round the farms and do my share of the work as usual. Then came silage-making and the rain fell nearly every day. The weather was still wet when the tower silo was full so we filled the first small silo too. By August we had enough good silage to feed our cattle during the winter, and some moderate quality hay as well. The wet summer did not disorganize the farm as it would have done in our early years at Carneddi, bringing confusion, anxiety and big bills for purchased hay. I had developed some judgment, now backed by experience, and thirteen years in the hills had taught me much.

We made more progress that year. Paul bought a second-hand tractor at a bargain price and, for the first time, our mechanization was independent and efficient; we could do our cultivations and mowing at the right time and without having to wait for the hired tractor. Paul was pleased to feel he was contributing towards the farm which interested him so much and he was also able to do a small amount of contract work. The tractor's arrival was timely as, after film work and twelve years' service in the mountains, the jeep's end was obviously near and it could no longer be relied upon to do heavy haulage on our steep gradients.

That wet summer brought some advantage with it. The heavy downpours rutted our road; little trickles became rivulets, the rivulets became streams and the streams bore a

225

debris of leaves, dead bracken and mud into the drainage channels, blocking them up. With no outlet the water poured on down the road in an ever-increasing torrent, carrying with it first the fine grit, then pebbles, and at last rooting out big stones from the road's bed and tumbling them downhill until at last there were channels eighteen inches deep scored down the surface and a great delta at the bottom of the hill. The road was now impassable for traffic. The Rural District Council were responsible for its repair and, after a while and when the lengthsman had reported on its condition, a lorry and road-men arrived to open the drains and to fill in the ruts with hardcore. After a day or two the road was tidy and serviceable again and they departed. A few days later there was another night of heavy rain and storm and the ground, now no longer so hard packed, was channelled deeper than before. I telephoned the County Surveyor and complained sadly. Even in exceptionally bad weather we needed the road; eggs must pass down, feeding-stuffs be carried up, Mr. Gardner must come for his monthly inspection of the strawberry plants, and often other officials from the Ministry of Agriculture. The County Surveyor reassured me. The loose grit and hardcore, satisfactory as it was in dry weather, was proving too expensive to maintain in wet, and it had been decided that a permanent surface must be laid. This was good news, for a tarred road would increase the usefulness of our acres. In thirteen years our way home would have changed from a track that was scarcely wide enough for the jeep, and where it was impossible to walk in anything more elegant than boots or Wellingtons, to a proper road suitable for cars, lorries and stiletto heels.

One day a diesel roller arrived, throbbing purposefully at the bottom of the hill. It was huge. It looked as incongruous in that narrow lane, with the little old stone walls and stunted oaks on either hand, as would an express train from Paddington stranded on a mountainside. We watched its inching progress up the crazy angle of the slope. The engine thumped deeply as it dragged itself forward at perhaps half a mile an hour while the surface of the road rippled in an unwilling wave before its ten-ton weight. Loose stones were crushed downwards, splintered into fragments and locked into the pitching of their granite bed. Behind the ground was a uniform perfection of smooth pressed stone, in front was the water-worn rockery which led to Carneddi. It was strange to see our lane so transformed—the track where generations of feet had climbed to the mountain holdings above, where Mrs. Owen had stepped in clogs with her butter basket or William Owen passed with a sack of coal in his cart, where the feet of Griffiths children had hurried to school in earlier days or walked to Chapel on Sundays, where horses' hooves and cart wheels were the only scanty traffic to the hill homes above.

After many days and when the roller had finished its preparatory work, tar barrels and gravel were brought up and the final surface laid. When it was finished we had a beautiful road winding up between the stone walls to within a hundred yards of the farm. Shallow drains still crossed it at intervals but these caused no hindrance to cars except for a slowing down. The last hundred yards were, for some reason, our responsibility and the Council stopped their work abruptly at the foot of the final rise. Although this was now much rougher than the rest, it kept its surface fairly well in heavy rain for it was mostly solid rock. My father and Paul had chipped out and widened it laboriously ten years earlier as part of the Hill Farming Improvement Scheme and they had done their work well.

In the autumn we bought a small new van and the jeep was sold for caravan towing. With a tractor on the farm and a tarred road, a jeep was no longer essential. I did not regret its going particularly. It had been very useful for twelve years but, though its powerful engine and rugged looks had fitted our hill farm, the now constant breakdowns and high petrol consumption were a cause of anxiety. The little van seemed luxurious by comparison. Rain and snow no longr beat on our heads as we drove along and it was possible to reach a destination looking tidy and civilized instead of arriving, weather-beaten and scarcely human, in a shroud of raincoats and sou'westers. I found it strange to have the steering on the right, and strange also that every control worked and produced the desired results immediately. There was not, perhaps, the eccentric holiday atmosphere of the jeep but a van was now more suitable to the state of development of my farming.

The jeep had been housed in the old cartshed and, with windscreen lowered on the bonnet, it had just fitted in. The roof of this shed was too low to admit either tractor or van, and now we should have to begin building again if both precious vehicles were not to stand out in the weather. On an expanding farm, however small, earnings get ploughed back and there never seems to be any money in the bank. One development leads to another and the time for saying, 'I've finished' never comes. I had just paid for the new roof of Ty Mawr; now I must begin paying out again. The proposed building must be solid, lasting and convenient, and so it would not be cheap. I applied for a 50 per cent Hill Farming Grant and was relieved when it was approved.

About Christmas time we began to build. Paul and I were quick and experienced now and, although the new shed presented some new problems, these we solved after thought. The shed was a lean-to on the long north wall of the deep-litter house, was thirty feet by sixteen and divided into three bays. When it was finished there was ample room for the van and tractor with one bay for machinery and room for a work bench, tools and shelves on the walls. The proportions of the building were pleasing and, for the first time, we had space to do maintenance jobs under cover in tidy and convenient surroundings. William Owen liked our work. 'Very nice carriage shed,' he said. Although the building was officially described as Tractor and Implement Shed, after this we always called it the carriage shed.

The months at Oathill had given me a more business-like outlook and I knew that the farm's gross output should be increased to make the tractor worth while. This was not easy now at Carneddi, with the land fully stocked and in the limits of the rugged hills. I thought, however, that we might try growing seed potatoes as an extra crop. They would provide more work for the tractor and more income for the farm, while Carneddi with its high healthy land and nearness to the sea was a suitable site for them. We had space for only half an acre but this was a sufficient area to qualify for the Grade A Certificate, and at least a step in the right direction. Now the kindness of our neighbours helped us again. I was able to borrow a ridger and had the promise of a spinner for lifting the crop at the end of the season; there was no need to spend more money in buying specialized machinery for the new crop.

We planted the seed potatoes where strawberries had been the previous year and by the end of April green tops were appearing along the rows. The year was 1959. We had thought the summer when Fred came home was very dry but the months which now followed were almost tropical in their heat and drought. The spring air was filled with sunshine and cuckoos, and June came in with flaming skies. One hot day Mr. E.G. Williams came to show me how to recognize any undesirable potato plants—the rogues. There could be wildings or bolters in the rows, or plants with mosaic and leaf roll, and the tubers from such plants must not be used again for seed but dug up and thrown away. I had already looked for rogues but none of the waving green tops seemed to have gone wild or bolted and none seemed to have virus symptoms. But I was inexperienced in potato growing and did not really know what I was looking for.

We walked the baking rows. The potatoes did not seem to be suffering from the drought. The peaty humus-filled soil held the water and green haulms dazzled in the sunshine while the roots were in a moist manure bed below. Mr. Williams could find no rogues. Our purchased seed had been healthy and Carneddi's land was proving as good for seed potatoes as it was for strawberries.

No rain fell during July and hay-making was quick and easy, with the hay drying as fast as we could cart it away. We made no silage that year. The damp Welsh summers of our usual experience were forgotten as the sum blazed down through the days of August and the fields turned a tawny gold. Water became short and we practised one economy after another. Still the arable crops did not seem to be much affected by the drought, though the aftermath did not grow. When we came to lift the potatoes at the end of the month there was a huge crop, with some of the tubers of a monster size. A large proportion were too big for seed and I would have preferred more and smaller potatoes but, as we filled sack after sack and carted them away to be stored and sorted in Capel Anwes, I was pleased to see such an abundance. The field carrots did well too, and some of the coral-coloured roots, crisp and tender, were as large as one-pint milk bottles. Later in the season I sold a good weight of the big potatoes for eating and the seed was bought by a local merchant. We prepared to weigh it out, forty pounds at a time on the milk scales to save the cost of a new weighing machine, and fill hundred weight sacks. These were good quality Australian jute, but bought cheaply as salvage from a wreck. It now remained to label the sacks before filling. Paul was not content with any unprofessional method and said we must make a proper stencil. He found one of the celluloid windows from his old Austin 7 and, with a sharp knife, cut the lettering through it. I procured my father's second best shaving brush and trimmed it short and bristly. Then, with black sheep-marking fluid as ink, Paul lettered the sacks.

Welsh Highland Grown
ARRAN PILOT
Cert A

The result was extremely professional; the means had cost us nothing and the seed potato venture had been, in its modest way, a success.

The drought continued and one shower only fell in September. Our water supply diminished and finally dried up. There was just one water hole for the cows in our lowest field and nothing for the house and all the other stock. At one time I should have been anxious, harassed and hurrying, now I had found that thought and energy could put most things right. Mrs. Staunton's spring still flowed and, as often as was necessary, Paul and I took the tractor with an eighty-gallon tank to her tap and carried home a supply. Water carrying took time. Once the full tank was at the farm, endless buckets must be lugged round to the hens, turkeys and calves. Our house grew grimy and piles of unwashed clothes and sheets mounted, but it was impossible not to enjoy the heat and beauty of those late autumn days. The woods and mountains glowed in the fire colours of the fall, the amber, gold and burnt sienna of dying vegetation. Early in October the weather was still warm enough for us to sit outside at night in shorts and thin shirts, playing chess by lantern light, while bats flitted in the dusk and big feathery moths tapped against the lamp glass. The moon would rise silver over the waterless mountains, but we knew that rain must come at last. In the meantime we could afford to enjoy the strange dry beauty of the golden days and silver nights until, in its own time, the weather changed at last.

Finally, in the middle of October, the rain came—real Welsh rain driving up the valley in wind-whipped squalls. Water chuckled in the gutters, a sound we had almost forgotten, and gushed through the downspouts into our buckets and basins beneath. We carried it eagerly indoors. Soon two lines of washing were flapping out in the storm and the red tiles of the kitchen were bright with scrubbing. Later we heard the cistern filling in the bathroom. We were nearly back to normal.

There was another improvement to the farm that summer. Mary made the flower garden. In common with many other farm gardens, ours was mostly neglected; it always came last and was frequently not attended to at all. There had been a small area of bald grass in front of the house, covered with the undesirable playthings of the sheepdogs, a big pile of rubble left over from the building and a pretty fuchsia hedge along the garden wall. Now, Mary, Girton graduate, was to be seen in a pair of my dungarees rolling huge boulders along what was rapidly becoming a paved terrace, wielding a pick-axe, cutting turves in the field and laying them along an extending area of lawn. For years it had been my intention to tidy up the garden, but the farm seemed to occupy all my time and the tidying was never done. Farm mud and animals continued to encroach on our doorstep until Mary set to work. Her plans were far more ambitious than ever mine had been. When she had finished, the garden was lovely. A paved terrace stretched from the garden gate along the front of the house and a lawn was laid, level and green in contrast to the rugged hills all around. She brought a touch of the exotic to that stark landscape with the largest, choicest flowers she could grow. It was surprising to see a massed bed of crimson and gold tulips flaming half-way up the mountainside. Later in the year cascades of deep purple and magenta clematis flowers encircled the bardic sign over our front door. She waged a constant war against straying hens from the deep-litter house, and it became a familiar sound to hear Mary making rude noises at them, while the sheepdogs dashed gleefully along to help and snatch a feather or two from fleeing behinds. She also painted woodwork and whitened stucco, and the house changed from a grey austere building at the foot of the cliff to a pretty place of greenery and flowers.

We had now lived at Carneddi for fourteen years. It seemed a long time since we had first arrived light-hearted and ignorant, and longer still since the days of the hens and goats in a city back garden, and Fred's tales of a country life. There had been many changes in the state of farming in that time. Poultry, most profitable in our early years, could now be made to pay only with very careful management and experience. The turkeys still showed a varying profit, never so good as in our first year of keeping them or so hard won as in the second. I had found a regular market with a local butcher who bought as many as I could rear and, after friendly haggling, we usually arrived at a price that was about right. Strawberry propagation continued to be a useful and unusual side line but Carneddi was still essentially a hill sheep and cattle farm, and we had not deviated too far from the old methods and the old way of life. To the uninformed shepherding hill sheep seems a simple enough job but to the learner it becomes filled with mystery, requiring almost magical powers on the part of the shepherd. For years the secrets of shepherding baffled us. How, we would wonder, can Tom know that this ewe, which is so wild we can hardly get near enough to see her, has lost her lamb; how can he know that this lamb, bleating so miserably, is really quite all right with its mother just over the brow of the hill; how can he be so confident in driving a bunch of panic-stricken yearlings down unfenced lanes and through flocks of other people's sheep; how can Jones, with his hand in the dark mystery of a ewe's womb, untangle this misplaced lamb and bring it safely to birth.

'We must be at school all our days,' Jones's father told me, and of course he was right.

Gradually the awesome task of shepherding over broken hill land seemed easier, and we grew a little more competent. Then the time came when we could do without Tom's help, and Mit and Ruff, two of Dash's sons, worked the flock for us. They were born on the farm and we trained them ourselves. The training of Welsh sheepdogs is not difficult, but again it needs the subtle touch which Welsh shepherds take as a matter of course, and which we had to discover by trial and error. The dogs are extremely sensitive and they are born knowing their job. Their instinct for shepherding develops as they mature and this uncanny inborn knowledge needs only to be directed. The quality of dogs' work may vary a little but much depends on the shepherd. Some men never have a bad dog; some never have a good one. Fully trained sheepdogs are difficult to buy, very expensive and often unsatisfactory after a change of master.

I found it an immense satisfaction to have a good working dog. After the feelings of utter helplessness we had known when sheep dashed off in all directions despite our precautions—complicated barricades and members of the family at every strategic point—it seemed miraculous to be able to drive the sheep where I pleased, with just one dog and the flock, as it were, on an invisible thread. An odd little sense of superiority comes while working sheep with a dog. It is the same feeling that a man has on horseback. Fleetingly, man and animal, working in harmony, become superman for the normal plane of physical powers has been transcended. This feeling is much heightened if there is an audience of uninitiated hikers. But, though I had progressed—and my increased knowledge of shepherding gave me more pleasure than any other single advance on the farm—I knew there was a long way to go before I approached the wisdom and seeming clairvoyance of the sheepmen around me.

Many ex-town's people have taken farms and most of them

have written books about it. Some are stories of achievement, others hilarious tales of the mistakes an innocent towns-man can make in the wilds of the countryside. These last amateur farmers usually have a fair amount of capital behind them because farming blunders and mild disasters become unfunny when there is no cash, and no one wants to write or read about them. But all these new farmers, successful and unsuccessful alike, are attracted to the countryside by a deep longing. A family farm is man's oldest settled occupation. Among the permanent urban population too, there seems to be a growing movement towards the fresh air. As towns become more intolerable, more people escape temporarily to the coasts, country and mountains. They want to look at the sea, green fields and hills—the splendour of the natural world—and live there for their holidays.

Though I had always been interested in farming, our move to Wales was not part of a calculated plan. I have been asked why, if a farm was my aim, I did not choose a district that was more favourable for farming. The answer is that I did not choose at all. Our family had come to a sort of crossroads, and instinctively we were drawn along the present way although we could not see what was at the end of it. Chance brought us to Carneddi, inclination kept us there. Land was cheap and the capital invested in our hill farm gave us wide acres of adventurous land when it would have bought us only five or six in a more fertile district. The type of farming was simple and almost timeless, mostly connected with stock, and it was within my powers in a way in which a mechanized arable farm would not have been. The people of the district were kind and helpful. I came with no special love of the moun-tains but, through shepherding and rock climbing, I found the strength which comes from the hills. Fred's spiritedness smoothed the great change between town and country life, and my father's firm belief in the importance of the farm backed my efforts. Perhaps the influence of the Hendersons was the biggest single factor that helped me. At Oathill I learnt more of the practical skills of farming but, of greater impor-tance, I learnt their way of thinking. I often fall short of their standards of energy and self-discipline, but perhaps there is more latitude for dreaming on a woman's farm on the mountainside. It is undoubtedly Henderson methods, so far as I have achieved them, which have kept the farm solvent. Then, as we made progress, I had Paul to help me and, with his encouragement, ingenuity and strength, I was able to do many things which otherwise would have been impossible. There is much yet to do of a work that will never be finished. 'We must be at school all our days'—but it is a happy education in the hills.

Not everyone can be a farmer and, as a means of livelihood, I consider that farming is ethically neutral. So long as there are enough farmers to feed the population, that is sufficient, and the food they produce is eaten by the just and the unjust alike. What, to me, seems important is that country living is most natural to the state of man, and man in his natural state is better able to know himself, and may be less distracted and more creative. This natural balance and self-knowledge seems vital if the present alarming acceleration of the birth-rate is to be peacefully reversed; for the world is already over-peopled and scientific knowledge is dangerously powerful everywhere. A modern sage has said that the human race is the cancer of this planet. It is hard to think in terms of hundreds of millions of other people, and one can notice only the increased noise and dirt, the new housing estates, the new factories, the nose-to-tail streams of traffic on the roads, and the tensions and anxieties which are near at hand. As the mass of humanity grows, the individual is valued less and the Image and Likeness seems fainter. Though scientific knowledge has tamed Nature, it may yet despoil the natural world. Meanwhile the hills remain precariously unspoilt for all who can lift their eyes to them. Their gospel is unchanged—'Raise the stone and you will find Me, cleave the wood and I am there also.'

DIARY OF A MEDICAL NOBODY
by Kenneth Lane

In 1929 Dr Kenneth Lane, newly qualified and mortgaged up to the hilt in order to buy himself into a practice, set off for a small country town in Somerset. He was to spend his medical life there and, from his beginnings as the new young doctor (whom nobody wanted to consult), was to become the much loved 'Old Doctor' . . .

His practice covered a kaleidoscope of English life . . . miners in the nearby colliery, farmworkers and gypsies in the surrounding countryside, and monks from the Abbey. He worked before penicillin, the National Health, or widespread birth control, and at a time when rival practices fought neck and neck for private patients.

A warm, wonderful book, rich with characters from rural England.

0 552 12033 2   £1.75

ANY FOOL CAN BE A PIG FARMER
by James Robertson

A walloping, rollicking, trotter's eye view of life as a pig farmer in North Wales

Cats, dung, and overdrafts are the three things you can be sure of finding on every farm. But on James Robertson's farm there were also rats, bats, and a boa constrictor. And of course there were the pigs . . .

Sow Number Seven, Queen of the Pen and winner of all the porcine gang wars.

George, who was supposed to father piglets on all the tribe, but fell in love with Number Eleven and wore all the hair from her back.

Duke, whose idea of being sexy was to come galumphing up and take a jump at the sow of his choice. As he weighed the best part of a ton several promising romances were squashed until he was put on a diet.

James Robertson was kicked, bitten, piddled on, and infected with pig lice. But he survives and lives to tell the tale in *Any Fool Can Be A Pig Farmer*.

0 552 12399 4   £1.75

HOVEL IN THE HILLS
by Elizabeth West

A warm, funny, moving account of the simple life in rural Wales.

She was a typist. He was a mechanic. One day Elizabeth and Alan West did what many people spend a lifetime dreaming of doing – they took to the hills. *Hovel in the Hills* is the story of the first nine years of their new life in a semi-derelict farmhouse overlooking Snowdonia. It is a heart-warming and salutary tale that abounds with the joys, and the dilemmas, of opting out of the rat race.

'Mrs West writes in a lively, humorous, down-to-earth style . . . an absorbing account of a brave experiment'
Sunday Times

'I don't think I have read a better book of its kind . . . Mrs West writes remarkably well with just the right element of humour'
Daily Telegraph

'The best book I have read about getting away from it all'
Western Mail

'Conveys the joy in the countryside, in wild things and in coping for oneself'
The Times

0 552 10907 X   £1.50

SUFFER LITTLE CHILDREN
by Elizabeth West

School secretaries are always middle-aged and wear old jumpers and tweed skirts that don't show the dirt. They sit surrounded by elastoplasts, wet knickers in plastic bags ("Angela has done it again. Have you a spare pair in your cupboard?"), confiscated lead-weighted coshes and obscene magazines, and tins of dinner money. They cope with threatening parents, infant sadists, leaking toilets, head lice, and the Education Authority.

At St. Claude's there was also the staff (mixed adults) and the children (mixed infants) who included Marlene, an enchanting five year old sex maniac, and the Hulberts, a three generational clan of affectionate criminals.

School secretaries are capable, cheerful, enterprising, resourceful, and also – after the first five years – very very mad.

0 552 12513 X   £1.75

A SELECTED LIST OF TITLES AVAILABLE
FROM CORGI BOOKS

While every effort is made to keep prices low, it is sometimes necessary to increase prices at short notice. Corgi Books reserve the right to show new retail prices on covers which may differ from those previously advertised in the text or elsewhere.

The prices shown below were correct at the time of going to press.

ORDER FORM

All these books are available at your book shop or newsagent, or can be ordered direct from the publisher. Just tick the titles you want and fill in the form below.

CORGI BOOKS, Cash Sales Department, P.O. Box 11, Falmouth, Cornwall.

Please send cheque or postal order, no currency.

Please allow cost of book(s) plus the following for postage and packing:

U.K. Customers—Allow 55p for the first book, 22p for the second book and 14p for each additional book ordered, to a maximum charge of £1.75.

B.F.P.O. and Eire—Allow 55p for the first book, 22p for the second book plus 14p per copy for the next seven books, thereafter 8p per book.

Overseas Customers—Allow £1.00 for the first book and 25p per copy for each additional book.

NAME (Block Letters) ....

ADDRESS ....

....